# AFRICA
# DOESN'T
# MATTER

# AFRICA DOESN'T MATTER

## HOW THE WEST HAS FAILED THE POOREST CONTINENT AND WHAT WE CAN DO ABOUT IT

### GILES BOLTON

 ARCADE PUBLISHING / NEW YORK

Copyright © 2007, 2008 by Giles Bolton

FIRST U.S. EDITION

First published in the United Kingdom in 2007 by Ebury Press under the title *Poor Story* and revised for this edition

*Library of Congress Cataloging-in-Publication Data*
Bolton, Giles.
  Africa doesn't matter : how the west has failed the poorest continent and what we can do about it / Giles Bolton.
      p. cm.
  Includes bibliographical references.
  ISBN-13: 978-1-55970-865-4 (hc)
  ISBN-13: 978-1-55970-878-4 (pb)
  1. Poverty—Africa. 2. Economic assistance—Africa. 3. Africa—Commerce. I. Title.
  HC800.Z9P6238 2007
  337.6—dc22                         2007039962

Published in the United States by Arcade Publishing, Inc., New York
Distributed by Hachette Book Group USA

Visit our Web site at www.arcadepub.com

10  9  8  7  6  5  4  3  2  1

EB

*For my parents*

# CONTENTS

# AFRICA DOESN'T MATTER

# INTRODUCTION

It was the singer Michael Bolton who smoothed my first entrance into Africa.

In 1996 I'd gone to visit a friend in Kenya whom I'd met in college. The flight path into Nairobi is truly spectacular. If you ever happen to take the overnight Kenya Airways shuttle from London, try and get a window seat on the left as the plane faces forward. Dawn breaks at about the same time you pass west of Mount Kenya, and if you're lucky you get to see its three peaks printed onto a mustard sunrise. From there you follow the Rift Valley south until the arid beige land rises suddenly underneath and you flip over the ridge of the Ngong Hills and cruise down gently over the khaki contours of Nairobi National Park into Jomo Kenyatta International Airport.

Inside the terminal, things were neither as sweaty nor as chaotic as the stereotypes had taught me to expect. But the abrupt immigration official who eventually deigned to consider my passport wasn't doing much for international relations . . . until he read my name. He looked up for the first time.

"Ah, Bolton. Like Michael Bolton!"

"Um, yes, I suppose so."

"Are you related to him?"

"No. Sorry."

"Never mind. His music is very good. Enjoy your stay."

The purple stamp thwacked down onto a clean page and I was in, vowing never to mock soft rockers again. My friend Alex had come to collect me, and as we drove out of the airport into a cool, bright morning, he flicked on the radio. In the thirty minutes it took to reach his house we were regaled with songs by Phil Collins, Bryan Adams, and Rick Astley. Michael Bolton notwithstanding, my first impressions of what the West had brought Africa weren't impressive at all.

Two weeks later, however, I was hooked. Back home I was about to start what I hoped would be a long career in the aid industry—a journey that in a few years would have me running the largest aid program in Rwanda, one of Africa's poorest countries—and my vacation was enough to persuade me that, music scene aside, this was the place I wanted to be.

I'll be honest: some of the attraction for a palm tree–addled mind was the vacationer's glamorous lifestyle. We'd made ramshackle camps in the most mind-blowing of expansive rocky landscapes, spent long, hot days scrambling through leopard caves to emerge into blinding blue-skied panoramas, and savored star-swamped evenings around dancing flames. Privileged Africa is truly something to experience.

But I'd also long wanted to do Something Constructive, and equally fascinating to me had been a glimpse of everyday Kenyan life. Here was a country totally different from my own—with different rules, dreams, expectations, and desires. And often astonishingly poor, from the rag-clothed community we'd seen cutting salt from a baking-hot crater in Kenya's barren north to the cramped slum's corrugated roofs that stretched rustily across a whole Nairobi valley, only to disappear from view entirely at night for lack of electricity. Surely these were problems the rich world could do something to address?

Three hours before my plane left, I stood looking over the scrub of the Athi plains, with a beautiful holiday romance in my arms and a dust-dyed sunset warming our faces. (Note: every book written by westerners about Africa has to feature a beautiful sunset, so it's good to get this out of the way early.) I was going to make a difference. I vowed to return as soon as possible.

The idea that westerners hold the key to Africa's development is, of course, a myth—not to mention patronizing. As I quickly learned, most of the answers lie, as they should, in the hands of African countries themselves and especially their governments. Corruption, conflict, and lack of democracy: all three are primarily internal problems, and the frequent failure of the continent's governments to achieve progress in these areas is depressing.

But if it's up to African countries to get their show on the road, it's the duty of America, Europe, and other rich regions to ensure there's a road to travel down—because it's they who set the rules both for the aid Africa receives and the system of international trade it must abide by. How come none of the forty-eight nations south of the Sahara have made sustained progress since most achieved independence in the 1960s, bar one or two states with exceptional natural resources? They haven't *all* been run badly, *all* of the time; more than thirty are now democracies. It was the one region of the world to decline economically in the 1980s and 1990s, and though the last few years have seen a welcome return to economic growth, thanks largely to a surge in prices for the few basic commodities the continent supplies, the overall numbers in absolute poverty have increased. The fear is that our era of globalization simply isn't working for Africa.

This book is written for people who are concerned about Africa but don't understand why it's still so poor. While there is quite a bit of good academic material out there, most of it isn't very accessible and it doesn't answer the direct questions most of us want answered. Is Africa's poverty all down to corruption? What actually happens to our aid money, and how do trade rules affect us at the checkout line? Can the United States and other rich countries really make a difference in Africa? These are the practical concerns I want to tackle. And I want to explain why, for all the campaigns, concerts, and politicians' promises to make poverty history, Africa will remain poor and we in the West complicit in its plight unless we change the way we're allowing globalization to develop.

On July 8, 2005, George W. Bush and the leaders of the world's seven other most industrialized nations, the G8, sat down to morning coffee in the bay-windowed Glendevon Room of the prestigious Gleneagles golf hotel in Scotland. What happened next was startlingly unusual: the leaders began a detailed discussion of Africa's problems and the West's part in their solutions. Never before had they devoted so much time to considering the predicament of the poorest continent. Never before had they acknowledged so openly that current arrangements, including the West's part in them, weren't working.

The G8's focus on Africa was no fluke, no sudden outbreak of altruism in a foreign policy world that nowadays feels so gloomily full of threats. The run-up to Gleneagles had seen hundreds of thousands of people across the West join protests demanding fairer aid and trade terms for Africa, despite the fact that the majority had never been there. Millions attended rock concerts from Philadelphia to London to Tokyo that sang from the same hymnal (though Stevie Wonder was, it's true, a big draw), while billions more watched on TV.

The remarkable scale of public support was matched only by the unprecedented consensus for change between lobbying groups, celebrities, and politicians. Bono shared a platform with Bill Gates, Bob Geldof was caught hugging Tony Blair, and Brad Pitt's video message supporting reform followed one from Nelson Mandela. Fighting poverty had become as clear-cut as fighting apartheid: every right-thinking person was for it. This was the world's last easy win, something both terribly wrong and encouragingly simple to rectify. (Remarkably, the cause has stayed fashionable right into 2008, with presidential candidates forced to give far more details about their planned overseas development policies than in any previous election.)

In the face of such overwhelming pressure, the G8 leaders did not disappoint, announcing a genuinely radical package of promises on Africa: doubling aid, canceling the entire debt of the poorest countries, reforming trade. Even the United States, long the skeptic of big new aid initiatives, signed up.

Yet the astonishing thing is that most of 2005's promises *weren't* new—nor indeed are some of the initiatives the Bush administration has announced since. Many had been made by Western governments before, including the doubling of aid and the reform of trade: it's just that no one had delivered. Others, including the extension of debt relief, had long been demanded by African governments and development campaigners alike: it's just that no one had listened.

As the G8 leaders left the airy Glendevon Room at the end of their meeting, leaving behind a detritus of half-empty cups of fair trade coffee, bottles of Scottish mineral water, and the crumbs of locally made shortbread, the question was obvious: would the promises be kept this time? Three years later, the answer is already starting to feel like the movie *Groundhog Day*: apparently, many of them will not.

Africa's failure to access the benefits of globalization isn't just a matter for gray-haired politicians on Capitol Hill in suits of matching color. As individuals in America and other wealthy countries, it's a worry for us too. Globalization, especially global trade, leaves us all more affected by each other's actions than ever before. Distilled to its essence, the prices the world's poor get for the few things they produce—such as cotton, coffee, and chocolate—are ever more directly linked to our day-to-day decisions about what to buy. In addition, the political decisions our leaders make about things like trade rules can have huge impacts on people far away who have no ability to influence those decisions. If globalization isn't working for Africa and the trade rules apparently aren't fair, does this mean we as individuals need to change our behavior as well?

Must we now start to "think, act, and shop" as if we're part of some vague-sounding global community, or else be complicit in any problems that ever-spreading globalization causes?

. . . And pigs will fly. The problem with such a pretty vision of caring globalization has always been that none of us can imagine it working in practice, especially if it means spending more money or seeing our own economies suffer. And I'd have to agree, if it wasn't for the fact that it's not just Africa that is losing out from the West's aid and trade arrangements: the other, untold scandal is that we're being ripped off too.

First of all there is the aid money from your hard-earned

taxes, which apparently isn't producing the results—lasting improvements in poor people's lives—that we are led to believe it will. Admittedly, this may not be as much money as many of us think (America spends less per head on foreign aid than any other developed country bar Greece), but you can add to that amount any extra donations you make to charities, drop in a collection box in the street or in church, or pledge in response to a TV appeal. You've already got quite a tidy sum invested in this game of African assistance: some might argue not enough, but still quite significant.

Next there's the extra money you've spent at the supermarket because you haven't been given the chance to buy low-priced products from places like Africa. You're not allowed to buy some of these at their real, low prices because of tariffs our governments impose on outside goods, such as sugar and cocoa products. That's another chunk of your money gone.

And then you discover that not only can you not buy the cheapest products but even more of your taxes are going to surprisingly high subsidies in your own country, set out in the new farm bill as well as its foreign equivalents. Are you American? In 2006 you spent nearly as much money subsidizing the U.S. cotton industry, $4 billion, as the entire value of the cotton it produced (while 10 million African cotton farmers would have seen fewer of their children die from preventable diseases if your taxes hadn't been spent on a few thousand farms in the Midwest). Are you European? You're paying to subsidize every cow in the European Union at $3 a day (while 300 million Africans live on less than $1 a day). Are you Japanese? You recently spent more than 1 percent of your annual income—at least $600 per household[1]—on rice through a combination of high prices and farmer support (while farmers in countries like Ghana couldn't even sell their own rice in local markets, let alone abroad, because of subsi-dized imports from rich so-called competitors).

Something is wrong here, something that doesn't work for Africa but doesn't seem to work for us either. This certainly isn't the benevolent relationship between the West and poor countries I pictured when, two years after my first visit, I found myself back in Kenya as a fully fledged aid worker.

It may have been a junior position, but my new job meant everything to me.

Based in Nairobi, I was tasked with helping to manage the British government's assistance to neighboring Uganda, a coun-try widely regarded as one of Africa's relative success stories. The issues were remarkable even if the tasks were mostly bureaucratic. I didn't get to travel to Uganda very often, but when I did there were awe-inspiring moments. Visiting the north to review some small-scale rehabilitation programs, for children once abducted by the terrifying Lord's Resistance Army and forced to become soldiers or underage wives, seemed more instructive and moti-vating than anything I'd ever done before.

Life in Kenya was somehow permanently new and exciting. I gained a diverse bunch of friends and lived in a pretty house in town, complete with a jacaranda tree whose lavender, bell-shaped blooms dropped gently onto my small terrace. I'd sit out there on Sunday mornings reading the local papers, happily embarrassing Stephen, the security guard, with my attempts at Swahili, and listening to the chaotic tooting and touting of Nairobi's *matatu* minibuses at nearby Dagoretti Corner—which took its ultracool name from a Kenyanization of "the great corner." I felt incredibly lucky.

Then, abruptly, my Kenyan reverie ended. In April 2000 I was brought back to London for a quick briefing and then was posted to Rwanda, a country unmade by genocide only a few years before. A small, landlocked state, and still one of Africa's poorest, it faced almost inconceivable challenges in trying to build a new society and economy. I was to run its largest aid program, funded by the British equivalent of USAID.

After my overnight flight from London via Brussels, a car picked me up at Kigali's small, efficient airport and whisked me across town to the office. Britain had taken on an ambitious responsibility as Rwanda's biggest financial supporter and closest ally. Many questioned the commitment of the country's new regime to its promises of reconstruction and reconciliation. Working closely with the United States, the next largest donor, my job was to monitor how aid money was being spent and lead discussions with ministers and other senior figures about current and future assistance. I felt—and was—young to be taking on such a responsible position in a culture where age is all but a synonym for wisdom.

You can't arrive in Rwanda without some apprehension. I didn't know what to expect. Did day-to-day life go on as normal where the worst acts of human depravity had been carried out only a few years before? (Answer: Of course.) Were the people I was passing on the road from the airport into town survivors, or would they have been involved in the slaughter? (A: There were very few survivors, but most of the leading suspects in the genocide were in jail or in exile.) What tribe were the baggage handlers at the airport, Hutu or Tutsi? (A: Everyone is officially Rwandan now.) Had any atrocities happened on the street my house was on? (A question I never sought an answer to.)

That evening, I joined one of my new colleagues for an enormous bottle of Primus beer on the terrace of Hotel Umubano, an underappreciated monument to 1970s design on the ridge of a hill. We watched as half of Kigali's small business and political elite turned up to meet and greet each other, while their children vacated the pool after a long afternoon's aquatics. My first day had been a sleep-weary blur of meetings of which I could remember little, bar the country and western tape playing in the car as one of the drivers, Pasteur, rushed us between appointments, a turgid dirge repeating, "I believe in love, I believe in babies, I believe in Mom and Dad, and I believe in you." First impressions were thus even worse than in Kenya. But then the hotel band struck up with a noisy rendition of "Eye of the Tiger," segued into some Sinatra and Bob Marley, and finally settled into the joyously bouncy guitar sound of Congolese soukous. I sat back and hoped that my understanding of the country would improve as quickly as had the music.

During my two years there I worked with some extraordinary people both inside and outside the Rwandan government. I discovered a great deal about the difficulty for outsiders in trying to provide useful support to a destitute country, amid a complex and fragile political situation where you can never presume to understand everything that is going on. And I learned a disturbing amount about the wider flaws in the way the United States and all Western countries deal with Africa.

I returned to London in 2002, via a long drive home across Africa and the Middle East and onward back to England with an American friend who had been toiling in humanitarian camps in Burundi. There I worked for a year on the UK's cooperation with the World Bank and the IMF, the two most influential global development institutions, traveling frequently to

Washington and supporting efforts to improve their effectiveness. Then, on short notice, I was transferred to work on British and American aid plans for Iraq before the war of 2003 and subsequently on their implementation.

Iraq may not have been a conventional aid scenario—nor, by African standards, was the country particularly poor—but politically it was riveting. The responsibility was to do the best job we could do in protecting humanitarian concerns and longer-term development plans, whatever the circumstances. I sat in meetings in Washington, Whitehall, Baghdad, and Basra and worked with the American and British militaries, diplomats, policymakers, and NGOs. The difficulties of trying to achieve reconstruction in a desperately insecure environment were enormous—perhaps the greatest example of aid agencies' good intentions being undermined by reality—and the frustrations deep.

Yet it wasn't Africa. And, frankly, I felt it was less important. Though this assignment taught me much about how big aid and foreign policy decisions are made and influenced in the West, what still ate away at me were the inefficiency and hypocrisy I'd seen during my time in Kenya, Uganda, and Rwanda.

Did I really want to spend a whole career in a global aid industry so badly structured and managed that it might simply never be able to achieve its aims? Did I want to continue collaborating with dedicated Africans and aid workers while the West's trade policies undermined so much of what we were trying to do? Was globalization as a whole ever going to give Africa a chance?

Exhausted too from my assignment on Iraq, I felt I couldn't go on without answering these questions. It was time for some time out. I left my job, determined to stand back from the day-to-day and explore the system of support to poor countries from the West of which I had been part.

*

I count myself genuinely lucky to have worked with a large number of intelligent, highly committed colleagues in the aid industry, Africans, Americans, Brits, and others alike. I have no desire to undermine their efforts. Yet what makes it vital that we question the industry itself when it comes up short is precisely the importance of its aims. I have long since learned to forgive the occasional Africans at airport check-ins or hotel reception desks who, to this day, continue to profess their admiration for Michael Bolton and inquire about my heritage. But it still seems to me a great pity that—if Nairobi radio stations are anything to go by—globalization has delivered to countries like Kenya a legacy in music so middle-of-the-road not even my father would listen to it but not useful things like lasting economic growth or longer life expectancy.

What if this great goal of reducing African poverty isn't actually achievable the way the world has been going about it? What if the aid industry has been, in effect, a token gesture that makes all of us living in the West feel as if we are Doing Something while concealing the reality that we're not really doing anything of the sort? Worse yet, what if, unintentionally, the very same international rules that we in the West evolve to manage our own globalizing economies make it ever more difficult for the poorest countries to develop?

This book answers these questions in five sections: Poverty, Aid, Trade, Globalization, and Change. They explain the basics of how America and other rich countries engage with Africa, with a particular focus on what actually happens to your aid money and how *you* too are affected by the trade rules that do so little for the world's poorest continent. They assess what is likely to happen next in Africa and in our own communities and whether Washington's promises, and those of other countries, have made a difference. They also provide a personal account of some of the lessons I learned firsthand. But above all, they tell a story of how we in the West fail to listen: and since we're in an era when the world is more interdependent than ever and Africa has the quietest voice, this has terrible consequences.

You, the reader—taxpayer, charity donor, consumer, and voter—have a right to know about all of this. You have a right as a taxpayer and charity donor whose money may be being wasted on halfhearted aid gestures for Africa, while more of your taxes are spent on unfair trade subsidies that continue to shut poor countries out. You have a right as a consumer prevented from buying cheaper products in the supermarket that would both save you money and benefit poorer-country producers. You have a right as a voter who may care about relations with Africa that are being carried out in your name.

And you also have a *need* to know that—as a taxpayer, consumer, and voter in an increasingly interdependent world— you may be among the only people who have the power to do something about it.

# POVERTY
## IMPOSSIBLE CHOICES

# CHAPTER 1
# A LIFE QUITE ORDINARY

If you drive about forty miles west out of Kenya's capital, Nairobi, along the old highway to Lake Naivasha, there's a right turn onto a long dirt road signposted to Kijabe, a small town in the middle of nowhere in particular. From Kijabe a rough, potholed track climbs between some trees and emerges after a mile or so into a quiet, gently sloping village called Machani, made up of several widely spaced houses with small plots of land between. On one of the lower plots, marked out with a few young eucalyptus trees and enjoying a view over the haze of Africa's great Rift Valley, live Lucas Muragi and his wife, Nancy.

I met Lucas and Nancy because I'd set out one morning, in early 2005, to drive into the countryside and try and find out what one random life in that part of Africa happened to be like that day. After meandering around the hills for a while I met Anne, a good English speaker and owner of a small, yellow-painted store called Kijabe Cereals. I told her I was hoping to visit someone local, neither especially poor nor rich, whom I could ask a few questions about day-to-day life (Anne, as a store-owner, was relatively wealthy). She took me up to Machani, and I followed her down the path to Lucas's house.

Too many years as an aid worker looking at poverty statistics—telling you facts such as that Kenya's average life expectancy is forty-nine[1]—had perhaps made me forget that no one is ever average and that everyone has their own story. Lucas was seventy-three and Nancy sixty-four. Given that I was researching a book about the inequities of Africa's relations with the West, I'd hoped perhaps to meet a young small-scale coffee farmer who might have an opinion about Western trade tariffs, or a single mother of five with strong views on the price of foreign-produced medicines. But instead here was a friendly, distinguished-looking couple whom Anne had presumably chosen for the wisdom of their age. So I ducked my head inside the house and, as directed by my hosts, sat down in the living room on one of the smart chairs covered in pristine blue-and-yellow-flowered nylon upholstery.

Lucas begins his day at around 6:30 a.m. The mornings are cold. He gets up, puts on a couple of sweaters and a woolen hat, and goes out to check on the cow and the two goats kept to the side of the solid, concrete-walled house. Usually he'd feed the chickens too and collect any eggs, but this is January and the coop is empty from Christmas celebrations. Meanwhile, Nancy chivvies the fire from yesterday's embers. Surrounded by blackened pots and a couple of Africa's ubiquitous yellow plastic jerry cans in the outdoor kitchen, she begins to prepare some cornmeal for breakfast.

Lucas is slightly stooped but in reasonable health, his formal manner backed up by an arresting glimmer in his eyes and a broad gummy smile. Later in the day he will go and work the three acres of land on which they grow the corn, some potatoes, and a few beans. But for now he sits down away from the fire to exchange morning greetings with neighbors passing by on the road. Nancy is a few inches shorter than her husband, a resilient-looking woman with an air of friendly efficiency and a taste for bright headscarves. The one she wore the day I visited was a riot of red and yellow, topping off a long black skirt and a faded blouse with broad collar. Occasionally stirring the cornmeal, she also prepares some tea, heated with some milk from the goats (the cow isn't producing much at the moment).

Nancy picks out some of the plastic plates and calls to Anthony, their grandson, who lives with them. Like many seventeen-year-olds, he doesn't manage to appear until breakfast has started to go cold. The three of them chat about the day ahead, the goat that seems to be in pain and made a bit of noise last night, the news on the radio about fighting between two nomadic tribes in the north, the boy who broke his leg at yesterday's school soccer match in Kijabe, the neighbor Anthony is going to help later with some harvesting. The sun has already started to burn off the thin morning mist and it looks set to be a bright day. With the food finished, Nancy clears up and Anthony goes inside. In the living room, alongside a poster of Christian proverbs, a Chinese-printed cartoon proclaiming that "Mother is the Dearest One on Earth," and a big faded sticker for Samay Quartz New Generation Clocks, there is a small mirror. Anthony gets his comb out and checks the new hairstyle a friend gave him earlier in the week.

Some two thousand miles away on the other side of Africa, once dawn has flitted far enough west to reach the riverside city of Kinshasa, it will soon be Marie Mawemba's turn to get up. Kinshasa is the capital of the Democratic Republic of Congo, a vast country with an eccentric and tragic history. Created by a rapacious Belgian king, it used to be called Zaire and is best known variously as the setting for Joseph Conrad's novel *Heart of Darkness*, for Muhammad Ali and George Foreman's 1974 "Rumble in the Jungle," for despotic decades of state looting by its former president, Mobutu, and, since 1997, for a civil and regional conflict estimated to have cost around four million lives.

None of this is on Marie's mind as she and her five-year-old son, Jean Baptiste, start the morning routine. When I visited them, in mid-2004, this began with a quick wash for both of them from a cupful of water poured from another of those yellow plastic jerry cans. Marie had purchased the water at a standpipe earlier in the week, determined that Jean Baptiste should not use the filthy liquid of nearby streams-cum-sewers, a major cause of the diseases suffered by so many local children. There's not much privacy in this sprawling suburb of close-packed shacks, yet nor is there much space in the small one-room hut they share with Marie's aunt Josephine and her three children, with its mud-brick walls and rusty corrugated iron roof whose gaps are filled with plastic sheeting. So Jean Baptiste is stripped down just outside the house and rather miserably subjected to a thorough scrubbing, while Marie makes do with a more circumspect wash while still wearing a threadbare baggy old T-shirt that has the words "Blue Marlin Soccer Juniors, Fla." printed on the back, and the dusty long cotton skirt that goes with it.

Ablutions over, it's time for breakfast, in theory at least. Usually there's only one main meal a day, in the evening. This morning, Marie brushes together some scraps of cassava loaf left over from last night and mixes them with a little water to make a couple of mouthfuls for Jean Baptiste. Marie has a generally genial countenance, offset by a phenomenally withering look she directs at her son whenever he misbehaves. She is surprisingly healthy-looking aside from a couple of lesions on her arms, most likely a symptom of poor diet. When Jean Baptiste only eats half his small breakfast, still morning-grumpy and with a bit of a cold, Marie berates him and finishes off the rest. All this is conducted at speed so that, well before 7 a.m., Marie is ready to leave for work. Jean Baptiste is left with Josephine. When he is older, Marie hopes to send Jean Baptiste to school, though she will need to earn more money to do so.

But for now he will spend the day with Josephine in the usual five-year-old adrenaline rush of play, exploration, getting shouted at, laughing, crying, and occasionally running home, tempered with a few periods of inactivity resulting from an undersupplied belly. Marie, meanwhile, will be out in the center of the city, a few kilometers' walk away, until dusk, either doing small jobs or looking for other bits of work. Her most regular employment comes from occasionally helping to clean a small factory that makes foam mattresses—work a friend of hers passes her way as often as possible. But she takes whatever is going: other cleaning jobs, city-paid work picking up litter on some of central Kinshasa's broad leafy avenues (you need to have an in with the foreman), filling in when another friend breaks off from selling her small stall of vegetables (paid in leftovers, albeit often rather rotten).

Marie is a strikingly bright woman with big ambitions, even though she's only ever had a year and a half of schooling: she wants to give Jean Baptiste a secure upbringing, find a regular paid job, and get a home of her own and stop the landlord berating her and her aunt for being late with rent. If she finds no work in the city today, as often happens, she'll end up spending what's left of her time bantering with her friends about the latest events and gossip, deciding which of the men

they know are the most attractive, and running for cover whenever the clouds burst, which happens most days with some
violence—the kind of things any nineteen-year-old would do,
even one with a five-year-old child. Both Marie's parents died
several years ago. Something about her suggests a streak of
ruthlessness, perhaps even viciousness, if you ever rubbed her
the wrong way. I couldn't help thinking, when I met her, as we
sat talking in a local roadside bar with crates for seats amid the
cacophonous bustle of early evening, that you definitely would-
n't mess . . . At home, pride of place in her shack goes to a
mint-condition magazine picture of Sean Combs/Diddy,
replete in white vest and bling. When I point out that Diddy is
a dead ringer for D.R. Congo's young president, Joseph Kabila
(which he is), she laughs and says the president would never
wear clothes like that.

The best part of Marie's day, she says, comes around sunset,
as long as she's managed to find work and make some cash.
Then she heads for home and Jean Baptiste. They have a meal,
often with a couple of the neighbors next door, and swap stories
about the day. Not so long after, given the absence of electricity
and the high cost of paraffin for lighting, it's back to the shack
for sleep on the rickety wood-and-sisal cot she shares with
her son.

## Five Myths about Africa

**"Famine is due to food shortages."** Drought or conflict can certainly lead
to much-reduced food production in particular areas. But it's rare that a
country as a whole has insufficient food, and the market can always bring
supplies in from other places, or even from abroad. Famine occurs
because individuals can no longer afford to buy food, so there's no point
in traders bringing in any to sell. Famine is really the result of fragile,

poor lives, where just one bad harvest—or the death of your cow, a collapse in crop prices, the loss of a job—can leave you with nothing, and no means to provide for your family.

**"Africa is overpopulated and they keep having too many children."** For its size, Africa is relatively underpopulated. India is barely a tenth as big and supports more people. Rwanda has the heaviest land pressure in Africa yet still has fewer people per square mile than England.[2] The problem is that economic growth too often lags behind population growth, land use is inefficient, and pressure on good land intensifies in the absence of other opportunities for employment. With stable growth and the new jobs it brings, Africa's population could afford considerable expansion. But in any case, birth rates tend to fall where growth, education, and health care improve.

**"Africa has many killer diseases."** No, it doesn't—or at least, little more so than other parts of the world. Most deaths in Africa don't occur elsewhere simply because there is treatment available in hospitals and clinics, drugs we can afford, and inoculations we have as children. Some of Africa's big killers?

- HIV/AIDS (over 2 million a year). It's pretty simple. If you get HIV in the West, you take antiretrovirals, which have a very high success rate at keeping you alive and healthy for years. If you get it in Africa—and 70 percent of the people in the world with HIV live in Africa—you probably don't, and you will soon die once full-blown AIDS takes hold, unless you're one of a lucky few.[3]
- Malaria (about 1 million a year). Aside from the deaths, malaria takes a massive toll in sickness and loss of productivity, with hundreds of millions suffering bouts every year.[4] But with proper treatment and use of bed nets, it could be reduced enormously. Southern Europe used to suffer from malaria; it's now all but extinct there.
- Diarrheal diseases (about 700,000 a year). Yes, people die from diarrhea, especially the vulnerable, such as young children, all for want of simple treatment like oral rehydration and access to clean water.[5]

And so on and so forth. More than 4 million children in Africa under five die every year; two-thirds of their deaths could be avoided with low-cost solutions like vitamin A supplements, insecticide-treated bed nets, and oral rehydration tablets.[6] Want to know how easy it is to stamp out a disease if you put enough effort behind it—and enough resources? In a rare success story, polio is close to being wiped out in Africa, largely due to a mass inoculation campaign since 1988. Nearly all disease is about poverty.

**"Africa has many dangerous animals."** In some ways this would be quite romantic if true, even though frightening. But elephants don't rampage through backyards on a regular basis, and leopards don't make a habit of chewing farmers in their fields. Most wild game is confined to relatively few reserves; there are thought to be only around 23,000 lions across the whole continent, a decrease of 90 percent in two decades.[7] They kill only a couple of hundred people a year (and barely ever a tourist).[8] In killing terms, it's the malaria-carrying mosquito that is the true king of the jungle.

**"The climate isn't conducive to development."** People tend to forget that much of Africa is in the tropics and receives lots of rainfall. It is, after all, the continent we're all descended from, so people have been living there successfully for millennia. Even on dusty plains, livestock can survive well as long as there is reliable access to water. It is thought that Uganda, a smallish country of around 25 million people, could still probably feed the whole of Africa if commercially farmed. If you can irrigate, almost anything will grow with all that sunshine. The bottom line is that if you are able to extract enough water—substantially an issue of cost—climate is hardly a problem: look at the agricultural heartland of the American South (though it has been pointed out that part of the reason the American South got rich in the first place was African slave labor).

Marie and Jean Baptiste in Kinshasa and Lucas and Nancy in Machani are four random individuals on a vast continent. While the people of that continent have wildly differing lives, they share with the rest of the world the same basic aspirations, day-to-day joys, and sadnesses: a good or bad week at work, a desire to provide for the family, see friends, keep up with local events.

Where they differ, particularly from those of us in the West, is in the near-impossible choices with which they are often faced. It is these choices that are the hallmark of poverty: dilemmas to which sensible solutions are simply not available. They encapsulate the predicaments that keep people like Marie, Jean Baptiste, Lucas, and Nancy trapped in poverty, unable to break out.

With Marie, the problems of poverty are obvious. She is young and optimistic but lives perilously and permanently close to the edge of crisis. She calculates she can manage three or four days without finding any work before she runs out of money for food for her and Jean Baptiste completely. Her cousin Josephine would and does help where possible, but she has little to spare. Marie has no assets, and even the small shack they occupy is rented by the month.

What are the impossible choices? This week, Marie chose to buy that jerry can of clean water: it's much healthier, for both her and her son, but it has meant even less food, though she's had a reasonable couple of days finding work. Earlier in the year she chose to try and cut her minimal costs elsewhere in order to start putting money aside each week for future school fees for Jean Baptiste, but in March she caught malaria. After two days of being unable to go to work, she had to choose to buy medicine, so the first few weeks' savings were gone. In theory she ought to choose buying a bed net to prevent malaria, to save on future medical costs and help ensure she's always fit to work, but that might mean going without either food or water for nearly a whole week. And on it goes. Jean Baptiste never had all the inoculations he should have had as a baby because his father was saving up to travel to his home region of the Congo to take over his own dying father's land; Marie hasn't heard from him in two years.

Marie's biggest fear is not being able to afford treatment for Jean Baptiste if he becomes seriously ill. Her country, at war for so long, has almost nonexistent health care and she cannot rely on clinics to provide even the most basic of medicines. I ask her, rather lamely, what she would do in such a situation and she answers immediately: anything. I admire her optimism about what is ahead of her—she is determined to break out of semislum life—but it's difficult to share it. Almost no one escapes Kinshasa's graspingly poor suburbs, and unless the country's economy finally starts to improve it's hard to see where opportunities will arise. She is trapped: starved of chances to improve her skills and demonstrate her talent, unable to maintain consistent health and strength to work more effectively, burdened with the blessing of a child who should never feel a burden. And Jean Baptiste, in turn, is trapped too: denied an education, denied opportunities, already significantly underweight for his age. Presuming he does grow up in reasonable health, he is likely to live the same kind of life as his mother.

Both Marie and I have finished our beers in the small bar by the side of the road. It is dark and the early evening activity has quietened down considerably. I start thinking about getting back to my friend's house and how to find the taxi driver who brought me here. Already a little bit merry—she doesn't often get to have a drink—Marie asks for another beer. I give her the money. Instead of buying another bottle, she pockets it, says thank you, and gets up to say goodbye. If anyone can make the right choices, perhaps it is her.

If Marie's poverty is conspicuous, what about Lucas and Nancy, far away to the east in their house near the edge of the Rift Valley? By African standards they are not especially poor. Despite little cash income (a pension would be a distant dream), they have a valuable asset in their reasonably fertile land and relative security in the food it provides. Their diet is fairly balanced. Lucas used to have a regularly paid job in the kitchens of Kijabe's mission school (a job in which, Nancy noted with a smile, he'd had little to do), which helped them through their childrearing years. They may wish they could afford a water tank to collect rain, which would enable them to farm cabbages and other green vegetables, they may worry about not being able to help family in a crisis, but many Africans—including Marie and probably every one of the 315 million others who live on less than one dollar a day—would take what they have.

Indeed, after an hour chatting away with Lucas and Nancy in their spotless living room on the day that I called, I wondered if I'd stumbled across the most benignly content couple in Kenya. But then Lucas broke off for a sip of the luminescent orange drink brought out especially for my visit and Nancy asked whether I'd like to hear about their family. Beneath the proud surface their dignity had first presented to me, a more complex picture soon began to emerge of how poverty had defined their lives too.

It wasn't just the fields in Machani that were fairly fertile, nor were they the only place Nancy labored. She had borne twelve children, which seems astounding to me. Of these, four had already died, two or three of them (it was speculated by others) from AIDS-related illnesses, while Anthony, the grandson who lived with them, had lost both his parents. Three of their remaining eight children now lived elsewhere in the village: two of these were "doing okay" in Nancy's opinion, farming their own plots of land and bringing up families, but the third, a son, was ill with typhoid and the cause of much worry. Three more children were "struggling" in Nairobi, apparently working in textile factories for little pay and living in slums because no one had been able to afford land for them in Machani or anywhere else. One more of the children they had lost contact with several years ago.

### A Quick Note on Typhoid

Usually caused by poor sanitation or hygiene, typhoid is fairly easily curable. When I got it once in Rwanda I went to the doctor, was prescribed some antibiotics, and got better in a couple of days. Yet it kills around 130,000 in Africa every year,[9] largely for want of the money to treat it. It's as good an example as any of what poverty can mean. I never found out what happened to Lucas and Nancy's ill son.

All in all, it became apparent that Lucas and Nancy are better off than any of their children, a sad outcome for any parent and emblematic of Kenya's own story of decline over the last couple of decades. But there was another surprise to come. If your math is better than mine, you'll have worked out that Lucas and Nancy had only accounted for eleven of their twelve offspring. I hadn't, so it was completely out of the blue about twenty minutes later, when the conversation had drifted onto the subject of the mobile-phone mast that was being erected nearby and creating some brief paid employment, that Nancy mentioned that one of their children still lived with them and would I like to "see" her?

Nancy disappeared to a small extra room at the side of the house and returned a couple of minutes later holding the hand of a smiling, haphazardly dressed woman who looked much younger than her thirty-eight years. As the newcomer murmured happily to herself, making sounds she'd never learned to turn into words and gazing off into the distance, it became clear that this daughter, Helen, was mentally disabled. Nancy revealed that she had looked after Helen every single day since she was born, and so had never been able to find work or help Lucas much in the field. As parents, they'd known Helen wasn't "right" from an early age, but the doctor in the clinic never identified the problem.

Most of the choices Lucas and Nancy have had to make during their lives may not have been quite as immediate as Marie's, but they are just as impossible. When they were younger, they could not afford to send all their children to school and had to choose who should go; in the end they managed to send eight, denying four (all girls) the opportunities a basic education provides. When Helen was born, the doctor hadn't known what was wrong but said he thought nothing could be done for her. In an ideal world, Lucas says they would have taken her to Naivasha, a nearby city, or even Nairobi, for a second opinion, but the rest of the family, food, and education all would have suffered.

No family is ever average.

Nowadays, primary education is free in Machani and the rest of Kenya (a policy the government was able to implement with the help of international funding—and has managed to maintain despite the country's recent troubles). This is good news for all but the poorest, who can't even afford the cost of uniforms, lunches, and a small contribution for building maintenance that parents are still often required to pay. But to give your child a really good chance you need to send them on to secondary school. The cost of fees, uniforms, books, and other necessities for one year is about $1,300, roughly the same as one acre of land in Machani, which will help provide reasonable security for a family's future. Which do you choose?

Anthony, the grandson, takes me on a quick tour of Machani before I leave. This village is fantastic: one of the few places in the world where you can genuinely find Faith, Hope, and Charity living next door, not to mention Wisdom farther up the road.

But while I'm admiring the names and the views, Anthony tells me that his grandfather suffers from high blood pressure and is diabetic, like many in Machani (probably because of local dietary deficiencies). The medicine he needs costs over $30 a month, about the same as local monthly earnings. Lucas can generally get by without it, but it leaves him struggling to work the field. And the cost for anyone seeing the doctor in Kijabe is a flat fee of $20.

It's frustrating hearing about the choices people like Lucas and Nancy have had to make throughout their lives (let alone the day-to-day struggle faced by Marie and Jean Baptiste). No one can parachute a golden goose into their chicken coop to increase their income overnight. But if their governments provided even the most basic services in things such as health care, education, and clean water, their lives would be hugely improved and their chances of breaking out of the poverty trap for good would increase enormously. Instead, the reality in Africa has been governments—and many other groups who've tried—that have failed for decades to do so, with few exceptions.

I call back in on Lucas and Nancy before I get on the road for Nairobi, to give them *kitu kidogo*, as it's known in Swahili—something small—to thank them for their time. Lucas, the diabetic, grins broadly and says he'll use the money to buy some sugar . . . As I get ready to take a photo to remember them by, he nips inside the house for his best jacket, palms his hair down, and reminds me to take the lens cap off. Then he puts his arm around Nancy and gives his best smile.

# CHAPTER 2
# AFRICA SCRAMBLED

The map of Africa has more straight lines on it than that of any other continent. Marking numerous national boundaries, these lines betray the extraordinary way most present African countries were brought into being, carved up arbitrarily between Europe's late-nineteenth-century powers in ornate conference rooms thousands of miles to the north. Never before had so much been decided by longitude and latitude rather than tribe or topography.

Thus began a hectic journey for the modern state in Africa, from imposed invention through joyful liberation to today's unfulfilled expectation. It is impossible to understand Africa's present plight, and especially the failure of its governments to perform better, without at least a whistle-stop tour through this unconventional and engaging recent past. Yet, as far too much non-African writing continues to overlook, African history goes back far beyond colonial interference.

It's easy to forget how young most current countries on the oldest continent are. The landmass from which mankind originated was dotted with various realms and territories up until the 1870s, but these bore little relation to subsequent borders. The few European spheres of influence were little more than trading posts along the odd stretch of coast, plus the longer-established British colony of South Africa at the tip. The rest of the continent got on with life as usual, having escaped the colonial march of Europe's powers across other parts of the globe over previous centuries. There were powerful kingdoms at various different times, such as Ashanti, Dahomey, and Oyo in the west, Kanem-Bornu in the center, Abyssinia and Buganda in the east, and the Zulus in the south. Meanwhile, the detail in European atlases tended to peter out as soon as they covered any distance inland in Africa, and whole rivers, lakes, kingdoms, and mountain ranges failed to bother the illustrators' pencils.

Then came Europe's mad scramble for Africa. This was the era of eccentric explorers and compliant cartographers, backed by the incomparable force of modern weapons. Gaps on Western maps were filled in apace. A small and reckless breed of land-grabbing adventurers traversed their way across the continent, establishing "facts" of ownership by signing treaties with bullied or gift-flattered local leaders, or through the direct imposition of force. The resulting paperwork made its way back to European conference rooms, where it was considered and contested until pretty much the entire continent was divided up between Britain, France, Portugal, Germany, Italy, and Belgium. Then the mapmakers were called in to transpose these rough agreements into indelible ink, agreements that owed everything to imperial bickering, bribery, and the gun and little to the logic of landscape or ethnicity. Thousands of miles of borders ended up in geography-defying straight lines purely because they were nice and easy for Europe's hungry aggressors to negotiate. It's a strange situation when cartographers have a greater influence on the birth of countries than the inhabitants of those regions themselves; and it would come back to haunt much of the continent.

In the space of fifteen years, thirty new colonies and protectorates were established. The birth of many African countries was thus a sort of immaculate conception, lacking as it did the usual passions of creation. It was all a source of much pride in the salons of London, Paris, and elsewhere, where few voices could be heard worrying about their credentials as midwives, or whether the pains of labor had been borne by any Africans unfortunate enough to be standing in the way.

What did Europe want so desperately from Africa? Its coastal trading posts had long enabled the exchange of goods for items craved back home, including gold, ivory, peanuts, palm oil, and, until not long before, slaves for the New World's cotton and sugar plantations. But then the explorers began to penetrate the interior of the continent, claiming the discovery of lush new lands and far greater riches. These discoveries, combined with the late-nineteenth-century rivalries of empire-obsessed European powers, gave rise to a semihysteria that resulted in the rapid division of the whole continent, including vast tracts still unexplored by outsiders.

The PR campaigns of the time claimed grand motives for this seizure of new colonies and their 110 million, largely oblivious residents. The first great foreign explorer, the British missionary David Livingstone, had pleaded for the three Cs to be brought to Africa: commerce, Christianity, and civilization. Undoubtedly well-intentioned in his case, the reality of Europe's ravenous appropriation of the continent was better reflected in the bluntly mercantile names of some of the British organizations soon holding concessions for these vast new territories: the British South Africa Company, the Royal Niger Company, and the Imperial British East Africa Company.[10]

Bar the odd change of ownership rights—most notably the

Versailles Conference following the First World War, which saw Germany's dominions casually shared out between the victors—African statehood remained relatively settled for several decades after the big bang of its creation. National boundaries were useful for defining which colonial power got to exploit and rule what realm. But they remained an irrelevance for many Africans, who owed no loyalty to these foreign administrators and their randomly drawn borders, unless they were unlucky enough to find themselves pressed into labor for some commercial or military venture.

Some countries received an influx of foreign bureaucrats, missionaries, and businessmen eager to experience life overseas or simply live in servant-studded sunshine. Others were ruled by proxy through local leaders, sometimes exacerbating long-standing resentments between different ethnic groups (a harvest Rwanda was to reap decades later). Overall, Africa did not yield the riches Europe's powers had hoped, certainly in comparison to their Indian and Far Eastern colonies. As such their occupation of the continent remained a little halfhearted. While there were certainly heated arguments over ownership rights, and even battles fought on African land as part of the First World War, little effort was put into developing the countries and building institutions and infrastructure, and there were only a few, belated attempts to engage Africans in the running of their states.

Then, almost as suddenly as they'd arrived, the European powers left. The late 1950s and early 1960s saw liberation and independence spread like wildfire across the continent, starting with Ghana in 1958, decades before the colonialists had expected it. A generation of African heroes of independence triumphed after years of struggle, reclaiming their land for African rule: Nkrumah in Ghana, Kenyatta in Kenya, Senghor in Senegal, and countless others. Lest we forget, this was one of the most joyous, inspiring periods of modern history: whole peoples seizing their most basic right of being able to rule themselves and celebrating it gloriously. Africa had stolen a march on the West, appropriating its enlightenment ideals of human rights and the entitlement to self-government but dumping the racial filter with which Europe had applied those ideals overseas. For those of us who can only remember the last country to transfer to black African rule, it was the equivalent of South Africa, Mandela et al. in the 1990s writ large across almost the whole continent.

Countless states emerged blinking into a new dawn: fully fledged, self-ruling countries, albeit still in the sizes and shapes designed by the departing powers. It was a hugely optimistic time. Freed from the colonial yoke, blessed with natural resources, Africa was going to develop rapidly and join the rest of the world as a continent of plenty within no more than a couple of decades.

## Moving Kenya's Goalposts

Legend has it that on the momentous day Kenya achieved its independence, December 12, 1963, the country's new flag became momentarily stuck as it was being run up the flagpole. The Union Jack had been brought down for the last time at a large midnight ceremony attended by tens of thousands in Uhuru ("freedom") Park in Nairobi, the drums were rolling, and the spotlights shone on the top of the pole, awaiting the bold fluttering of Kenya's new red, green, and black dawn. At this point, Prince Philip, there to represent the Queen, is reputed to have leaned over to president-elect Jomo Kenyatta and observed, "It's not too late to change your mind."

While this story always tickled the expats, I am not so sure Mzee Kenyatta and his countrymen found it so amusing. Kenya's independence day is now celebrated every year at Nyayo stadium, not far from Uhuru Park. Soon after I had moved to Nairobi in 1998 and started playing for the British High Commission's soccer team, a game was arranged at Nyayo with a team of MPs from Kenya's parliament. Playing in a stadium was a dream for an amateur soccer player more used to rusted goalposts in scruffy West London parks. For the MPs, however, it appeared to be an opportunity to avenge Prince Philip's effrontery thirty-five years before, not to mention preceding decades of colonial subjugation.

By halftime the High Commission team was winning 2–0, a testimony to our advantage in relative youth and what looked like some of the MPs' greater skill at lunching. It was thus against expectations when the second period produced a complete turnaround: the ultimate game of two halves. Each time we attacked it seemed as though the referee would immediately blow for a free kick, and the game ended up being conducted entirely at our end. Playing as goalkeeper, on one occasion I caught the ball and was promptly steamrollered by a politician carrying considerably more gravity, not to mention gravitas, than I will ever manage to accumulate. Penalty to Kenya, obviously.

The game, remarkably good-natured despite its unconventionality, ended 2–2, and honor was shared along with a few beers. I could well understand the MPs' desire, in this small way, to even the score with the former colonial power. But the really interesting thing for me was realizing that probably none of the MPs had asked the referee to "adapt" his neutrality at the halftime break. The official would have decided for himself that the impending outcome was unacceptable. Thus came to pass the least important possible instance of corruption in Kenya's history, a problem that sadly has produced far more serious results in the country.

## At Work with a Hangover

Before you buy anything, it's always a good idea to read the small print. Beneath the headlines, the detail of Africa's circumstances at independence wasn't so good . . . In fact, it was pretty awful.

Africa was certainly freer, but that didn't mean material improvement was going to be easy. Fresh from the success of independence, Africa's new leaders faced a stunning set of challenges. Three stood out above the others.

First, the entire continent remained desperately poor and grossly ill-equipped to thrive as a bunch of newly independent nation states. Few of the colonial powers had done much to educate their subjects in the running of the territories they had claimed. In Marie's country of the Congo, that vast million square miles of land in the middle of Africa, there were thought to be only sixteen people at independence who'd completed university degrees. In Burundi the number was said to be two. Most Africans hadn't received any school-based education at all.

There was little transport infrastructure to connect different regions and peoples in the same country, not least because what roads and railways there were had been designed to deliver raw materials to the coast for export rather than enable people to get together. Entire constitutions were created in an instant, sometimes copied word for word from other countries. State institutions, modeled on idiosyncratically European systems, were handed over in a job lot, with vacancy signs hanging over every senior post. In former British colonies, African judges dispensed sentences wearing eighteenth-century-style London periwigs. In French ones, communications between African civil servants were written in the highly formalized legalese of old-fashioned Parisian government. The surrealism of Europe's arrogance in trying to rule Africa in the first place was outdone only by the inevitable culture clash of the legacy it left behind.

Second among Africa's standout challenges was the lack of a sense of national identity in most countries, to help bind them to face the complex trials ahead. Only three countries in sub-Saharan Africa were blessed with ethnic uniformity: Somalia, Lesotho, and Swaziland.[11] The rest were mostly arbitrary collections of different groups, sometimes traditional rivals, most of whom would never have asked to coexist in the same state. Now they needed to help rule over each other. Inevitably, some groups thrived and others suffered.

Kenya was as good a case as any. There the Kikuyu, Lucas and Nancy's tribe, were in the happy position of being able to dominate proceedings at first as the largest group and the lead protagonists of the independence struggle. The Masai, on the other hand, were split down the middle, one side in Kenya, the rest in Tanzania, a minority in both. The one common experience of all Kenya's groups—rule by the British from the city of Nairobi they'd built at a convenient railhead only a few decades before—disappeared when the Union Jack was lowered for the last time. Despite the good intentions of many involved, was it realistic to expect all these groups to come together seamlessly in this invented city and work for a common, "national" interest?

Nigeria, meanwhile, made Kenya look like child's play. This enormous country, created in the 1890s by the ambitious wheeling-and-dealing British head of the Niger Company, Sir George Goldie, was home to a myriad of tribes speaking up to two hundred different languages: hardly an ideal recipe for stable, consensus rule. The reality was that too many of Africa's new independent states were nations in name only.

It wasn't just that people wanted power for its own sake. Africa's first two great problems, poverty and lack of national identity, were exacerbated by its third: the benefits of office were massively disproportionate to the countries' overall wealth. This is perhaps one of colonialism's most damaging and overlooked legacies, sketched out by the Polish journalist Ryszard Kapuscinski in his brilliant book *The Shadow of the Sun*. In order to tempt minor officials from Bristol, Bruges, or Bordeaux to work in the colonies, regal qualities of life had been created: large houses, lush gardens, servants, swimming pools, allowances, cars. It was hardly likely that Africa's new rulers, inheriting these privileges overnight, were going to renounce them, not when a life in poverty was fragile, not when it gave an opportunity to provide for your family, to give something back to your own community, to secure your position in power in uncertain new times through the use of patronage.[12]

What happened next in many countries should therefore not have been much of a surprise. While many thousands of new politicians and public servants across the continent were inspired by their new responsibilities to build a fresh future, for thousands of others the brief celebrations of independence were soon superseded by more practical questions of securing their own status. People's loyalty to a state that had done little or nothing for them to date was too often overtaken by attempts to get the best deals for traditional allegiances of family and tribe. In many countries, a struggle for power and a culture of corruption took root.

## Brown Roots, Green Shoots—The 1960s and 1970s

Desperate poverty, lack of national identity, hugely disproportionate rewards of office . . . not exactly a great foundation on which to build a brave new future. Plunged headlong into a global economy on a competitive basis just as Southeast Asia was beginning to thrive, Africa lacked a workforce educated and skilled to compete, let alone the contacts and guaranteed custom of colonial powers. Freed from foreign rule, it was also

cut off from the capacity to control access to the rich markets it
needed to reach, or to influence international prices for the few
exports on which so much now depended—exports that were
attractive to the West but not essential enough to give Africa a
strong voice at the negotiating table. Against this fragile background, the first couple of decades for many countries should
really be viewed as a relative success, though falling well short
of optimism's expectations. Income per person in Africa grew—
by an average of 1.2 percent a year in real terms in the 1960s
and 0.8 percent in the 1970s.[13] Many countries remained
largely stable. Education became a realistic aspiration for
millions.

The story varied, of course, depending on where you were.
Some countries were beset by military coups: Africa experienced
forty in the 1960s, 1970s, and 1980s, along with twelve civil
wars. Others had a more sedate existence. Yet even where stability reigned, the challenges were enormous. One of Africa's most
lasting problems is the simple one of capacity. Not only were the
administrative systems inherited by the continent's new powers
often alien, but where were the qualified staff to run national
health systems supposed to come from, let alone the money to
pay them? What about all the new teachers for the schools, the
accountants and auditors to ensure transparency of systems, the
lawyers for the courts, or the journalists to monitor the politicians and keep the public informed? The abuse of power is so
much easier with a population that has not had access to much
education and where no tradition of independent media or questioning leaders has been established.

While Africa struggled to make a success of its future, the
international community hardly covered itself in glory. The
enthusiasm of cold war powers for compliant support for their

cause saw them provide assistance to a number of dubious African rulers, which was often as inept as it was inapt. The Soviet bloc, short on cash, handed out arms shipments to favored leaders across the continent, even though most were communist only to the extent of quotes crafted for Kremlin consumption. Conflict boomed. Almost as inappropriately, the West courted its own set of shady allies with large loans that bought immediate loyalty but left rising debts and nourished corruption. Western companies were happy to make deals to exploit the continent's raw materials even if they were signed by evidently crooked leaders with no intention of sharing the rewards with their countrymen. In most Western countries, you could even get tax breaks on the cost of bribes to win contracts in the first place.

By the 1980s, President Mobutu Sese Seko of Zaire, the boxing fan who spent $15 million staging the 1974 Ali vs. Foreman "Rumble in the Jungle," was thought to be the fifth richest man in the world thanks to his own knockout combination: the rape of his country's resources and the reliable flow of poorly monitored external loans (and other aid: by the late 1970s the United States was splurging nearly half its aid budget for sub-Saharan Africa on Zaire). Mobutu built monuments and personal bank accounts but little else, while the West, especially the U.S., found itself in the absurd position of encouraging ever more loans for fear that Mobutu's previous failure to use them responsibly left Zaire increasingly fertile ground for a socialist backlash. The irony was only deepened by the fact that Patrice Lumumba, the leader who probably had the best chance of leading his country smoothly through independence, had been murdered back in the 1960s in a crime widely thought to have been carried out by Belgian agents with CIA support for fear he might not prove sympathetic enough in the fight against Marxism.*

Zaire may have been one of the more extreme examples of corruption and ill-advised Western efforts, but it was these kinds of loans that did so much to give aid a bad name and make Western taxpayers skeptical their money would ever be well used. The ongoing civil war that has beset Mobutu's country (now known as D.R. Congo) since his eventual departure and death in 1997 is a reminder of what can happen when people receive no benefit from their citizenship of a state for too long: they are much more likely to fight to get their own hands on the few assets left lying around.

## Mobutu's Chef and the Perfect Omelet

Visiting an American aid worker friend of mine in Kinshasa in 2004, I was delighted to discover that one of Mobutu's former chefs now worked at her house. Monsieur Roger is a dignified man in his fifties, with a troublesome hip and a polite, professional manner. In a country as poor as D.R. Congo has always been, the ultimate desire is a stable paid job. Notwithstanding the evils enacted on the rest of the country at the time, M. Roger's stints with the president were his personal golden years, during which time, he told me, he was even given a car.

The villa in which he now cooks is a testament to the brief period in the 1970s during which Mobutu tried to build the façade of an African renaissance (even a man as intelligent as Muhammad Ali fell for it,

---

* *Mobutu's country always had pronounced potential for tragedy, created as it was by another megalomaniac, King Leopold of Belgium, in the 1890s. Leopold traded on the sympathy of European and American antislave campaigners to persuade Europe's more established powers to let him "bring civilization" to the million square miles of territory left over in the middle of Africa once they'd claimed all the coastal regions; surely the most unwieldy invented state of all. Leopold then pillaged the country of ivory and rubber by the systematic use of slavery long after other powers had banned it. Half the population is estimated to have died as a result.*

apparently commenting, "Zaire's gotta be great. I never seen so many Mercedes").[14] It's a mildly decaying building of wonderful kitsch, with a sweeping staircase rising from the middle of the living room, a curved swimming pool and tropical trees outside, complemented by an eccentric parrot that wanders flightlessly around and tries to eat your feet while you type.

On most of the days during my visit, my friend and her roommates, also aid workers, would come home from their offices for lunch and we'd eat together. But one Thursday it was to be just me, and around noon M. Roger floated unobtrusively over to ask what I'd like him to cook. He rejected out of hand the suggestion that I fix something for myself, so I tried to think of something simple and settled on eggs. Twenty minutes later, an extraordinary confection arrived, at once the most architecturally spectacular dish I'd ever seen—fluted tomato skins and a Picassoesque arrangement of vegetables—and by far the most delicious omelet I'd ever tasted.

It was a breakthrough moment for me in understanding the temptations of office and corruption. I'd never really been into black limos. And Mobutu's choice of official mistress, plumping for the chubby identical twin sister of his wife in a statement of power-crazed weirdness, left me uninspired. But if an omelet could taste like this, imagine what a three-course meal would be like . . .

## Decayed Decade—The 1980s

Despite many countries' promising early progress, including the likes of Kenya and Côte d'Ivoire, nowhere in the 1960s and 1970s had managed to make a decisive break from poverty. But it was the 1980s when the remains of post-independence optimism dissipated entirely. At a time when most of the rest of the world grew, income per person declined by 1.2 percent a year in Africa. Civil wars dragged on, corruption festered. Far too many flawed leaders entrenched themselves in power. Appalling famine raged in Ethiopia.

Western involvement wasn't improving much either. There were some welcome new moves in Europe to allow former colonies privileged access to their markets for certain produce. But while the most spurious and corruptible loans of the cold war era thankfully began to diminish (though Mobutu was spooned money right through to the 1990s), the predicaments of Africa's highly stressed societies were worsened instead by a new ideological stringency. The good news was that the West realized it needed to pay much more attention to what its loans and grants were being used for. The bad news was that the "structural adjustment" policies it now insisted borrowers follow were overly prescriptive and frequently ill judged.

Optimistic about the power of markets to provide solutions for populations too poor for the market to have any interest in them, structural adjustment policies generally included rigid diets of privatization and severe cuts to essential services like health and education in order to balance budgets. While the desire to get the books in order was understandable, in business terms this was the equivalent of selling off many of your best assets at the same time as cutting spending on training and research and development and guaranteeing a large increase in sick days taken by your staff. Many economies declined further, debts continued to build, and budgets still weren't balanced.

What was the effect of these difficult years on Africa's great nation-building challenge? Unsurprisingly, faith in governments and the nation-state failed to grow in many places as people gained little from their still-new capitals, while tales of pocket-lining politicians gave even the good guys a bad name. The temptation to vote for your local big man regardless of his policies or honesty—who at least promised your town a tangible new road or school or paid you directly for your vote—grew bigger than ever, compounding the calamity of corruption. The conundrum of state employees in poor countries (pay them reasonably to reduce incentives for corruption and to hell with the budget; or pay what you can afford and increase the corruption) took another turn around the vicious circle.

Back in the West, taxpayers grew ever more cynical about their aid money achieving anything, seeing little evidence of success, hearing too many stories about overflowing banquets for the elite and ever-emptier bowls for the masses. The shame was that, while no one except Africa's elites could shoulder the blame for misrule and corruption, there was no need for so much aid to be so badly designed. Africa was stagnating, and the Western taxpayer was being shortchanged too.

The problems continued into the 1990s, as HIV/AIDS in particular started to exact its terrible toll. Despite the difficulties of the 1960s, 1970s, and 1980s, overall human development over that period—measured by the UN as a combination of income, life expectancy, and literacy—had actually grown. In the AIDS-afflicted 1990s it fell in twenty-one countries.[15] By the turn of the millennium, income per person was fully 10 percent lower than in 1980[16] and had actually returned to its 1960 levels— before most of an impoverished continent had even embarked on its supposedly brave new future, and when couples like Lucas and Nancy had started out with such hope. At a time of global plenty, Africa was the only region of the world getting poorer.

## A Theory of Relativity

This history sounds pretty depressing. And of course it is: continuing poverty means bad health and early death for millions, hundreds of thousands of mothers dying in childbirth, millions of toddlers never reaching their fifth birthday, constant hunger and lack of opportunity, the torture of never being able to provide for all your family's needs.

Yet perhaps we're simply starting off from the wrong place. When the outside world looks at Africa, the question always seems to be: why are things always going wrong there? We might do as well to ask why things haven't actually been worse.

With hindsight, the expectations of both Africans and the rest of the world at independence were hopelessly hopeful. Democracy, capitalism, and the nation-state had emerged hand in hand over centuries in America and Europe, carefully balancing and complementing each other; Africa was expected to adapt to these radical social changes overnight. Even though it had far longer to adjust and develop, Europe had suffered numerous upheavals, revolutions, coups, and conflicts—including the small matter of two world wars, the east–west partition of the entire continent over several decades, and the persistently periodic fighting in the Balkans—in the twentieth century alone; yet Africa was somehow going to progress peacefully. The United States had experienced serious trouble with corruption during the early decades of its own independence (not to mention a full-blown civil war sometime later); Africa was supposed to run cleanly and smoothly from the word go.

None of this was realistic. Were most African states ever really viable in the first place, in terms of being able to deliver stability and security, and meeting all the basic needs of their people? They had the same, tiny budgets to spend as had the colonial powers, sometimes even less, only now they were required to meet the vastly expanded expectations of their people, some-thing the hastily departing colonialists had never attempted. Why expect people to hold faith with alien systems and structures of government when they received little or no benefit from them? Why show patriotic loyalty to a concept of nationhood imposed on you? More pragmatically, why presume that a country will blossom from trade when the traditional colonial customers have withdrawn the guarantee of their business, when there is minimal transport infrastructure, and when the costs of getting produce to market, whether local, national, or international, have long been considerably higher than in Asia and elsewhere?[17]

In some ways it is easy to comprehend much of post-independence Africa as a set of states mostly conjured out of nothing in an extremely short space of time that have not had the economic means to fulfill all the duties required of them. If African countries were businesses, nearly all of them would have gone bust, no matter who the CEOs. But of course countries don't go bust: people just struggle even more, debts just keep rising. It's a giant version of the poverty trap faced by Marie and Jean Baptiste, with whole countries unable to meet their needs and thus being unable to stimulate growth.

There are some interesting debates about why Africa has remained so poor and why much of Asia has done so much better over the last forty years, though there is little consensus. It's evident that the greatest day-to-day causes are Africa's own failings: misrule, corruption, and instability. But it's not enough to stop there: we must ask why Africa has been so susceptible to these problems. Everyone has their own ideas. The economist and special adviser to then–UN secretary-general Kofi Annan, Jeffrey Sachs, argues that Africa suffers from a uniquely multifaceted poverty trap, including the endemic diseases of malaria and AIDS, difficult geography, environmental degradation, climatic vulnerability, and more. Others offer various other explanations, including cultural and family structures, lack of water sources, minimal urbanization, the absence of high-yielding crop strains, and so on.

I would add only that most Asian countries had histories of nation-statehood and central government in one form or another before colonization, so that when independence came there was greater political stability. Many Asian countries— including India, for example—were also left better administrative structures to rule on a national basis. In comparison to Africa's three standout problems at independence—poverty, lack of national identity, and grossly disproportionate rewards of office—an argument can be advanced that the latter two were not as bad in Asian countries, most of which in any case have had longer to find their feet. And, of course, once a few countries started to make progress, especially in Southeast Asia, they tended to help pull up their neighbors. Africa has never achieved that critical momentum.

## Present Improvement?

In many ways, it doesn't really matter what the reasons are for Africa's failure compared to Asia's success. All regions of the world are vastly different, not to mention the countries within them. Why did America progress when it did, Europe when it did; why did South America's progress stall for so long? The bottom line remains that Africa has never even taken off. Yet it's not all bad news. The last few years have seen something of an upturn in many places. Average annual growth was around 6 percent between 2004 and 2007,[18] partly on the back of increased global commodity prices. There are thirty democratic heads of state where thirty years ago there were three.[19] Several countries have been on an upward path for many years: Uganda, scene of gruesome dictatorships under Milton Obote and Idi Amin until the mid-1980s, reduced the proportion of its people living in absolute poverty from 56 percent to 38 percent between 1992 and 2002, lifting millions of people out of the worst of circumstances.[20] Mozambique has been equally impressive, against the backdrop of an appalling history of civil war. Botswana, AIDS levels aside, has long been a bright beacon of hope, able to take advantage of its diamond-studded natural resources where others have seemed to become all the poorer for their riches.

The key question is whether this is the start of a better trend or simply a cyclical reaction to a period of decline. A significant number of countries seem to be pointing to a new way ahead, primarily by mastering their own problems but also by harnessing more useful support from the West. Only a few can yet boast a solid record of consistent achievement, but the determination is clearly stronger.

Nothing can make you more optimistic about Africa in the new millennium than reading about the horrors of the 1970s and 1980s. The declining number of wars, coups, and dictatorships suggests a growing stability, borne of countries and people becoming more used to the states bequeathed them, making them their own and demanding more of them. It also reflects the extinguished desire of cold war powers to shore up unpopular regimes in return for continued loyalty. If AIDS can be controlled, if trade can be increased, if aid can be harnessed effectively, perhaps Africa is beginning to have a real chance to move forward . . .

These are big ifs. As Africa's recent history shows, it is African actions that do most to determine Africa's prospects. Only they can change the reality on the ground. But as that history also shows, whatever the West does—whatever is done with your money—has an impact, from cold war loans to trade policies. The simple reality is that since Africa is very poor, what the rich West does matters.

The big question is whether we are set to fan oxygen onto the sparks of an African renaissance, thirty years after Mobutu first staked a claim for it, or supply a wet blanket. But first we need to know whether corruption, as many people claim, is so bad in Africa that there's nothing anyone can do to help anyway.

# CHAPTER 3
# PRESIDENT FOR A DAY

The abiding image most of us have of Africa and its poverty is that the biggest problem of all is corruption. Yet the trouble with understanding corruption is that it is both cause and symptom: cause of inefficient and ineffective government, inflated prices, wasted aid; symptom of weakly developed institutions, low salaries, fragile existences.

Corruption can't be ended by Africans or outsiders overnight. But change needs to come from the top. What we can ask is, would things be a whole lot better if Africa had proper economic and political reform? To test this, we need an idea of the scope of challenges facing African countries, and a leader of absolutely unimpeachable integrity to try and meet them: someone with intentions as pure as the snow on Mount Kilimanjaro rather than as dark as the tinted window of a Mercedes limo.

So, Mr. or Mrs. President, do you feel ready to rule?

Welcome to the Republic of Uzima, a fictional state based on the average conditions and statistics of all forty-seven countries in sub-Saharan Africa, excluding South Africa (*uzima* means "reality" in Swahili).[21] The swearing-in ceremony is over, and you've made a short speech vowing to focus relentlessly on improving day-to-day life for all Uzima's people. The jaded few thousand citizens in front of you have no more faith in these promises at present than in those of your predecessors, but you are determined to prove them wrong.

Now that you've assumed control, you need to be briefed on what you're in charge of. So you call all your ministers and senior officials to a meeting at State House, and, one by one, you watch them arrive in their cars, looking nervous about what their new leader may have in store. With everyone in place, your prime minister commences with an overview.

## Basics

Uzima has 15,380,026 citizens on a landmass of 189,330 square miles (roughly the same size as Spain, or a bit larger than California). Average life expectancy is forty-seven, and the population is growing at around 2.2 percent a year,[22] which means an extra person for you to rule over every two minutes or so. Only a small proportion of your people have salaried jobs, denying most the security of a regular income. Two-thirds live in rural areas, mainly farming small plots a bit smaller than Lucas and Nancy's. But the increasing population means increasing pressure on the land, so more and more people are moving to the cities, despite the fact that three-quarters of all city dwellers live in slums and unemployment there fluctuates between 15 and 35 percent.

Gross national income (similar to gross domestic product) in Uzima is the local currency equivalent of $8.36 billion a year, working out at around $540 per person in 2006 (these figures have been boosted by the recently weakening dollar: in constant 2000 prices, income is only around $390 per head). The period from 1990 to 2002 saw average growth of 0.02 percent,[23] but this was far outstripped by the increase in population, resulting in overall decline. The last few years have been better, however, seeing growth of around 6 percent a year from 2004 to 2007 (largely thanks to improved international prices for the few commodities Uzima exports), even if this only translated into real growth per person of just under 4 percent a year.[24]

Not yet an expert in all these economic facts and figures, you ask what the numbers mean in real terms for the Uziman people and day-to-day life. The prime minister replies that, out of a population of 15 million, just under 7 million live below the internationally agreed measure of absolute poverty. These are the extreme poor, the ones who can't afford simple drugs or school fees, who struggle through fragile lives, who lack access to clean water, who go persistently hungry, who die young: people like Marie and Jean Baptiste in Congo, or Lucas and Nancy's children living in Nairobi, the ones you are most determined to help. They have been mired in poverty for generations, despite the brief hopes brought by independence.

Those real growth rates of 4 percent in recent years point to some optimism that progress can be made. But they also mark the scale of the challenge: under your stewardship, Uzima needs to do even better than this—easily its best stretch for decades—and keep doing it every year, if you are to halve the proportion of Uzimans living in extreme poverty by 2015.

## The Millennium Development Goals

In the late 1990s, thirty-odd years into African independence and after decades of aid agencies working away at their various agendas, someone had the bright idea of agreeing upon some universal goals of what poor countries and the international aid community were actually trying to achieve. Though it seems an obvious plan in retrospect (and it says a lot about how poorly coordinated efforts were before), it proved radical and has been significant in getting all the different players to work together better. It has also enabled economists for the first time to start calculating what it would cost on a global basis to start reducing poverty, as seen later in this chapter.

The MDGs, as they are often known, were formally subscribed to by Western and poor country governments alike at the UN Millennium Summit in September 2000, providing a useful guide to the sort of progress Uzima needs to be making. They represent a powerful dream—if they can be implemented. The world's leaders pledged to achieve the following by 2015:

- Reduce by half the proportion of people living on less than a dollar a day and those who suffer from hunger.
- Ensure that all boys and girls complete a full course of primary schooling.
- Eliminate gender disparity in primary and secondary education (at the moment many more boys attend school globally than girls).
- Reduce by two-thirds the number of children who die before their fifth birthday.
- Reduce by three-quarters the number of women who die in childbirth.
- Halt and begin to reverse the spread of HIV/AIDS, malaria, and other killer diseases.
- Ensure environmental stability, including halving the proportion of people without access to safe drinking water.

## An Unhealthy Situation

The prime minister's scene-setter has proved a little intimidating. Yet you are determined that, with real effort and the right intentions, progress can be made. In any case, it's not just economic growth that will defeat poverty in Uzima. Simple improvements in health would make a big difference too. So you turn to your health minister and ask for a checkup on the nation's well-being.

She starts abruptly by telling you that Uzima's biggest killers are AIDS (about 21 percent of all deaths), lower respiratory infections (flu and the like—about 10 percent), malaria (9 percent), and diarrhea diseases (7 percent).

- AIDS is an epidemic: more than half a million Uzimans have the disease; 131 die from it every day, while another 177 contract it, 29 of whom are babies. Still only a fairly small proportion receive antiretroviral drugs, which, among other things, are excellent at preventing mother-to-child transmission.

- AIDS has a huge impact on Uzima's productivity, as it hits those of working age worst (though it's not as bad as in Malawi, where it's rumored AIDS has killed teachers faster than new ones could be trained,[25] or Botswana, where it was reported in 2002 that only attendance at funerals came close to the illness itself as a cause of teacher absenteeism);[26] 250,000 Uziman children have lost one or both of their parents to the disease.

- Uzima's mothers have five children, on average; this makes them rather brave, since they have a one-in-thirteen chance of dying in pregnancy or childbirth. Part of the reason for this high mortality rate is that only two of the births of those five children will be attended by a qualified health worker. Presuming the mother does survive, however, it's very likely one of her children won't: nearly one in five dies from preventable diseases before family and friends get together for a fifth birthday party.

- Uzima loses 20,833 children to malaria every year (two a minute for Africa as a whole), even though this figure could be slashed if everyone had cheap bed nets and simple treatment drugs.

- Nothing reveals the absurdity of your people's poverty more than the fact that 7 percent of all deaths in Uzima are caused by simple diarrhea diseases. These diseases result from a lack of clean water, and most deaths could be prevented with simple treatment and essential drugs. As your minister observes, the irony is that while more than half your people lack access to such drugs, they need them much more frequently than their counterparts in rich Western countries because they get ill much more often.

- Then again, it's not all about access to drugs: 34 percent of the population is simply undernourished, and hunger contributes to more deaths than AIDS, malaria, and TB combined.

You haven't been briefed on the budget situation yet, but you're outraged to discover that Uzima's current annual health expenditure—combining both government and people's personal spending—is only $20 a head, compared to around $7,000 in the United States.[27] Although $20 may mean Uzima is five or six times a bigger spender on health than Ethiopia, you know that to have a hope of meeting internationally agreed health goals by 2015, you will need to triple the number of health staff, vastly expand the provision of clinics, and make far more drugs available. You ask the finance minister to make a note: it's obvious we are going to have to do far more on health.

## Yearning to Learn

Next up is the education minister, himself a former teacher. You tell him you are particularly committed to improving Uzima's education. Quite apart from it being a basic right all your citizens should be entitled to, it is probably just as significant as health in determining Uzima's prospects. Given that an astonishing 44 percent of the population is younger than fifteen years old, perhaps it's even more important. Not only does future growth depend on a competitive workforce, but the more education a nation has, the better its health becomes and the fewer children each mother conceives. Even AIDS rates tend to fall.

- There's quite a bit of good news here. The current adult literacy rate is 65 percent, up from around 38 percent in 1980. Enrollment in primary school is on the rise. Better still, there's certainly no problem with a lack of enthusiasm among pupils or parents for school: all kids want to go and almost all parents want their children to be there.

- Enrolling is one thing, staying and learning another. Fewer than half of those enrolling in primary school complete their years there, let alone go on to secondary school or college. Too many families can't afford the fees or—where the fees are paid—the lunches, uniforms, or books. That's why more than one million primary school–aged Uziman children don't currently go to school at all. Indeed, 28 percent of children aged between ten and fourteen are actually part of your country's workforce.

- The education minister knows you want to make primary education free for all, but he warns you it will be an impossible stretch to find the money within his current budget. While primary education is vital, you also need to get a good number of children through secondary school and on to colleges if Uzima is to be better able to compete internationally. It's especially important to carve out university slots at home, because many students who can afford to go abroad to study and never return. Yet each slot in a university costs around thirty times that of a primary school slot, and even secondary school is considerably more expensive.

*

If you are going to make Uzima more competitive, it's obvious you need a massive ramping up of expenditure here too: thousands of new schools, tens of thousands of new teachers, funding for maintenance budgets, lunches to attract the poorest children into attending, the lot. Whatever the financial implications, it is clear that every child needs to start primary school, and finish it, and a significant proportion must go on to secondary and college education. You ask your finance minister to make another note: you are going to have to at least double your spending on education too, probably more.

## Farm-to-Factory Frustration

It's not all about education and health, of course. Your ministers and officials move dutifully on to agriculture, which provides most Uzimans' employment, half the country's exports, and one-third of gross national income.

- Much of your country's land is overstressed, its soil stripped of nutrients. Deforestation is widespread and desertification increasing—a trend likely to accelerate rapidly if global warming continues.
- Only 3.8 percent of the land is irrigated, a major problem in Uzima's warm climate with unreliable rainfall.
- Subsidizing fertilizer would help, as it would radically improve crop yields; at present the vast majority of farmers can't afford it, partly because it costs more in Uzima than in any other global region.

Meanwhile, Uzima's infrastructure is in a shocking state of disrepair, and the rehabilitation needs are enormous.

- Only 13 percent of Uzima's roads are paved, and the vast majority of rural roads are in a terrible condition. This isn't just about giving your citizens a faster, less bumpy ride: Uzima's local and national transport costs are around twice as high as those of the average Asian country, hitting hard at your citizens' ability to buy cheap produce and your country's ability to export competitively.

- Business leaders are rightly pressing you to invest in much more electricity generation so firms can have a regular, reliable supply and increase productive hours, not to mention that this would enable children to study at home at night.

- Investment is urgently needed in ports, telecommunications, and new information technologies through which the rest of the world now is operating.

- There's also the need to improve the availability of clean water and sanitation. Forty-two percent of your public lacks access to "improved" (reasonably clean) water sources, and 47 percent, to improved sanitation, resulting in the spread of many diseases.

The briefing goes on . . . various ministers stand up for what feels like hours at a time, outlining defense demands, police, the revenue service, customs, diplomatic posts overseas to try and attract more support, the civil service, and so on. Finally the presentations draw to a close and you break for a modest cup of instant coffee rather than the traditional buffet (a result of expense cuts you have already instituted, a move that seems to have cost you quite a lot of goodwill). Only the finance minister remains to speak, to set out the budget with which the Uziman government has to meet these challenges.

## Political Interruption

It's still the coffee break, and the finance minister is huddled in the corner with his officials, putting together the last points of his presentation. So you take the opportunity for a chat with your political adviser, that friendly stereotype of a large, middle-aged, and no-nonsense African lady we will call Mama Ekevu (*ekevu* means "sensible" in Swahili), a woman you know you can trust. You want advice on some of the reforms you intend to implement. What she tells you is at least as important to Uzima's future—and to yours—as anything the finance minister will have to disclose.

Although you have yet to hear the financial figures, you confide in Mama Ekevu that you expect to make big cuts in the less poverty-related parts of the budget. This will enable you to channel more money into education, health, and so on. Defense will be your first target. After all, who can afford an army when schools and clinics are in such desperate need?

Mama Ekevu raises an eyebrow and counsels you to be careful. Not only is Uzima's military spending modest by international standards, contrary to most people's perceptions, at around 1.9 percent of GDP—compared with 3.2 percent for Europe and Central Asia, 3.9 percent for the United States, and 6.2 percent for North Africa and the Middle East[28]—but there is a need to keep a reasonably strong army because of the risk of trouble from the four countries sharing your borders. In the years since independence those countries have experienced several wars and coups.

Uzima itself has also been at war fairly recently, one of twenty-eight in Africa between 1980 and 2001. And there has been at least one coup since independence, so you may need the army to help maintain stability at home, let alone abroad.

Incidentally, Mama Ekevu observes, the coup that did take place was carried out by army officers, which suggests an extra reason to keep the military on board.

The risk of instability on Uzima's borders raises another problem that doesn't appear in the official presentations. On top of all your own people, Uzima is currently playing host to nearly 100,000 asylum seekers, refugees, and internally displaced people. Mama Ekevu says she always smiles when she hears angry debates in Western parliaments about their burden of immigration, when it's the world's poor countries, like Uzima—those who can least afford to help others—who have the weightiest load to bear. Africa as a whole plays host to more refugees, asylum seekers, and internally displaced people than does Europe.[29]

The greatest threat to your great plans, however, is a more mundane one of political survival. After all, you're not going to achieve much if you can't stay in power. Much of the public is skeptical about your promises and whether you have the entire country's interests at heart, rather than just those of your own tribe or the international community. You can't really blame them. Although Uzima is now democratic, as are most African countries, your people experienced years of autocratic rule and rigged elections. Because previous national leaders have delivered them little, many will still vote for whichever local politician promises them the most tangible benefits.

There's another constituency of vitally important people you also need to keep sweet: those around you. You may want to bring in a new, impartial team of ministers, but you must be careful about who you throw out. They all have power bases and access to state resources, which they could abuse fairly easily if they wish. You must pick a new government based not just on

merit but also on ensuring a geographical mix and the appease-
ment of figures who might cause trouble from outside. And you
can't clamp down too quickly on the lifestyles of MPs and ministers you think live too luxuriously. They may turn around and
exact revenge.

Finally, in whatever plans you instigate, Mama Ekevu says you
must be careful how you treat the public service, from civil
servants to the police, nurses, and teachers. There is no chance
you will be able to apply radical reforms or cost savings overnight.
Although many public-sector jobs are sought after because of
their reliability (not that the government always manages to pay
nurses and teachers on time), actual salaries for junior positions
are often very low. Many officials struggle as much as other
Uzimans to support their families and make ends meet. The low
salaries make it difficult to stamp out corruption. But neither has
anyone yet found the resources to pay them more.

## Dressing to Meet a Real Minister of Finance

On my first day in Rwanda as head of the British aid office, having come
straight from an overnight flight, I only had time to drop my bags at my
"Eye of the Tiger"–soundtracked hotel before being taken to a meeting at
the Ministry of Finance. On one side of the table sat the minister himself,
accompanied by a number of his officials, and cramped around the other
were teams from IMF and World Bank headquarters in Washington. The
topic of the meeting was Rwanda's proposed annual budget and how
realistic the visitors thought it was—in particular, whether it created too
high a deficit. The UK had been invited because it was a significant
contributor to the budget. With discussion already under way, I squeezed
my way into a chair at the back.

Dr. Donald Kaberuka, Rwanda's likable and widely respected finance
minister, who was to become my closest interlocutor in the government,
was probably the smartest-dressed person I'd ever seen. As I came to know

him over the next two years, including at some interminable conferences in humid, congested meeting rooms, I don't think I ever saw him with so much as a cuff link out of place. He was a sort of African economist James Bond. Where 007 could come out of from a ten-minute fistfight in an alligator-infested swamp needing only to flick a leaf from a perfectly tailored lapel, Dr. Kaberuka would emerge coolly from stuffy, daylong meetings appearing as fresh as he had in the morning, while his officials and foreign diplomats staggered out behind, all of us dripping with sweat and unbuttoning shirts more creased than an IMF official's brow.

Though I didn't fully realize it at the time, this particular meeting had begun to reveal some of the persistent contradictions African governments can find themselves in with the international community. On the one hand, donors like the World Bank and the UK were pressing the Rwandans to make serious, funded plans capable of reducing poverty. On the other, organizations such as the IMF were demanding a balanced budget.

None of this worried me too much on my first day. I was still wearing the rumpled shirt and trousers in which I'd traveled from London; my main objectives for the meeting were not to make a bad first impression, try and pick up the key issues, and otherwise keep a low profile by stifling any yawns after my sleepless night. I thought I'd succeeded until, back at the office after the meeting, I received a discreet call from a senior Finance Ministry official who mentioned how highly the minister regarded personal presentation. My unsuitably unsuited appearance had made exactly the wrong kind of impact.

Back in the hotel that night, I opened the window and rang down for an ironing board. In from a warm night came several friendly mosquitoes and the hotel band's latest dubious effort. My first personal contribution to Rwanda's economy comprised a quick trip to the hotel shop for insect repellent, earplugs, and a couple of new ties. Dr. Kaberuka, meanwhile, has gone on to become president of the African Development Bank, the continental counterpart to the World Bank. It is a prestigious role, in which I hope he will be able to play a significant part in improving the quality of aid.

*

Mama Ekevu's counsel has been educative but alarming. It's a relief that the finance minister's presentation, finally about to start, will be the last of the day. Having received a crash course in Uzima's problems and in its political landscape, you're on the edge of your seat as you begin to discover how your government is set financially to respond.

## Bottom Lines

With a gross national income (GNI) of around $8.36 billion and an average African tax-to-GNI ratio of around 28 percent, the government has a basic budget of $2.34 billion. Or around $152 per person. You stare at the finance minister with incredulity: you have to meet the Uziman public's needs in education, health, water, road building and maintenance, agriculture, infrastructure, policing, national defense, customs, revenue collection, foreign representation, environmental protection, and civil service with only $152 per person?

Well, not quite, replies the minister. About $800,000 is spent every day servicing debt—or $290 million a year.[30] This figure would be higher still if Uzima was meeting all its debt obligations, and if some of its debt hadn't already been written off under international initiatives (there are promises of more to come, but it's the poorest African countries that have benefited most so far). The finance minister acknowledges that paying debt may seem harsh given that most of it was built up by previous, unelected regimes in Uzima whom you personally opposed. But there it is: the money still has to be paid back to those who should really have had better judgment than to give loans to such undemocratic regimes in the first place.

So it's actually more like a budget of $2.05 billion, or $133 per person.

How far is this $133 per person going to go? Standing back from Uzima for a moment, the simplest way to answer that is to look at three African countries for which the UN, a couple of years ago, calculated the cost of meeting the Millennium Development Goals on poverty, health, education, and so on.

The three countries the UN Millennium Project looked at were Ghana, Tanzania, and Uganda. They have an average GNI per capita of $400 against Uzima's $540, and are thus nominally poorer. But as a group in recent years they have performed better than average for Africa, and therefore Uzima, in key areas: similar life expectancy, fertility rate, and population growth; better than average economic growth, higher literacy and primary school completion rates, lower under-five mortality. All three have been widely regarded as relatively well-run countries. Most important, all three have been making significantly better progress than average in reducing poverty, and thus provide useful—though of course rough—benchmarks for the kind of investment required, with sound management, for Uzima to make better progress.

What did the UN's research show it would cost to get on track to meet the MDGs in these countries? Health costs would be most expensive, working out to around 7 percent of GNI. If we assume a similar percentage requirement for Uzima, this would amount to $38 per person. The costs of getting all kids into primary school, and other education costs, come in at 4.5 percent of GNI—$24 per person. Already, your precious Uziman budget is down from $133 per person to $71 ($2.05 billion to $1.09 billion overall).

The next biggest demands are investment in roads and energy production, bringing cheaper food to markets so Uzima's people find it easier to meet their families' basic nutrition requirements, and boosting the economy. Roads take up 3.8 percent of GNI, or $21 per person, and energy 3.5 percent, or $19. This leaves you with only $31 left per person in your budget, or $477 million overall.

The other sectors for which the UN Millennium Project projected costs were water supply and sanitation, improving the lives of slum dwellers, preventing hunger, and promoting gender equality by eliminating disparity between boys and girls in education, plus a nominal figure for other areas not yet costed (large infrastructure projects, higher education, national research systems, environmental sustainability). These totaled an additional 6.1 percent of GNI, or $33 per person, leaving you with a deficit of $2 per person, or $31 million.

All this, of course, is before you begin to think about any of the other costs of government: the army, the civil service to run the country, local government, revenue collection, foreign ministry, customs, police, judicial system, and more. To put it in some kind of context, most low-income countries currently spend more on these areas than they do on health, education, and so on.[31]

The implication is horribly clear to you as president of Uzima: even with the best of intentions, there is no way you can reach your goals.

The costs estimated by the UN for Ghana, Uganda, and Tanzania to meet the MDGs, while providing only a rough guide to Uzima's needs, are borne out by research elsewhere. Indeed, the UN figures may be modest. At a World Health Organization summit in 2001, African leaders agreed that the required level of public spending on health was 15 percent of GNI, not the 7 percent suggested above (and America, a much healthier nation, now spends around 17 percent).[32] The government of Ghana's 2002 poverty reduction strategy, much admired by the international community, suggested a funding shortfall for that country of $75 per person per year, on top of existing expenditure.

For what it's worth, Uzima, being representative of the continent as a whole, doesn't have it as bad as half the countries in Africa, Ghana, Tanzania, and Uganda included. Uziman domestic revenues (mainly tax collection) of around 28 percent of GNI are much greater than theirs, meaning you can make a better effort to meet your people's needs. The UN researchers predicted their three test countries would have needed expenditure of around $78 per person in 2006 to be on track to meet the MDGs. Of this they thought those countries' governments were able to provide only around $23. African households themselves were projected to be able to meet around $9 (while most things like schools and health costs have been shown to need to be fully free if they are to be effective and reach the poorest, there are a few areas where charges can be introduced, such as subsidized electricity costs, fertilizer, and so on). This left a shortfall of $46, much more than half the required funds. Worse still, this gap was estimated to grow to $143 by 2015 (costs rise in later years once the systems are in place to absorb more investment: by way of example, it takes a few years until you can recruit and train all the new teachers, nurses, and doctors required, so they don't appear on the payroll right away).

Uzima's shortfall would probably be smaller. Following the UN examples, it would require nearly 25 percent of GNI to meet its MDG needs. On top of that you must meet all the other costs of government, plus debt demands. Yet you only have domestic revenues of 28 percent of GNI. All in all you are likely to be left with a gap of perhaps 10 to 15 percent of GNI, or nearly twice as much again as your existing budget.

All of this, of course, presumes you are managing government more effectively than your predecessors in Uzima—at least as effectively as Ghana, Tanzania, and Uganda, some of Africa's better performers. And it presumes you are achieving economic growth better than Uzima's best recent year, every year.

## Impossible Choices

Your mind goes back to the promises you made at your swearing-in ceremony to the people of Uzima. You now know the scale of the challenge, and the resources with which to try and meet it. What is going to give? In education, do your prioritize the building of more schools to create places for every child, or more teachers to teach them? Do you fund a university to create a more investor-attractive workforce and prevent the brain drain of students who go abroad and never return, or use the money to ensure that all primary-age children have at least one textbook between three of them? Do you make cuts to the military, hoping the neighbors won't cause any trouble and the army itself doesn't become discontented? Improve access to clean water for the rural poor, or sanitation facilities for disease-ridden city slum dwellers? Pave more roads or generate more electricity? Subsidize bed nets to reduce malaria, or concentrate on immunizations for babies?

Just as with Lucas and Nancy in their small house on the edge of the Rift Valley, poverty is about impossible choices. Even with the perfect leader, determined to do only what is best for his or her country, there is no way Uzima can meet its most basic needs.

Half of Africa is worse off than Uzima, half of it better. If you found it difficult, what on earth are the poorest countries supposed to do? Countries like D.R. Congo where Marie lives, Niger, Burundi, Ethiopia?

Just like individuals, countries become caught in poverty traps. As we will later see, bad governments play a major part and there is simply no point bringing new money in through aid if it won't be well spent. But if even the governments with the best rulers can't succeed, there is clearly more to it than just corruption. Unable to make sufficient investment, economies wilt, health stays bad, productivity suffers, families can't save, dissatisfaction festers, faith in government and democracy fails to grow. Meanwhile, those with bad intentions thrive: civil servants take a corrupt cut here and there, police and judicial officials do worse, local leaders entrench their fiefdoms through patronage. Insidious cycle. Vicious circle.

## Reaching Out

How do you, the president, escape the ruthless loop of under-investment and poverty, how do you help people like Lucas, Nancy, Marie, and Jean Baptiste to have a better life? You do all you can to manage your country more effectively, make savings where possible while walking a tightrope of stability, try and get people to buy into the reforms needed, gradually increase investment in certain areas. But it won't be enough to get you out of the trap and meet all the challenges you face.

Somehow you need to find extra money to spend on your people's basic needs and lay the foundation for future growth: you need aid. And somehow you need to boost people's incomes and your government's revenues: you need more trade. Aid and trade. This is where the West comes in.

It's time for you to retire as president and go back to your normal life. Aid and trade really matter. As taxpayers, charity donors, and consumers in the West, it is our money that is at stake. For many Africans, it is their prospects. So what are the rules?

# AID
## GOOD INTENTIONS

# CHAPTER 4
# WHERE DOES YOUR MONEY GO?

A new day in Kinshasa, the riverside city on the western side of Africa. Jean Baptiste careers around his cramped neighborhood with other small children, skillfully guiding a wire metal hoop with a stick up and down the passages between the makeshift houses. The idea is to keep the hoop upright and rolling, while going as fast as you can. Jean Baptiste is pretty good at it. His mother, Marie, is off in the city center as usual, looking for work.

Some of the measures to improve Jean Baptiste's prospects are simple: a school to go to, access to clean water, inoculations against key diseases, a bed net to sleep under at night to avoid malaria. Marie can't afford them. And the president of their country, Sean Combs/Diddy lookalike Joseph Kabila, hasn't got a hope of funding all of them either, even if he were to prove as good a leader as you were in Uzima, a much richer country.

You don't need to be Thabo Mbeki or Thomas Edison to figure out that aid ought to be able to help here. The biggest thing aid has got going for it is that the countries who most need help are so poor that a little money can go a long way: a few dollars a year to put a kid through school, provide some water pumps and sanitation, subsidize key drugs, and so on. This is what we give aid for—to help people out of poverty or disaster.

So far, so simple. So why doesn't it work better? Why do we hear so many stories about wasted aid and why hasn't it been more successful at helping African countries out of poverty? What has been happening with your money?

If you've been a good citizen paying your taxes for a few years now, you've probably spent several hundred dollars of your hard-earned salary on aid, perhaps even a few thousand if you're a big earner. Of course, in the context of your overall tax payments it's peanuts—the average share of gross national product in North America, Western Europe, and Japan going to aid in recent years has been about 0.3 percent.[1] But add to your tax contributions the donations you may have made to charities that work in Africa or other poor countries, dollars you have dropped in collection boxes, and so on. Feel good about yourself, give yourself a pat on the back. You've at least been doing a bit. The table opposite, using figures for 2005, shows how much.

As you can see, different countries spend very different amounts of money on aid, depending only slightly on how rich they are. Although aid spending through taxes has changed a bit in most countries since 2005, the broad picture remains fairly accurate. Given that only a third to a half of the population in Western countries pays taxes, if you're one of those who do you can at least double the figures in the table (and, obviously, the more tax you pay, the more you have invested).

The figures for charities are for spending in poor countries through what the Organisation for Economic Co-operation and Development (OECD), the West's leading economic think tank, classifies as Private Voluntary Agencies—though most of these are aid charities. The List of Shame table in chapter 8 shows how Western countries as a whole measure up to their promises.

## How Much Do You Have Invested?

| | Aid through taxes, per person | Aid through charities, per person |
|---|---|---|
| Australia | $92 | $31 |
| Canada | $110 | $34 |
| France | $164 | n/a |
| Germany | $123 | $16 |
| Ireland | $207 | $82 |
| Italy | $74 | $2 |
| Japan | $98 | $2 |
| Netherlands | $319 | $17 |
| Norway | $592 | n/a |
| Sweden | $397 | $1 |
| United Kingdom | $190 | $9 |
| United States | $85 | $30 |

Source: OECD/DAC[2]

## Humanitarian vs. Development Aid

Broadly speaking, aid can have two aims. It either provides humanitarian relief in response to emergencies, or it tries to stimulate longer-term development.

The first aim is the one we are most familiar with. Humanitarian aid seeks to give immediate assistance to people in desperate need—such as those affected by earthquakes, tsunamis, or, more frequently in Africa's case, famines and wars. The objectives are simple: keep people from dying and help them try to get their lives back on track. This is the aid we see most on our TV screens and in the leaflets of charities pitching for our support:

tents and food drops, emergency formula for malnourished babies, and so on. Being relatively straightforward, it's fairly effective too: we rarely hear about humanitarian aid workers who've gotten there in time, with sufficient money, being unable to save any lives. The main problems are mobilizing enough resources and doing so quickly.

Yet humanitarian relief comprises only 5 percent or so of total global spending on aid. Chronic emergencies are relatively few and far between (which is why Africans get so irritated that Western images of the continent are based almost exclusively on starvation, war, and suffering). Most of Africa gets on with day-to-day life without crisis, rather like Lucas and Nancy on the edge of the Rift Valley in Kenya: the continent may not be one large bed of roses, but nor is it an arid pit of despair. And this is where the vast majority of your money, development aid, is supposed to come in.

Lucas, Nancy, and most of Africa have been unable to make a lasting break from mundane, run-of-the-mill poverty. Development aid tries to create the opportunities for Africans to pull themselves out of poverty for the long term. In consumer language it's a bit like making an investment rather than an immediate purchase.

Because it's not as simple as handing out basic foodstuffs and blankets (though humanitarian aid workers would shoot me for simplifying the issues so much), development aid is harder to get right than humanitarian relief. It's also much better value if it works because it gives poor people control over their own lives and enables them better to withstand future humanitarian disasters without outside help.

The key test of development aid is, therefore, *whether it helps reduce poverty with lasting effect.* It's the test by which we can judge whether Africa is getting the help it needs from the various types of aid it receives, and whether you're getting value for your money.

## How Is Your Money Spent?

Leaving aside the small proportion of aid spent on humanitarian relief, your money is delivered in three broad ways.

- First, activities funded by your donations to charities and other good causes, which are mainly small projects in the field including water pumps, giving families goats, and so on. We'll call this Charity Aid.
- Second, larger-scale financial and technical assistance provided by American and other governments' aid agencies. This is what about two-thirds of your aid money through taxes is spent on. It can loosely be termed National Aid.
- Third, assistance from international organizations like the World Bank, IMF, and UN, which often takes the form of grants and subsidized loans straight to African governments. This is where the remaining third of your aid taxes ends up. We'll call this International Aid.

These types of aid are the subjects of the next three chapters. The distinction between the three is not quite as clear as I've outlined: large charities occasionally work on programs with African governments; national and international aid agencies sometimes fund small-scale projects. But by and large the separation holds and it's the easiest way to divide up the workings of what is, too often, a very opaque industry.

## Warning! What They Don't Tell You

As I hope will become clear over the next pages, aid can be done effectively and it can be done very badly (and some even defies basic common sense). Yet there is little honest public debate about the quality of aid. And this absence of feedback is a significant factor in why so much bad aid is able to persist.

Most of the information we get about aid is from charities. We trust them, and they are hypothetically well placed to tell us how inefficient some aid is. But they also need to convince us that aid is effective so they can get their hands on our money. It's almost impossible to do both. Indeed, most charities simplify and exaggerate how much effect aid can have—your $20 will buy a hoe, which will change a family's life forever; and so on. Even 2005's big Bono- and Bob Geldof–led Make Poverty History/One campaigns focused narrowly on getting governments to spend more cash. If they'd also tried to pressure governments on the equally important need to spend more effectively, it would have damaged the compelling simplicity of the message.

Many of our governments in the West, meanwhile, are generally quite pleased to avoid telling the public too much about how their aid is spent. This is partly because aid is a risk-taking business and it's impossible to guarantee all your money will be spent cleanly and perfectly if it's going to have an effect; there's a fear of bad headlines, especially here in America. But it's also because many governments know some of the ways they spend money are highly ineffective and they don't want to draw attention to it.

Our only other source of information on aid, occasional media reports, focuses almost exclusively on dramatic disasters. On the few occasions that journalists cover more everyday aid work, it is mainly when they've been flown out by charities to report on particular issues or projects, leaving them unable or unwilling to criticize, or to report on other perspectives. It's the same when celebrities are taken on whistle-stop tours of the very best of a charity's projects so they can help with fund-raising back home.

The outcome of all this is probably the most unaccountable multibillion-dollar industry in the world. This is a shame. Because it's also one of the most important.

## Flowers and Misunderstandings

One area where the aid industry has been unequivocally productive is in the proliferation of acronyms. Almost every organization and project in the aid industry becomes known by its short form, and it was no different for the agency I worked for, the Department for International Development, aka DFID. Unfortunately, as I was to discover in my first week in Rwanda, the gardener at my new house had learned of this acronym too . . .

Tuesday. One of my new colleagues came rushing up the stairs and burst into my office.

"Giles, you've got to come quickly, I couldn't persuade him to stop it."

"What is it? Stop what?"

"It's Sylvestre, the gardener at your house. He's cutting DFID in ten-foot letters into the lawn and planting them with flowers. It's supposed to be a welcome present for when you move in."

We drove across Rwanda's small capital, Kigali, to the house, an incongruously Swiss-style residence that was all small windows and big eaves, fronted by some ruthlessly pruned flowerbeds and a large flat lawn. Rather like the people, Kigali showed few surface scars of its violent past, and the journey from office to house was a pleasant one that took us from one of the city's two main hills to its other, via a poorer settlement in the valley between. Every spare bit of land along the way, from front yards to tiny patches of earth on street corners, was taken up with carefully tended cornstalks and banana palms, while the outlines of the hills were crenellated with lanky trees rising from the gardens of the bigger houses, like mine, that hogged the higher plots.

Two welcoming guards let us in through red metal gates and, true enough, there was Sylvestre planting away. The letters were now fully carved out, and he'd gotten halfway up the F with a series of small bushes. This was bad. I was already intimidated by the thought of moving to a house large enough to come with staff and desperately wanted to make a good first impression. But I really didn't fancy two years of seeing work initials inscribed in the home's soil, taking up almost the whole lawn.

Sylvestre had stopped working and had removed his battered straw hat, which he held humbly in front of him, revealing the lean, friendly, and nervous face of a man in his early forties. It was the first time he'd met the new boss, and he too clearly wanted to make a good impression. I suddenly felt much younger than my twenty-seven years. Adjusting an unseasonably warm woolen suit, bemused by the deference and unworthy of my new domestic responsibilities, I stepped forward to introduce myself.

After a fair bit of awkwardness and confusion (not much helped by my explanations about wanting to be able to play soccer across the lawn), Sylvestre and I eventually compromised on covering up the letters and agreed on a set of new flowerbeds elsewhere. It would, of course, have been unrealistic to expect Kigali's gardeners to understand a Londoner's taste in horticultural design. In just the same way, it is wrong to assume the West always knows what Africa needs. The difference is that while I could rush back to my displaced Alpine chalet and agree on a change of plans, the West doesn't have to listen to the poorest continent. Africa gets what we decide to give it, well intentioned or otherwise. So when we get it wrong, it really matters. As I learned during my time there, while my garden was efficiently tended and the imprint left by the grassed-over letters gradually faded, this happens far, far too often.

# CHAPTER 5
# PASS THE HAT—
# CHARITY AID

Saturday on Main Street or at the local shopping mall, some-where several thousand miles from Africa. Someone with a bright T-shirt thrusts a donation box in front of you and asks for help installing water pumps in poor villages. Back home, there's an email asking for support for AIDS orphans. On TV that evening there's an ad for one of the big charities—the Red Cross, perhaps, or Save the Children or Doctors without Borders—asking you to become a regular donor.

Sometimes we say no to these requests; a couple of times a year many of us will say yes. Of all the things we spend money on that day, aid will be the most worthy. But it is also the one most of us will know least about. For everything else we buy, we have a clear idea of whether it's value for money because of how it tastes, how it looks, how long it lasts, or how well it cleans. With our charity aid, we drop a dollar bill or two in the box, or write a check—and hope.

It's difficult to know from afar whether the aid we're paying for is any good or not. Is charity aid the kind of assistance that the Republic of Uzima, or Marie and Jean Baptiste, Lucas and Nancy, really need to make a difference?

every year in the West we give nearly $15 billion to aid charities,[3] probably around $4–5 billion of which goes to sub-Saharan Africa. Charity aid may only work out at about a seventh of the sum our governments spend on aid through our taxes, but it's probably the part we're concerned about most, where the link between what we give and what poor people far away get is most direct.

How much we give individually varies a great deal country by country, as the table in the last chapter showed. The Irish and Australians are generous private aid givers, Americans and Canadians aren't bad, while the Italians and Japanese aren't good. More varied still are the things we spend our money on. There are charities that give cows to needy families, flying doctors who treat eye cataracts, farm consultants dispensing agricultural advice, librarians collecting old textbooks to send to African schools, advisers teaching compost-making techniques, religious groups preaching abstinence while others distribute condoms . . . and on it goes. Pretty much anything you could ever think of that might be useful for Africa's poor, there will be a charity for it.

It is no surprise, given all this diversity, that the quality is extremely mixed. Charity aid is a bit like a lucky throw at the school fair: some of the prizes are great and some are junk. The problem is figuring out which is which, without being able to look. If all the box-shaking volunteers for the thousands of charities appeared in their bright T-shirts on the same day at the same shopping mall, we would be faced with a nightmare (and not just a visual one): how on earth do we know who has the best recipe for reducing poverty?

## How Does Charity Aid Work?

There's no great mystery here. Exactly how much aid charities spend on frontline assistance—how much actually reaches the end user—depends on the charity itself and what they do. But most well-established, reputable charities spend up to 15–20 percent of their funds on fund-raising, and another 15–20 percent on administration and "program support" costs: everything from offices and HQ salaries to toilet paper.

The rest goes to projects (or sometimes lobbying, if that is what the charity specializes in). Charities in most Western countries have to publish their accounts, so you can check this on their Web sites—there's advice later in this chapter on how to do so.

### Expensive Fund-Raising

It may seem excessive that 15–20 percent of our donations typically go toward fund-raising costs. But this reflects the way most of us give, making one-time contributions in response to television ads, mass mailings, or the volunteers on the street. All these approaches cost time and money. Giving through a regular commitment is far more cost-effective, as well as providing charities with a more predictable income.

While the remaining 60–70 percent of your donation—for reputable charities, at least—will be spent directly on trying to help poor people, it would, however, be wrong to believe that all that money goes toward tangible goods. Unlike humanitarian relief, development aid is about trying to create long-term change that may require training, regular visits, adaptation, and evaluation. Often the "raw materials" of a project—such as cows or goats provided to poor families or money to directly sponsored children—are a relatively small expense, even though fund-raising literature understandably tries to imply that your contribution of

$25, $50, or $100 will purchase something highly specific. It's good design, management, and monitoring of project aid that matter most.

## Life in the Projects

There are three concepts crucial to making charity aid—and indeed all kinds of development aid—effective. These are *ownership*, *capacity*, and *sustainability*. They may sound as though they were invented by granola-munching, sandal-wearing aid workers (though some of us prefer flip-flops), but each one is surprisingly important—and surprisingly difficult to get right.

*Ownership* is a particular challenge. The best way to find out what people want is to ask. Perhaps this sounds obvious, but the aid industry has long been full of well-meaning foreigners who think they know just what a poor community needs and set about providing it, only to find their efforts ignored, or their nice piece of equipment unrepaired and unused. Indeed, the whole way charity aid is advertised to us as potential donors feeds the idea that we can predict from afar what people require—a chicken, water pump, human rights training, school.

## Classrooms in Uganda

The best charities know that the process of identifying what a community wants and needs, and how best to provide it, can be a long one. The more careful the design, and the more local people are involved in it, the more effective it is likely to be.

When Uganda first embarked on a huge school construction program in the 1990s, supported by many foreign governments, the funds in several districts were stolen by officials. Meanwhile, local communities stood by compliantly, too used to bad treatment to complain. A change was needed.

Under the new system, communities themselves were obliged to build the first four feet of the school walls, whereupon government funding would kick in and contractors would finish the job and put the roof on. By the time those communities had sufficiently organized themselves to build the walls, there was no way they were going to allow officials to run off with the money. Forcing officials to pin the construction budgets onto the doors of their offices, where everyone could see how much had been received, helped further. There was no longer any question of who owned the new facilities.

Second to ownership comes *capacity*. It's obvious that there's no point giving aid unless the people who are supposed to benefit from it have the capacity to use it. Aid needs to fit with people's experience, expectations, and cultural habits. And it also needs to be technically appropriate: it's obviously worthless to introduce tractors to poor farmers who own small plots of land or whose expertise is all in hand techniques.

Yet capacity too is an underestimated challenge that has rendered countless interventions worthless. By definition, aid is trying to create a new, improved set of circumstances for people—so it is often likely to challenge them in ways they are not used to.

## Getting Your Goat in Kenya

Giving goats has become a hugely popular form of aid in recent years, appealing to charity donors as a form of aid that seems simple and direct. But even goats are stubborn when it comes to the issue of capacity. When the first goat projects began in Kenya, many of the animals soon suffered from abscesses, diarrhea, pneumonia, and worms and later died. This was partly because the aid projects were trying to introduce high-milk-yielding foreign breeds that the beneficiaries simply weren't used to looking after.

The key factor in improving these projects lay in training families how to look after the new breeds, giving them the capacity to make the aid a success. Yet even then many such projects require ongoing veterinary support, not to mention purchasing food aid for some of the poorest families when drought hits, to avoid them eating their wards. Such projects are not nearly as simple as they seem, and need constant monitoring and adaptation.

They are also much more costly than meets the eye: the goats themselves are a minor expense, with most of your funding going to veterinary and other support costs.

Most important of all in making aid a success is *sustainability*, the holy grail of development work. The ideal of all aid is to provide the one input that acts as a catalyst for wider progress to be made, long beyond the lifetime of any project. But it's rare that there is such a magical single ingredient, rather than a whole range of things that need improving.

Again, this is something that charities are not totally honest about with us as potential donors. Charity fund-raising literature, somewhat understandably, tells us that our donations will have a clear, identifiable, and life-changing effect. But the poverty of people like Lucas and Nancy, Marie and Jean Baptiste is rarely so easily transformable. Even with more limited aims to help people improve their lives gradually, charity aid's biggest difficulty is ensuring that a project's benefits will be felt long after the project ceases. Kenya's goats show how difficult this can be.

Nearly all aid is susceptible to being compromised by outside events. Charity projects, relatively small in scale and able to focus on only one or two aspects of people's poverty, are especially vulnerable. You can fund a health clinic, but what if there are no nurses or drugs? You can fund inoculations for babies, but what if there are no facilities to keep vaccines refrigerated, or the electricity supply is unreliable? You can put a standpipe into a slum, but what if the slum landlord takes it over and demands a price for anyone wanting to use it?

The obstacles to successful projects can come in the most unexpected ways: even subsidizing bed nets to prevent malaria is no use if half of them are then bought by wedding-dress makers as a cheap source of material—as happened in Uganda in 2005 (until the practice was outlawed). Aid must be very carefully thought through if it is to have a chance of creating lasting change.

## Congolese Breeze

It's only occasionally that a one-time aid contribution can be guaranteed to have a truly sustainable effect. I came across one such project in Marie and Jean Baptiste's city of Kinshasa.

The Association Congolaise Pour L'Assistance Orthopédique Aux Jeunes Handicapés treats children with polio. Polio has virtually disappeared across the world thanks to the discovery of vaccines in the 1950s. But not in war-torn Congo. Walk along Kinshasa's big-treed central avenues for an hour or so and you will see several children with telltale withered legs. Generally the cause is polio, though a limping child can also have been the victim of badly administered quinine injections, given by poorly trained nurses to kids with malaria. The children are seen as unproductive members of the community, incapable of work. Too great a financial burden, some are abandoned by their families and left to beg. With nothing to aid their mobility, they drag themselves along the streets with their hands, come dust or downpour.

The ACAOJH provides basic corrective surgery (required in about half of cases) and then fits the children with leg braces. This is backed up with accommodation and three to six months of schooling to help the children adapt back to mainstream society. It's remarkably simple. And remarkably effective. Suddenly the children are mobile, self-confidence rises, and they can work and have a much better chance of taking care of themselves. In 2004, the charity treated 238 new kids. Each one is an astonishing transformation to watch.

Inevitably, no aid intervention is perfectly sustainable: equipment needs repair or adaptation; it's impossible to know what other trials these children will face as they grow up; the project (funded by a U.S.-based organization) depends entirely on donations and will never become self-financing. But even if it finished tomorrow, this example of charity aid will have made a radical and lasting change to the children it has treated.

If only all interventions could be so happily self-contained.

aid isn't easy. But with careful design and some good luck, your money can make real, important differences to people's lives . . . Which is why it is enormously frustrating when so much of our charity aid is actually delivered by amateurs with far too little expertise for their efforts to have any success.

### Aid's Sunday Drivers

Passion is not the same as expertise.

The extent of Africa's poverty means that those of us coming in from outside with money have great power to second-guess what we think is needed. Yet there are no great standards that need to be met to qualify an organization as a charity. And there are no set qualifications required to be an aid worker, which makes aid singularly unlike any other comparable "social" profession, such as nursing or teaching. Almost anyone with a bit of enthusiasm or cash can interfere in the workings of a poor society.

In short, all you really need to be able to do is persuade a few people to write a few checks, and away you go. The quality of fund-raising literature thus seems to matter far more than the quality of work.

*

The problem with trying to draw conclusions about the effectiveness of charity aid is that the quality of charities is so varied.

The best charities know how difficult aid is and are professional, committed, and experienced. They take time to design projects carefully, and back up their efforts with thorough monitoring and evaluation. They work through local staff rather than expatriates wherever possible. They know that you can only provide inoculations for babies if the mothers aren't suspicious about the contents of the needle; that a water pump will lie disused if no one has the means or knowledge to mend it; and that a pristine new school will stand empty if there are no teachers (it is ownership, capacity, and sustainability again).

The worst charities—aside from the direst few that exist only as an excuse to keep expatriate staff in tropical comfort—are those that believe aid is simple and all they need to do is turn up and "make a difference": aid's Sunday drivers.

Regrettably, the charities most likely to fall into this category are sometimes the most well-meaning: small-scale organizations started by one or two good folk with unlimited goodwill but minimal experience. Raising money to send to a village—because someone "got to know a waiter while on vacation in Tanzania and he took us to his village"—is human and understandable. But for the time, money, and effort expended, you'd be very likely to make a far greater impact by fund-raising for an established charity with a track record of running successful projects; and there will be one less foreign organization trying to intervene in other people's lives.

Also ineffective are the charities that are overly prescriptive from afar about how people will need to change their lives "forever," making the mistake of thinking that the lives of people with little must be simple. After all, would you ask a farmer from rural Mozambique to tell you where to build a new school in, say, downtown Detroit or Dublin, how big it should be, or what books the students most need? So why presume it works the other way around?

Such a lack of professionalism is damaging not only to the image of aid, but also to the recipients, not to mention that it is a waste of money. It perpetuates the idea that aid is all about foreigners coming in from outside, rather than people taking charge of their own problems with outsiders bringing in support to help them do so. I vividly remember, when visiting Lucas that day in early 2005 in his village near the Rift Valley in Kenya, that his first question was "Have you come to help us with something?" It spoke plenty for his expectation of foreigners and aid, based on decades of experience.

Of course, there are also numerous examples of enthusiastic individuals managing to achieve extraordinary things in tandem with local people. But there are doubtless many individuals out there with a natural talent for medicine: I'd still prefer to be treated by a qualified doctor.

## Scottish Hospital Beds for Rwanda

I once heard in Kigali about an offer from a thoughtful Scottish health authority that was disposing of some robust old hospital beds for newer stock. Rather than trash them, they wondered if it would be useful to send them to Rwanda.

It was a typically generous idea. Yet the staff in Rwanda's few hospitals would probably have struggled to put the beds together without the right tools or instructions in a familiar language. And the cost of shipping the beds from Clyde to Kigali would have far outweighed the price of having new ones made locally, which would also have benefited the local economy.

## Unaccountable Aid

Aid's great problem is that it is unaccountable. There is virtually no oversight of what charities (or any other aid organizations) do: they are continents away from the people who've entrusted them with their cash.

I wouldn't want to imply that many charity aid workers do questionable things with our money: the best thing the industry has going for it is that most people involved in it are far more passionate and sincere about their work than people in most other jobs. Yet there is almost nothing to ensure that good charities thrive and receive more funding, while ineffective ones go out of business. After all, when was the last time any of us chose to give money on the basis of project evaluation reports rather than heart-tugging leaflets? We have a bizarre tendency to donate money for issues we don't know much about, either because we feel sympathetic or we know that the people asking for the money are "good people." And then we get aggrieved when we read stories about corruption and aid being misused.

Meanwhile, the people who do have a real stake in the quality of aid, the Africans who are supposed to benefit, have virtually no way of making charities accountable, short of refusing bad assistance altogether.

So is charity aid capable of providing the help that Africa needs to pull itself out of poverty? Unequivocally, the answer is no.

Think back to your stint as president of Uzima and it's clear that charity aid has no chance of filling the manifold gaps of underinvestment the continent faces. Charity aid at $4–$5 billion a year works out to roughly $6 per person in Africa, when Uzima's annual needs were estimated at $50 and upward. Most Africans will never benefit from a charity project.

But it's also because of the structure: even if the quality of aid charities was consistently good, if you were inventing an aid system from scratch to respond coherently and strategically to African poverty you wouldn't do it by establishing several thousand different charities operating across the continent with smallish sums of money. By 2003, there were thought to be 39,729 branches of international charities across Africa, according to a study by the London School of Economics.[4] What's more, most charities have their headquarters thousands of miles away, pursue overlapping objectives, and make few attempts to coordinate with each other. (The ideal, for what it's worth, would probably be a small number of much bigger charities that use their expertise to fund smaller African organizations for specific projects—which is the approach some of the best, more established charities already take.)

Yet if charity aid is never going to help solve Africa's problems as a whole, there are many individual Maries and Jean Baptistes, Lucases and Nancys, who can be assisted. The better charities understand the constraints of project aid and will often work inspiringly hard, with local people, to have an impact. Charities may be able to do little to address the underlying causes of poverty. But they can take big strides in targeting specific symptoms in localized areas, making a real difference in the lives of individuals, families, and communities.

If we want this to happen, we must donate intelligently, bearing in mind that the challenge of aid is a hard one that requires professional, dedicated work. Getting value for your charity aid money requires a little bit of effort. There is a happy coincidence of interests here: if we take more care in which charities we give to, spending a little time to check that they are likely to be effective, it increases the incentives for those charities to improve their performance.

## So Who Should I Give My Money To?

There are a great many good charities that use your donations wisely and bring real change to the lives of poor people. The difficulty is knowing who they are. Here are some things to look for:

- Make sure it is a registered charity with the IRS: it should say up front in the literature.
- Do they give credible information about their track record and how they spend their fund, rather than just the heartrending stuff about how much your cash is needed?
- Are they open about what proportion of their funding is spent on administration and operational costs?
- Try not to choose charities based on your own views of what might help most—look for organizations that sound like they find out what poor people themselves want.

If you have time, look at annual reports or request evaluation material for some of their work. Use Google to find their Web sites: charities with nothing to hide will encourage your interest, and many of the best provide lots of information. Also very useful are charitynavigator.org and give.org (both U.S.-based).

If you don't have time to look into this yourself, or you feel you don't know enough about it to judge, there are two shortcuts to making a reasonable guess about whether your money is likely to be spent usefully:

- Is it a large, well-established charity? If it is—like Oxfam, Save the Children, and many others—there's a pretty good chance they have sound expertise and implement reasonable lesson-learning, monitoring, and evaluation processes. (There are several excellent smaller charities out there, but unless you have time to research them, you are better off giving your cash to established names.)
- Does the charity receive funding from large donor agencies, such as your government or the UN? If they do, they are likely to have a

reasonable track record. Governments have the resources to check on charities' performance in the field as well as oblige them to follow core audit and accounting standards.

Finally, once you've decided who to support, give usefully:

- Try to ensure that the charity gets tax relief for your donations. Most Western countries have good tax-relief programs in place (the charity will tell you how). It makes your donation worth that much more.
- Make a long-term commitment so charities can budget sensibly, have to spend less on soliciting your funds, and don't just get money in times of emergency.
- Give money, not stuff: if you want to clean out your closets, then sell the contents and donate the proceeds—or give to a charity that will do so on your behalf. Sending things overseas for secondhand use is expensive.

## Project End

While it *is* worthwhile to support good charities, we should be realistic about what our money can achieve. The limited sums available to charity aid, the huge scale of needs, and the uncoordinated scattering of resources across thousands of organizations mean that this form of aid can never coherently address the real roots of poverty. By and large, it can only treat some of the symptoms. The importance of doing so isn't to be underestimated—at the least, providing poor people with some relief from their struggles—but nor should we pretend it's the long-term answer Africa needs.

The real opportunities for us to make a difference in Africa, as we will see, lie not in the detail of charity donations but in changing the nature of the West's whole relationship with the poorest continent.

*

The key test of all types of development aid, as set out at the beginning of this section, was *whether they help reduce poverty with lasting effect*. Charity aid can't do this on a significant scale. It can create islands of excellence, and the grassroots expertise of many good charities can make them useful delivery agents in wider processes of change. But it will never be the main medium with which to help reduce poverty, as most charities themselves acknowledge. That's why many good charities have strong campaigning arms alongside the running of projects: they know the big game is in trying to influence the much larger amounts of aid that are spent through our taxes.

As president of Uzima, committed to improving a country's entire health, education, and water provision, small projects in a few different localities are not really going to be much use to you. What you need to do is improve your country's overall systems—but, as we have seen, you lack the resources. So the big question is whether larger-scale aid can be used to help African countries and their governments improve their own systems.

## Helping Jean Baptiste

Let's focus on helping just one small child in Africa, Jean Baptiste. As a charity, you don't remotely have the resources to tackle all his basic needs: health, education, water, and so on. You need to focus on one area. You decide on health, remembering that around one in five African children dies before even his or her fifth birthday: Jean Baptiste could really do with better services in this area.

The charity is quite big, so the first proposal is to build a few basic health clinics to reach children like Jean Baptiste in Kinshasa's many downtrodden districts. But then someone points out that there is no one to pay the nurses' salaries year after year to staff them. So you take on the salaries too, despite the detriment of such a recurrent cost to your coffers.

With salaries covered, the problem of drugs emerges: who is going to pay for them? Parents like Marie certainly can't. There's little choice but to fund the drugs too.

Project costs have now expanded so much that you realize you can only fund one clinic rather than a couple. It's a shame, as you will obviously be reaching fewer children like Jean Baptiste than you had originally intended. But it's the sensible option.

The clinic gets under way. Marie brings Jean Baptiste in for a couple of inoculations he never had as a baby, and for the first few weeks it feels pretty good. Then you discover that the clinic keeps running out of drugs because people are soon coming from all over Kinshasa to take advantage of the free medicine, which isn't available anywhere else (and there's no system of registration for most homes you can use to ensure that only local people benefit).

Worse, a bad fund-raising year back home coincides with a humanitarian crisis to which your charity needs to divert money urgently. Unfortunately, the emergency needs are simply greater even than the needs of people in Kinshasa. Funding ceases, the drugs run out, the nurses don't come. The clinic, still pristine, empties as quickly as it filled, and the people are left with the same problems as before. So is this the best way of helping Jean Baptiste?

•

Experienced charities, of course, would not have built the clinic in the first place. There's plenty of better work they would be doing, such as the polio project elsewhere in Kinshasa. But what Jean Baptiste really needs is a better-functioning health system, where the recruitment of doctors and nurses, the budget for building clinics and procuring drugs, and the strategy for expanding basic health care to the worst affected are all carefully planned and reasonably funded.

It's the kind of thing you were trying to do as president of Uzima. It's the kind of thing that bigger, national aid ought to be able to help with.

# CHAPTER 6
# BUDGET OR FUDGE IT
# —NATIONAL AID

Rwanda's favorite foods are grilled tilapia, a large white fish found in the country's numerous rivers and lakes, and goat kebab. Although the vast majority of Rwandans can't afford meat and fish even on a weekly basis, these dishes appear at most celebrations or major events. They're usually accompanied by French fries, quite probably the best legacy of the country's colonial Belgian past.

A few weeks into my time in Rwanda and I was still adjusting to having abruptly become a big tilapia in a small aid pond, the representative of a very poor country's biggest donor. Then the prime minister convened a meeting of all heads of mission to brief them on an emerging drought in the northeast, and Jean de Dieu, one of my agency's drivers, took me to the prime minister's offices early enough to watch all the ambassadors' incongruously large and shiny flag cars arrive. While we waited, he made a detailed case as to why we should upgrade from our already impressive Land Rover Discovery.

The meeting was a first insight into the extremely peculiar workings of the diplomatic and aid world in Africa. My responsibilities in Kigali were to follow and report on what was going on in the country, monitor how British aid money was being spent, and hold discussions with Rwandan ministers and senior civil servants on current and future assistance. Meanwhile I had Dutch, Swedish, French, Belgian, American, Canadian, German, and Swiss counterparts, among others, all with their own offices, all trying to do exactly the same thing—as indeed were various UN agencies, the World Bank, the African Development Bank, and several other donors. The result was all of us spending our aid separately, with widely differing procedures and conditions attached, and only cursory attempts at coordination.

As I drove among Kigali's hills between various lunches and cocktail parties that were proving unexpectedly essential for keeping track of what other donors were up to—and at which grilled tilapia and goat kebabs were always available—I began to wonder: was this really the most coherent support the international community could provide to Rwanda or any other African country?

**n**ational aid—assistance provided directly by Western governments' own aid agencies rather than spent through international donors like the World Bank and UN—accounts for around 70 percent of the aid money funded by our taxes, or four to five times as much as we spend through charities. Around a third of this sum on average goes to sub-Saharan Africa (though only about a sixth if you're American).[5] All told, it amounted to just over around $18 billion net for the region in 2006.[6] And it's due to go up for the next few years.

## How Does It Work?

There are a wide number of options available to national aid donors in how to spend your money:

- *Consulting*: funding advisers to help change the way anything from education programs to sewers or tax-collection systems is run.
- *Buying and building*: drugs for babies, computers for ministries, bridges for rivers, and so on.
- *Funding charities*: more projects like those funded with private donations, or using charities to manage particular donor initiatives.
- *Financial transfers*: direct funding for African governments' own programs and budgets, if of course their plans are sufficiently well organized and transparent (a very big if).

Having such a large menu of options to choose from, and sufficient resources to implement them on a large scale, gives national aid a clear advantage over its charity counterpart. In theory, it means donors can assess the nature of any problem and use whichever form of support is most effective. And they can try to address that problem across a whole country, rather than just in one locality. In other words national aid can do what charity aid can't when responding to a challenge such as providing lasting, better health care for children like Jean Baptiste: it can help to tackle everything from the provision of drugs to the construction of clinics to the training and recruitment of doctors and nurses, and everything in between.

National aid is where the big money is. If any type of assistance you fund has a chance of really helping to reduce poverty, this is surely it.

*

The ideal of aid is to strengthen the ability of poor people to meet their own needs, thus laying the foundation for independence and development. Outside agencies can always step in to provide a few things in an emergency, whether it's the UN distributing food or charities providing limited health care and so on. But it is only if people themselves become able to meet their needs that change will be lasting.

Most such needs—such as schooling, health care, water, and roads—can only be met on a comprehensive basis by Africa's governments, rather than nongovernmental groups like charities and foundations. Sadly, as we saw with Uzima, most African governments lack the resources to do so. So the aim of aid, where possible, must therefore be to try and strengthen African governments' ability to deliver.

Why isn't it possible for donors to create lasting development without working with African governments, given that so many are corrupt? It's not just that it's only African governments that have the scale of resources to even begin to meet national needs (African government revenues dwarf any one donor's resources), but even if you run great projects on a national scale your efforts can be entirely undermined by developments or deteriorations elsewhere. The history of national aid is littered with isolated islands of excellence that end up having zero bearing on the whole.

## The Good, the Bad, and the Ugly

This means the first of what can be known as the Clint Eastwood lessons of international development (and apologies for not taking them in order). Here's the *bad* news about national aid:

> *There is very little that can be done to help badly run African countries.*

Vast amounts of research—as well as common sense—show that little progress can be made in African countries unless their governments are strongly committed to development rather than, say, personal enrichment. This may be pretty depressing, but you are best off walking away from a badly run country and investing your money somewhere it will get a better return. The alternative—giving badly run countries money anyway, as happened frequently during the cold war—just tends to see the elite's Swiss bank balances grow while Joe Mpublic's crops wilt.

It means there's little we can do for places like Zimbabwe under its icon gone rotten, President Mugabe. You could try and train teachers, but you have no idea whether the government would pay them once trained. You could ship in essential drugs, but you don't know whether the government might impound them or charge for them at high prices. In fact, it's often only charity and emergency aid that can be of use in such circumstances: providing direct help for some of the population worst affected by failing systems, and grassroots projects supporting democracy and advocacy groups that might help in a small way to build the foundations for future change.

Here's the *good* news about national aid:

> *Amazing things can be achieved by supporting systems in better-run countries.*

The dream of development is for an African government and its donors to agree on some core aims—such as making primary education free for all children—and work together to improve African systems' lasting ability to deliver them. The super-dream is for African systems to be sufficiently robust and monitorable for donors to channel donor money straight through African

budgets. It's so much more effective than everyone doing a separate little bit. If you think back to being president of Uzima, with
pure intentions but paltry resources, this is exactly what you
would have wanted.

As taxpayers in the West, it may be counterintuitive to have our
aid fund systems in an unspecific way, rather than knowing it buys
something tangible like a hospital or some livestock. But maybe we
should view it in the same way as how we don't fund other services like schools back home in a piecemeal fashion, with a few families agreeing to pay one teacher's salary for a semester, while
hoping various neighbors will remember to pick up the janitor's
bill, the building maintenance costs, textbooks, lunches, and so on.

Contrary to some common belief, systemic aid *does* happen
and it *does* work (though traditionally this is not America's favored
way of spending money—of which more later). By 1986, Uganda
had become one of Africa's very poorest countries, a legacy of
brutal leaders and years of war. But then a government arrived
that brought stability and a real determination to improve its
people's plight. In the thirteen years from 1992, the number of
Ugandans living below the national poverty line fell from 56
percent to 31 percent. Meanwhile, primary school enrollment
went from 62 percent to nearly 90 percent. The Ugandans even
achieved unprecedented reversals in the spread of HIV and AIDS,
with prevalence dropping from 18 percent to 6 percent in the ten
years or so up to 2005.[7] This was what development is all about:
real-deal, real-life improvements in millions of people's lives.

The credit for these immense advances belongs overwhelm-
ingly to Ugandans. But their ability to achieve them was helped
by large amounts of donor funding, much of it straight through
Ugandan government systems, plus a range of technical help from
experts with experience of what has worked in other places. By the

early years of the new millennium, donor money comprised nearly half the $2 billion Ugandan budget.[8] Without it, there would never have been so many children in school, babies inoculated, or people rising from poverty.

In Mozambique, recipient of the highest aid per capita in Africa and where donors also fund half the budget,[9] the number of people living in absolute poverty dropped from 69 percent in 1997 to 50 percent in 2004–5. Real GDP growth since 1993 has been over 8 percent a year, though the country was so destitute that it is still one of the world's poorest. Literacy is up; more than 90 percent of children are enrolled in school.[10]

There are similar stories elsewhere. Tanzania, a poor but now impressively governed country, was able in 2001 to abolish school fees with the help of donor funding, so that nearly 95 percent of seven- to thirteen-year-olds are now enrolled. Even in African countries that are generally perceived to be less well run (by their citizens as well as the international community), such as Kenya, major progress can sometimes be made where priorities can be agreed upon between government and donors. Kenya introduced free primary education in 2004 with the help of donor funding, and almost immediately 1.2 million more children were able to attend school—children like the offspring of Lucas and Nancy's own kids, not all of whom had been able to go to school a generation before.

In the right circumstances, it is unequivocally true that aid works.

## A Quick Note on Systemic Aid

Of course, just saying that donors need to work through systems is a simplification of a complex process. Take the aim of trying to expand primary education. An African government, with the help of donors, may need to: recruit and train thousands more teachers; find sites for, and build, thousands more schools; develop policies to try and ensure that as many girls attend as boys; consider free school meals to encourage the poorest children to attend; put in a training program to increase administrative and policymaking abilities in the education ministry; improve the payroll system so that teachers are paid regularly and ghost names are removed; overhaul procurement systems for textbooks to prevent corruption; review and reform often outdated school curricula; work out strategies to combat high teacher absenteeism through AIDS or other illness; and plenty more. And all that's before the vital issue of trying to improve the quality of actual teaching itself.

Just like charity aid, national aid needs experienced, dedicated, and professional staff working hard alongside their African counterparts if it is to have a chance of success.

So far, too simple? It's time for the *ugly*.

*Effective aid is a dirty business.*

I made good aid sound too easy, didn't I? If it was that straight-forward, why doesn't it work more often? Whatever happened to the problems of corruption and aid money not reaching the front line? The answer is, well . . . sometimes the money *doesn't* reach the front line. Channeling your funds through African systems means, by definition, spending money where organization can be weak, where there's a lack of qualified officials and accountants, where civil service salaries are low and the temptations of corruption high, and where there are plenty of bad eggs among the good ones.

In other words, it means there's a pretty firm guarantee that some of your money will not end up in the right places. Some will be lost in simple inefficiency before it ever reaches priorities like salaries, drugs, and schoolbooks. Worse, some of your money may be corrupted away.

What can be done about this? Well-designed aid will help African governments address all these areas (especially the strengthening of financial management), reducing the opportunities for corruption and having the double benefit of improving the transparency of African governments' own spending as well as donor funding. Good aid workers will work as hard as possible to minimize the losses on the way to the front line. Yet it remains unlikely your money will be spent with absolute spotlessness or effectiveness. Though there must be maximum effort to minimize corruption, it's a reality that must be accepted. How on earth do you help strengthen African systems if you permanently stay outside them?

Many critics of aid seem to have a problem with this obvious point, arguing that we should only provide aid when we're sure every cent can be accounted for. They risk cutting off their nose to spite their face. If African systems were so perfectly efficient, well staffed, and robustly accountable, they doubtless wouldn't need anyone's help anyway.

The public debate that donors engage in with their taxpayers back home on this subject is often immature. Donors who rightly do spend much of their money supporting African systems—including several European agencies—are scared of admitting that they can't be sure where absolutely all the money ends up. They risk patronizing their public. But it's the other aid donors, who primarily fund only their own, closely controlled projects—and this includes the world's biggest national aid donor—that are short-changing their taxpayers far more. You can only be sure every penny reaches its destination if you oversee every stage yourself, and administer it with your own, expensive expatriate staff. Such support is not going to form part of Africa's own progress. These donors may be saving pennies, but they've lost the point.

# CUT-OUT-AND-KEEP GUIDE TO CORRUPTION!

You're probably not convinced yet that corruption isn't such a big issue in aid. It's certainly important not to trivialize it: corruption is probably Africa's biggest obstacle to development. But it's important to draw a distinction between how much it is a blight for Africa as a whole and how much it actually infects the day-to-day aid spent with your taxes.

*How much aid spent through African systems is corrupted?*

I'll put my neck on the line here. What you *can* be fairly sure of is that most of your aid money provided through African systems is not spent corruptly, even though this is the kind of aid the United States remains reluctant to engage in. This is because managing aid is not rocket science—it's the work that I and my colleagues were responsible for in Rwanda. You seek close agreement on exactly what your funds can be used for; you access accounts to be able to verify expenditures; you have those expenditures monitored and checked by external auditors. If it can't be proved your money is going to the right place, you can cease payment.

So while it would be plain silly to claim that every cent of your cash spent through weak systems has arrived exactly where intended, the large-scale fraud enabled by the cold war lucre-for-loyalty era should be out (indeed it's the most stupid mistakes of this era that are still greatly responsible for the Western public's sustained, skeptical view of aid).

## Schools and Sleaze in Rwanda

During my time in Rwanda, two European donors started to work alongside the World Bank to give substantial direct support to the Rwandan government's budget—5 to 10 percent of its annual income—and checked it off against one of their main expenditure lines, teachers' salaries, which they could verify had actually been paid. Sure, a number of ghost names might still have been on the payroll, payments to some teachers might have been delayed while local authorities used the funds for other things, and there might have been some schools where one or two teachers were paid over the usual (incredibly low) rates because of special relationships with head teachers or officials. But overall this was effective, large-scale support, helping Rwanda toward providing an education for every child. Alongside the support to the budget, the donors provided technical expertise to help strengthen the quality of education and the robustness of financial systems, closing down the opportunities for corruption. And part of the agreement was that the Rwandans would also increase their own spending on education, in addition to donor resources. That was monitored too.

*So is corruption still a problem for aid?*
Yes, absolutely. You might be reasonably sure your own aid money is spent effectively, but the danger remains that you are supporting a government that could be wildly corrupt or otherwise unpleasant in other parts of its administration. Suppose, say, the Rwandan regime was happy enough to take donor money to boost education, helping its popularity with its people, but in other areas was corrupt, undemocratic, and became involved in unnecessary foreign wars (as some other donors indeed claimed). Surely it wouldn't be justifiable to strengthen such a regime, not to mention the fact that you'd be better off investing in education in countries with better overall prospects?

Systemic aid's biggest difficulty is not the direct threat of corruption, it's the political risk of supporting governments that turn out in various ways *not* to be truly committed to their country's interests— what donors broadly call bad governance.

*How do you decide who is worth working with?*
No easy answers here. Since not every country is as badly run as Zimbabwe or as well run as Mozambique, donors constantly need to make judgments about the true intentions of African regimes. Such assessments are inevitably subjective.

But by and large donors are too conservative and squeamish, far more concerned about not supporting a government that may eventually prove unworthy of it than making sure they support ones that *are* worthy (it's the fear of those headlines and questions from Congress about wasted money again). When you stand back from this business as usual, you can't help feeling that many donors have simply forgotten the extent of the crisis faced by Africa. Is it really more important to worry about housekeeping for every cent of our resources than to accept that you must be prepared to take a few risks if you are to win at all? Where are the venture philanthropists?—and I don't mean private individuals like Bill and Melinda Gates, who do not see their niche as funding budget support. The interlude at the end of this chapter about the international community's actions in Rwanda after the genocide gives an idea of the costs of such caution.

**S**o why isn't Western aid to Africa more successful, even if ugly? Why do many donors still fail to deliver useful, systems-based assistance to appropriately committed African governments when there is remarkable evidence that this is what is needed?

There are two problems. The second is what these donors spend their money on. But first there's the absurd structure through which they deliver it.

## Too Many Cooks
What do you think is the best structure for providing help to some of the world's poorest countries? Maybe three or four professional, dedicated organizations with a balance of expertise, representing a consensus position from the international community about what countries need to do to receive reliable, effective support? Think back to being president of Uzima. Regardless of whether you'd been able to convince donors to provide direct funding for your budget, this is the kind of straightforward system you'd want to deal with, right?

It's not what you'd get. There are now at least fifty-six countries with their own donor agencies dispensing aid worldwide, each demanding their own discussions, designing their particular approaches, and imposing their own procedures. And then there are dozens more international aid organizations. For every one donor representative like me in a country such as Rwanda—along with my British and Rwandan colleagues in the Kigali office, the policy and administration teams back in the UK, and the various consultants we'd bring out—there are lots of other donor representatives doing exactly the same thing. Ethiopia has more than forty donors. Twenty work in Zambia on education issues alone.

Coordination is often weak, and the strain on recipients huge. A country like Uzima submits 10,000 quarterly reports to donors each year and hosts more than 1,000 missions.[11] African government ministries have large human-resource gaps, which is partly why they need assistance, yet the few capable officials spend vast amounts of their time writing reports and sitting in meetings trying to maintain donor funding. It's such a problem that donors frequently fund expatriates to do these reporting and negotiating jobs for African governments instead, which hardly adds to the ownership or sustainability, let alone the building of capacity. Meanwhile, there is no competition to ensure that only good donors survive (see appendix for a current list of donors).

Perhaps it's unfair to call this donor structure absurd. It's easy to understand how it emerged: following the rush of the independence era, many Western governments converted their colonial ministries into aid agencies; there were a lot of traditional ties to maintain, and aid was often used as a way of advancing national interests. But we know better than that now, which is why most of the best donors spend vast amounts of time and effort simply trying to coordinate their work, in a desperate attempt to overcome the foolishness of the system.

I remember concluding in Rwanda—admittedly a country whose government had particularly few qualified staff, partly as a legacy of the genocide—that the Finance Ministry had only three or four senior officials with a reasonable overview of the ministry's work and the political context around it. For anything important, I needed to talk to one of these officials. For anything really important, I needed to talk to the extremely smart, extremely capable, Dr. Kaberuka, or it wouldn't be registered at high enough levels. It was the same for all donors. We were all running around duplicating each other's conversations, analyses, demands—and often overlapping each other's projects. Those few Finance Ministry officials scarcely had time for much else, such as their job running the economy or helping plan the rest of the government's work.

If aid were in the private sector, most of the donors in the world would have gone out of business long ago. Only the effective (and there are not many of them) would have survived. But there are no such pressures on the bloated donor world. Ironically, it's only when poor countries become less aid dependent that they feel strong enough to rationalize the system that is supposed to be helping them. In 2003, India announced that it would accept aid only from the six largest national aid donors in the country, forcing smaller agencies, such as the Dutch, despite being quite a good donor, to close down their programs.[12]

## Why Aid Isn't Better—The Part You Really Need to Know

The fundamental problem is a lack of accountability. The biggest challenge for public-sector institutions anywhere in the world is how to remain efficient in the absence of the private sector's disciplining bottom line of profit. What helps for the likes of education systems in our own countries is that the same taxpayers who pay for the service also use it. The media, our legislatures, and we ourselves are all relatively good at holding governments to account about their performance. Our governments know they must deliver reasonable services or risk rising criticism and possible ejection at the ballot box.

Aid, paid for with our taxes, is another public-sector service. The problem is that the people who pay for it aren't the same people who receive it. It takes place too far away for us to know whether we're getting value for money, with little real media or political interest. And the consumers of this service—poor people in Africa and elsewhere—have no vote or real influence to improve it.

In sum, the people who have a real interest in how aid works have little influence, while the people who have real influence have little interest. This may be neither surprising nor easily remedied, but it goes a long way to explaining why the structure and content of so much Western aid isn't delivered in the interests of the people it is supposed to serve.

Now it's time for the second major problem with national aid. It is partly the ridiculous duplication among donors that leads to bad day-to-day decisions about what to spend aid money on. Having too many cooks, in other words, leads to . . .

## The Wrong Ingredients

Don't get me wrong. There are several national aid donors who are working hard at trying to spend their money effectively, pioneering new approaches to supporting African systems, increasing accountability and pooling their efforts so as to minimize what are known as transaction costs for recipients. President Bush's new Millennium Challenge Account has, broadly, been a great improvement on the project-heavy traditional focus of USAID assistance, even if America remains stubbornly opposed to cofinancing work with other donors (but see the sidebar in chapter 16). And although most aid globally continues not to be spent efficiently, some of the assistance provided to countries like Mozambique, Uganda, and Tanzania, as we have seen, has been a success and shows that it can make a real difference.

Unfortunately, much other donor money (including a still significant amount spent by the United States) is compounding the already difficult job of providing effective assistance with additional distractions: a continuing obsession with projects, the overuse of expatriates, unreliable delivery, and downright bad prioritization.

### Bad spend 1: Projects, project, projects

Donors still spend most of their (your) money funding projects. Indeed, some donors still refuse *on principle* to spend any money through African budgets. Around 75 percent of donor support in Africa is still provided as project aid, rather than through African budgets.[13] Although donor projects are generally on a larger scale than charity projects, it still means thousands of separately run processes that are hard to coordinate, and duplication is sometimes rampant. Of course, this is partly because some African countries do not have systems robust or uncorrupt enough to work through. But even with those, it is possible to pool approaches and fund through common arrangements, something that happens far too rarely.

### Bad spend 2: Expatriates, expatriates, expatriates

Funding projects often leads to numerous expatriates being brought in from home to manage every item, thus guaranteeing high salary costs. The World Bank estimates there are around one hundred thousand donor-funded "technical experts" in Africa. Bringing in outside expertise is a valid form of aid but should only be used in moderation.

Most consultants are non-Africans, generally coming from the Western donor country funding the work. The rather shocking reason behind this is that many donors still "tie" their aid so that the consultants they fund (as well as any materials they provide) have to come from their own country rather than from the best available source internationally. It's partly because donor representatives like to read reports by people who speak their own language (in all senses), even though these reports are really supposed to be for African organizations to benefit from. But it's also seen as a way of supporting your own aid industry, despite it undermining the quality of the aid itself.

These consultants are nearly always sincere and hardworking, and they may just be able to show where every cent went. But they will struggle to tell a convincing tale about the wider impact.

## You Only Make a Bridge Where There Is a River

Talk to anyone who has worked in national aid and they will recite countless entertaining stories: of how they worked on a three-year project to get a country ready to change its inefficient tax system, only for a new regime to come in and alter the plans completely; of a multimillion-dollar new power station that was nearing completion when funding stopped because of political disagreements between donor and government, leaving the gleaming concrete to mildew; of an expensively trained team at the heart of a health ministry who briefly ran a much more efficient drug distribution system, only for all its staff to be poached to join other donor projects. In Rwanda, there were five or six different donor projects that were all supposed to be "capacity-building" in the Ministry of Finance, some with heavily overlapping objectives and responding to the requests of different influential groups in the regime.

Then again, I remember joining the office in Nairobi in 1998 and hearing of a flagship bridge-building project in Kenya. Several state-of-the-art bridges had been constructed to improve transport links for isolated communities. But the other donor responsible for building the roads joining the bridges never delivered and they now sat impotently over random rivers, connecting nothing.

There is a traditional Luyia proverb in western Kenya that says, "You only make a bridge where there is a river." It takes an industry capable on occasion of surreally poor coordination to need to add, "—and, obviously, a road."

Such inefficient, "jobs for the boys" behavior is, incidentally, exactly the sort of thing the West chastises Africa for.

One of the worst offenders in this area continues to be the United States. This really matters because, as the largest national aid donor, America could be the most effective. While there are some areas where it has particularly strong expertise (including initiatives to promote local democracy), it refuses to fund African systems directly, hamstringing the benefit it could bring. An astonishing 70 percent of U.S. aid is "tied" to U.S. consultants and materials[14] (Italy is even worse at 92 percent), and fully 47 percent of U.S. aid spending in one recent year went to consultants (other major culprits are Australia at 46 percent and Germany at 34 percent).[15] That's right: nearly half of U.S. national aid never even got anywhere close to Africans in terms of food, water pumps, or direct support for African systems: it went into consultants' pay envelopes, the vast majority of whom are American.

### Bad spend 3: Unreliable aid

Picture yourself as president, drawing up the Uziman annual budget. Donors have made various promises and you're trying to factor them into your budget so you can plan how many schools you can run or new roads you can build. Yet you are astonished when finance officials tell you that many donors are so appallingly slow to deliver on their promises that they routinely have to discount donor commitments. In Ethiopia, the Ministry of Finance in the past has discounted European Commission aid by 75 percent (expecting only 25 percent to arrive on time) and African Development Bank loans by 80 percent. American aid is usually perceived as a little more reliable, but is still often discounted by recipients. Uganda, a long-standing aid favorite, regularly discounts up to 50 percent on donor commitments. How can you plan with that?

What complicates matters further is that all donors are constantly reviewing their own political decisions about whether to maintain, decrease, or increase the aid they give you. Given the inherent volatility in most African countries, the lack of a uniform international position means fairly frequent and often uncoordinated withdrawals and reinstatements of aid by various donors. The result is unpredictable, stop-start financing from numerous different pots.

With a more streamlined donor system, donors could have clearer outline conditions and consensus decisions on when to freeze payment when those conditions are not met. African countries would be clearer where they stand and they wouldn't be able to play Western countries off against each other, as they sometimes seek to do, with the impact of aid freezes offset by continued flows from elsewhere.

### Bad spend 4: Getting your national interests in a twist

This must be the most shocking indictment of national aid of all.

You probably thought your aid money went to help the poorest people in the poorest countries, no? Think again. Only about $4 in every $10 of global aid goes to low-income countries (most of which are in Africa). The G8 at Gleneagles in 2005 promised to improve their targeting, but so far the shift is slow.

The problem is that many donors' aid still goes to "strategic partners" in support of Western national interests rather than need. As always, some donors are worse than others. Despite Africa containing most of the world's poorest countries, only three of the top ten recipients of U.S. aid are African; the European Commission also boasts only three. In fact, the two largest traditional recipients of U.S. assistance in the last couple of decades have been Israel and Egypt, which may come as a surprise to American taxpayers. More recently, Iraq, Pakistan, and Afghanistan have risen on the list.

## The Right Priorities?

Although American aid to Africa nearly doubled between 2001 and 2006, it still constituted only 22 percent of overall U.S. aid spending—less than a quarter. Most assistance still goes to middle- or lower-middle-income countries, and only one of the world's ten poorest countries features in the top ten recipients of American aid.

| 10 Top Recipients of U.S. Aid in 2006 (US$ millions) | | 10 Poorest Countries—with U.S. U.S. aid in 2006 (US$ millions) | |
|---|---|---|---|
| 1. Israel | $2,495 | 1. Burundi | $26 |
| 2. Egypt | $1,779 | 2. D.R. Congo | $93 |
| 3. Iraq | $1,637 | 3. Ethiopia | $329 |
| 4. Afghanistan | $1,011 | 4. Liberia | $156 |
| 5. Sudan | $906 | 5. Guinea-Bissau | $0.1 |
| 6. Pakistan | $763 | 6. Malawi | $50 |
| 7. Colombia | $580 | 7. Eritrea | $2.8 |
| 8. Jordan | $512 | =8. Niger | $23 |
| 9. Ethiopia | $329 | =8. Rwanda | $95 |
| 10. Kenya | $322 | =8. Sierra Leone | $30 |

Source: U.S. State Department[16]

Part of the trouble, again, lies in every Western country continuing to maintain its own donor agency (this may be more excusable for a large country such as the United States than it is for numerous small European states). It's a walking invitation for

Western foreign ministries, responsible for advancing other national interests, to interfere with aid priorities. A couple of Western countries even raid aid budgets intended for poverty reduction to pay for domestic immigration services. Around 2 percent of global aid flows are estimated to be used this way.[17] Take an especially low bow, Australia and France.

## The Final Product: Appetizers, Not Main Courses

Just as for charity aid, the key question for national aid is *whether it helps reduce poverty with lasting effect.* Unlike charity aid, it has a real potential to do so, to provide genuinely useful, coherent assistance to reach millions of people like Marie and Jean Baptiste, Lucas and Nancy. It's where the largest part of our aid money goes. And sometimes it really works.

Yet compared to what it could be, national aid is often a giant exercise in frustration and squandered opportunity. It's difficult to describe how surreal the industry begins to feel after you've worked in Africa for a couple of years. It's certainly the least effective major public service funded by Western taxpayers that I'm aware of. Using aid to try and stimulate lasting development is hard at the best of times. But when other priorities start to interfere with the ideal structure and content, it becomes exceptionally difficult to do well. It's rather like a can of white paint: it only takes a few spots of color and the whole lot is spoiled.

For all the excuses donors use not to provide coherent budget support to African governments that might be able to use it—excuses that focus mostly on fear of corruption—the greatest irony is that our failure to do so means we don't get to test whether those governments are really up to the challenge. Meanwhile, most Western taxpayers remain oblivious to the ineffectiveness of aid money spent with their cash. The UN Millennium Project itself has calculated that only 24 percent of aid actually finances real poverty-targeting investments on the ground. We are not getting value for money, and the Africans we aim to benefit from our aid are suffering as a consequence.

# INTERLUDE
# GAMBLERS REQUIRED

Most African countries are very poor, and we in the West must be prepared to take a few more risks to help them. This means moving toward coherent, systemic support as quickly as we can (through the budget wherever possible), ensuring that our assistance is much more predictable and reliable, and establishing with African countries clear, limited conditions for our help. Often, the risks aren't really that high. Rwanda provides an important and useful example.

## Rwanda: Back Story

It's hard to think of a country that better reflects the international community's failing of Africa than Rwanda. The genocide of 1994 was clearly signposted long before it happened. And when it did, the international community still did nothing. Nearly a million Rwandans died, in only one hundred days, out of a population of eight million.

The initial reaction of the West was guilt-stricken and large. Humanitarian aid agencies piled in. Charity appeals rightly elicited our sympathy and took our money, and it wasn't really the time to point out it would have cost us less in taxes and donations if our governments had bothered to intervene before the bloodbath rather than to clean up after it. President Clinton later admitted that the failure to intervene ranked as his greatest regret.

But it is the reconstruction stage after the humanitarian response that is always the most difficult. The men and women who had finally put a stop to the killing were the rebel Tutsi army who had fought their way in from Uganda in the north. They now found themselves in power over a destitute, destroyed country. What was required to make Rwanda a viable state again was to create security, rebuild institutions, and begin a long process of reconciliation. Staff had to be found to fill all the middle- and high-ranking jobs in the ministries, law courts, schools, hospitals, and everywhere else (these jobs had previously been held by the Hutu elite, most of whom had now fled or were compromised). Resources were needed to help the region get back on its feet.

Rwanda had become one of the two poorest countries in the entire world. For the international aid community, as much as for the new government, it wasn't just abject poverty at stake. It was the stability and security of a country with a continuing potential for the worst events mankind can manage to muster.

## Rwanda: Slack Story

The international community was understandably nervous about Rwanda's new rulers. Were they up to these massive challenges? It was still nervous when I arrived there in 2000. Only the UK had moved on to providing long-term support directly to the Rwandan government budget, though not without some soul-searching back in London. It's not hard to comprehend the anxiety: a country with a lethal history of ethnic conflict was now ruled by a minority elite with no track record of governance, plenty of grounds for feeling vengeful against the majority, and no inclination to listen to international "partners" who had so conspicuously failed to stop the killing of their kin.

Most donors, as a result, assumed the easy position: they'd do a few projects, continue to meet humanitarian needs, fund other bits and pieces here and there. This was the approach taken by the United States too. And if the new regime really appeared committed to reconciliation in a few years' time, if it was opening up to democracy and achieving economic growth, maybe they'd work more with Rwandan systems then.

In other words, having gotten it wrong with their support for the previous government in Rwanda under which the genocide was planned, most of the international community was reluctant to get too closely involved again, ironically punishing the new regime for the sins of the very one they'd overthrown. France was particularly distrustful. Its first major nonhumanitarian project after the Rwandan genocide was thus to rebuild the trashed French cultural center . . .

So what *was* really going on in the Rwandan regime? Could it be trusted with support? Was it moving in the right direction? I arrived in Kigali with an open mind on these issues, unsure that the UK's close relationship was very wise in the face of all the criticism.

And after a while I realized these simply weren't the right questions. Rwanda's new government was dominated by people who had gone into exile over the previous thirty-five years as a result of intermittent massacres, who'd grown up estranged from their homeland in refugee camps, unwanted by their hosts, who'd fought a long war to get back in and seen many of their brothers and sisters in arms killed in the process, and finally took power over a population many of whom were suspected of complicity or complacency in the genocide of their kind. It didn't take a genius to realize that there was no way this group of people was going to relinquish power for a long time—certainly not until they were confident that doing so didn't risk a return to the conflict and exile of the past. Ten, fifteen, twenty years minimum, who knows? Certainly, the very last thing they were going to do was listen to much advice from their failed friends in the international community.

In the face of such a situation, what should donors do? There were promising signs that many in the regime were trying to change and open up society, to create a reformed country without ethnic allegiance (Tutsis and Hutus had been abolished: you were allowed only to be Rwandan now) and build a future on mutual trust and opportunity—and who understood that since the majority was bound to return to power someday, their only hope was to change Rwandan society sufficiently that it would be a safe place in which their families could remain. But equally there were vengeful hard-liners in the regime determined to keep a tight grip on power, come down hard on dissenters, maintain a very strong army, and only pay lip service to reconciliation.

The usual donor question—can we trust this regime?—was hence redundant. Not only was there no clear answer, but one wasn't going to emerge soon. This government was the only show in town for the foreseeable future and there was nothing to be achieved by standing on the sidelines worrying. On the other hand, while there *may* have been nothing to be achieved by getting involved, there was at least a chance. Oddly, the United States seemed to understand this through the relatively close political and intelligence links it cultivated with the Rwandan establishment, but not with its limited, project-based aid.

I saw the role of donors in Rwanda as being to find mutual areas of interest where improvements could be made, and to support the regime's progressive elements in their efforts to open up. There were no demands the international community could make for its aid, no negotiations it could have that would affect the government's policy on core security, which included the speed of democratization. Instead, bit by bit, I and my colleagues began to have more open conversations with the Rwandans about a range of policies.

The UK had a ten-year commitment to provide assistance to the Rwandan government, as long as they too kept their own promises on a range of areas that signaled the direction of their administration, to be reviewed independently every year. This encouraged confidence that we were a genuine, long-term partner, and made their budget planning a bit more reliable. We found areas to which we were both committed—such as expanding education—and areas to which we weren't (we eventually canceled some of our support to the state broadcasting agency because of the regime's lack of interest in allowing it a more independent role).

## A Bet Worth Taking

I don't think I was naïve or overly optimistic about the Rwandan regime. It was responsible for some nasty things: the odd apparent disappearance, intolerance of criticism, involvement in a war in neighboring D.R. Congo that diverged from protecting its national security into exploiting that country's natural resources. But it also had some incredibly inspiring features: many officials' genuine attempts at reconciliation; demobilization and reintegration of former genocidal militias; impressive economic growth; achievement of basic security in the countryside (it's interesting to ask poor people in unstable countries what they most want: schools, health care, water?—the answer is always security). And it was the only hope that Rwanda had.

In my head I used to guess it was roughly fifty-fifty whether Rwanda would be a stable, relatively fair country in fifteen years' time. All donors could have remained at arm's length. But better to try and play a small part in encouraging the progressives in the regime, increasing the incentives to risk opening up society and perhaps give them a bit more confidence that the international community might be relied on to help if things ever got bad again (though I felt mixed about this last point as I wasn't really sure I believed it). Rwanda's approach to dissent and to its conflict in D.R. Congo would not have been substantially different if we had withdrawn our support, so we were not significantly reinforcing a dubious regime. Instead we were helping get more children into school, improving auditing and accounting systems, supporting and monitoring local elections, and more.

Six years since I left, it's still uncertain how things will turn out. It is certainly Rwandan actions that will do by far the most to determine Rwanda's future. But I'm sure we were right to take the risks.

Standing on the sidelines wringing our hands about politics achieves nothing. Standing on the sidelines sweating on every penny and running tightly controlled projects achieves very little. Taking risks with your eyes open *may* achieve nothing. But at least there is the chance it will achieve far more.

Contrary to apparent mainstream opinion, doing nothing in an exceptionally poor and needy African country is as political as doing something. When I think back to that first meeting I attended in my scruffy clothes, between the IMF team worried about the fiscal deficit and the Rwandan Finance Ministry team trying to create a budget capable of reducing poverty, it was partly the absence of braver donors supporting government efforts that had created the problem to begin with. Rwanda was far poorer than Uzima. There was absolutely no chance of reaching the Millennium Development Goals without more assistance. But there was a good chance that a broken society would remain unable to fix itself in its crucial post-conflict years and would return in due course to its fearful history.

Rwanda is, of course, an exceptional case. Yet the essential point is the same for all donors worried about whether or not to risk working with African governments. Since it is only through overall government efforts that African countries have a lasting chance of development, it is surely better to get involved, to risk backing a few dud horses and sometimes lose, than to gaze on, betless, from the protection of the project paddock. There do, of course, have to be limits: no point backing a ride if its jockey is as plump as Robert Mugabe. But we can certainly gamble more than many donors currently allow.

In an ideal world, the international community's question in Rwanda would have been: here is a country coming out of genocide and more than thirty years of instability, there are bound to be a difficult few years ahead as a new regime and minority group is in power, and it could go either way. What is the best role the international community can play?

And the ideal answer would have been for donors to come together, make substantial financing available as a group, have a single, coherent dialogue, and establish a clear agreement with the government on some core bottom lines about what constitutes acceptable progress, with regular review. Then would come careful support, not retracted in a knee-jerk fashion at the first sign of trouble, but clear and hard about pulling back if serious foul play persists.

Wouldn't that be a better way to help a country like Rwanda recover, and wouldn't it be a better reflection on the modern world and the West's role? Instead the international community, which failed Rwanda so signally during the genocide, continues to fail too many countries like Rwanda in the present.

# CHAPTER 7
# AIRILY CONDITIONED
# —INTERNATIONAL AID

In the run-up to the genocide in Rwanda, the commander of the UN forces in the country, General Roméo Dallaire, found himself making promises to people—that the international community would intervene to protect them—that he later found he could not keep. It is well documented in the movie *Hotel Rwanda*, encapsulated in a shattering shot of the last UN soldiers departing down the hotel drive to leave defenseless "locals" alone in the forecourt. General Dallaire subsequently suffered a breakdown back home in Canada, lived for a while on a park bench, and tried to commit suicide—one man carrying the weight of the whole international community's failings.

Albeit with less terrifying consequences, the problems of international aid are somewhat similar. The institutions that manage international aid theoretically provide a more coherent response to African countries' needs than national aid donors. Yet they are at the forefront of the contradictions in Western assistance to Africa, frequently promising what they cannot deliver. And unlike General Dallaire, they have no excuse that they don't know better.

**a**round 30 percent of the aid Africa receives comes through international institutions, compared to around 60 percent through national aid and 10 percent through charity aid. Western taxpayers funded these institutions to the tune of $25 billion globally in 2005, with $9 billion of that going to sub-Saharan Africa.

## Big Spenders—International Aid Institutions in Sub-Saharan Africa in 2005 (aid in millions)

| | |
|---|---|
| $3,511 | World Bank (through its concessional lending arm, International Development Association [IDA]) |
| $3,144 | European Commission (funded by EU member states only) |
| $1,278 | UN (through its various agencies including UNDP and UNHCR) |
| $836 | African Development Bank (through a fund similar to IDA) |

## International Footnotes

The European Commission practices, problems, and virtues are similar to those of national aid donors, albeit with a slightly more complicated bureaucracy and a decision-making structure that has traditionally led to sluggish response to African needs. I won't dwell any more on it here. Nor will I focus specifically on the African Development Bank, whose aims and practices essentially mirror those of the World Bank, by which it is dwarfed in both size and speed of response.

The United Nations, despite a high public profile, is a surprisingly small player in financial terms. It sometimes suffers similar coherence problems in African countries to those of national aid donors because it's made up of a confusing number of agencies, largely autonomous, whose agendas inevitably overlap. A country like Uzima might expect to host representations from UNDP, UNAIDS, UNHCR, UNICEF, OCHA, FAO, WFP, WHO,  UNFPA, UNIDO, and maybe UNESCO, UNECA, UNIFEM, ILO, OHCHR and others (see appendix for definitions). Their staff spend almost as much time as those of national aid donors in trying to coordinate.

The political influence of the UN should not be under-estimated and it does some good work, especially in humanitarian crises when properly funded. But in development aid terms, its blessing—high perceived political legitimacy because it represents all nations—is also its curse. Western donors, most notoriously the United States, are reluctant to channel as much of their money through the unwieldy decision-making structures of UN agencies, where they have one vote among many, as they are through the World Bank, where, as the major creditors, they control the board.

In terms of resources, the World Bank is the dominant international player in most African countries—and frequently the largest aid organization of any type.

In terms of influence, it is the Bank's sister institution, the International Monetary Fund, alone that can rival it, despite the fact that the Fund spends little money itself. The Bank and the Fund. It is these two organizations on which this chapter will focus.

## The World's Local Bank

The World Bank, great demon of many antiglobalization protesters, operates much like any local bank. It provides loans to borrowers if terms can be agreed upon, and in many ways it is unfairly maligned. It is intellectually the most impressive aid institution, with vast numbers of highly qualified, intelligent staff.

More important, there are plenty of surveys that show, dollar for dollar, that World Bank loans are among the most effective forms of aid expenditure, raising more people out of poverty than most other forms of assistance.

The effectiveness of the Bank is easy to understand. The loans it provides to poor countries, through IDA, are highly concessional: there's no interest and repayments don't begin for twenty years (imagine that for your next mortgage!). All told, World Bank loans cost poor countries about a third of what commercial loans would cost—with the difference met by donors who top up IDA finances every few years. In other words, two-thirds of a loan is effectively a grant. Helping decide and administer the UK contribution to IDA was part of the job I returned to after my time in Rwanda.

To you, the president of Uzima, World Bank loans are much more attractive than most national aid: the sums are substantial, the flow is reliable, and repayment is deferred. Most loans directly try to support your government's systems, and the use of consultants is relatively limited and focused. In other words, in terms of the tests of lasting aid we established in the chapter on charities, World Bank loans have a strong likelihood of getting *ownership*, they take *capacity* seriously, and their tendency to make commitments for the long term helps *sustainability*.

There's an obvious irony here. Why are the World Bank's major creditors happy for it to provide systemic assistance directly to African governments when this is exactly the kind of aid many of them won't provide through national aid donors? After all, the Bank's funding comes from the same Western taxpayers' pockets as do other types of aid.

The answer is that each country's accountability to its own taxpayers seems diluted by the number of other contributors, so no one is as worried about negative headlines concerning assistance gone wrong. Thankfully, they can thus afford to be braver in their aid. The United States is the best example of this: despite U.S. taxpayers being the Bank's largest single source of financing, and despite it being the only country on the board with a virtual veto on lending policy, the U.S. government is happy for the Bank to engage in the kind of systemic support to African countries it forgoes through its national aid. The Bank thus ends up with largely the right attitude toward supporting African systems, which, while not quite Monte Carlo or bust, is appropriately adventurous.

## The "345ers"

The common image of international aid workers is rather like the British view of American servicemen in the UK during the Second World War: overpaid, oversexed, and over (t)here. With their three-course meals, four-wheel drives, and five-star hotels, it's a picture that does considerable damage to both African and Western perceptions of the aid industry.

There is certainly some truth to it. UN, World Bank, and IMF staff in particular *are* overpaid, more so than most national aid staff and a lot more than charity workers. It's a sometimes sickening system that could allow UN staff in Kigali in 2001 still to be receiving daily payments of more than $100—on top of their tax-free salaries, housing, and other allowances—for being in an "emergency" location that had long before become safer than most African cities.

But, image aside, it's not a fundamentally important issue. If you want good people for important jobs, you need to pay at least reasonably at Western rates. Bloated aid officials in flashy hotels are more than anything simply the visible face of massive inequality between Africa and the West. If it jars—well, good, it should.

## The Accidental Policeman

Like the World Bank, the International Monetary Fund was established toward the end of the Second World War. It wasn't designed to serve Africa. While the Bank was to provide money for reconstruction, primarily in Europe, the Fund was to help maintain international economic stability: economic thinking of the time was still heavily scarred by the recessions and Depression of the 1930s, and the Fund would provide advice and finance to help predominantly Western governments through short-term balance-of-payments problems. The basic idea was that if countries ran out of money temporarily, rather than plunging into recession and defaulting on payments, they could borrow from the Fund.

Because of persistent macroeconomic struggles, however, the Fund has since become a permanent fixture in most African countries. It serves what, on the surface at least, is a useful and legitimate function, monitoring overall economic policy to ensure countries don't store up such balance-of-payments problems by spending more than they earn. This may sound like a largely technical, if important, role. Yet it has landed the Fund with enormous influence, because donors are understandably reluctant to provide aid to countries whose economies might be about to go down the tubes, and it's the Fund's opinion to which they listen. As Uziman president, if you want aid you *must* have the Fund on your side.

## Representing a Failing System

So why do both the Bank and the Fund have such bad reputations? I wrote at the beginning of this chapter that international aid institutions are at the forefront of the contradictions in Western assistance to Africa. I had the Bank and Fund particularly in mind.

Because it lends on a larger scale than any other donor, the

World Bank is the most powerful voice demanding from African governments that they adopt serious national plans capable of reducing poverty if they are to receive aid (these plans are known as Poverty Reduction Strategies—see box below). In doing so, the Bank is trying to act as a responsible lender, only agreeing to part with its cash if there is a good chance of a return on its investment. The benchmark is for African countries to reach the Millennium Development Goals by 2015, including halving the proportion of people living in poverty (from a starting point in 1990).

Yet if an African country writes such a plan, including the kind of large-scale investment required for countries like Uzima that we saw under your presidency in chapter 3, the IMF will step in and quite rightly say it's unrealistic because of lack of funds and would lead to a massive balance-of-payments crisis. At this point, as president, you would therefore turn back to the Bank and say, "We can't do it unless you and other donors give us more money." The Bank will then reply that not only does it not have enough money to give you, but unless you can make the Fund happy, it won't give you any cash at all.

In the end, African countries end up writing plans that they know can't really reach the MDGs (but dutifully say they can), donors provide some funding (though generally less than promised), and no one acknowledges the absurdity of it all. The practical result is a West that wants to have its cake and eat it too, without even giving the chefs enough ingredients to bake it in the first place. African governments are meanwhile let off the hook, postponing yet again a true examination of their commitment to deliver adequately funded, noncorrupt services to their people.

It was this debate that I had stumbled into on my first day in Kigali, untidy and sleep-weary, and it remains replicated in capitals across Africa. During my time there, partly at the behest of the

Bank and Fund, the Rwandan government developed its plans into what it called "high-, medium-, and low-case scenarios." In other words, this meant: a completely unrealistic plan requiring far more financing than was available; a very optimistic plan in case economic growth was fantastic and donors very generous; and lastly a plan based more or less on what they thought they'd get.

In his book *The End of Poverty*, Jeffrey Sachs recalls similar debates he witnessed as Kofi Annan's special adviser and head of the UN Millennium Project in countries like Ethiopia and Ghana, calling it a shadow play. He uses a nice turn of phrase to sum it up:

> *The IMF and World Bank reveal split personalities, championing the Millennium Development Goals in public speeches, approving programs that will not achieve them, and privately acknowledging, with business as usual, that they cannot be met!*

## Poverty Reduction Strategies

It's not all bad news! If sufficient resources can be provided by donors, there's more hope than there used to be that they will be put to good use. It lies in the introduction of mundane-sounding national Poverty Reduction Strategies (PRSs).

One of the greatest historical difficulties for poor countries has been being forced to sign up to numerous conditions in order to receive different donors' aid, generally set by bureaucrats in offices thousands of miles away. One of the great difficulties for donors, in turn, has been how to establish whether poor countries are sincere in signing up to these conditions, or how much they are just saying the right things to get their hands on the cash.

Over the last decade a new approach has emerged. Rather than having to agree to various donor-imposed demands, poor countries are expected to develop their own comprehensive national plans, PRSs, through a process of consultation with their own people and a serious analysis of their most urgent needs. As long as that process is generally agreed to have been credible, donors are expected to stop setting their own conditions and instead hold African governments to the commitments laid out in the PRSs. Donors should also deliver their own assistance in line with PRS priorities, creating a more coherent, unified effort toward development.

As with any initiative, there are teething problems. And the need for one credible set of objectives for all to follow in a country may sound as obvious as was the need for some global development targets through the Millennium Development Goals (it says much that no one adopted it before). But it has already brought more consistency to the work of donors while encouraging in African ministries the assumption that policy should be informed by an assessment of a country's needs, rather than partisan priorities alone. If sufficient resources can be found, Poverty Reduction Strategies represent a serious vehicle for progress.

## Airily Conditioned

There are, however, two areas in which specific Bank and Fund policies further undermine their own already difficult tasks.

### Market muddles

The first of these is an overenthusiastic faith in the market. Partly in response to Africa's emerging debt crisis in the 1980s, as well as to the ideologically driven agendas of the Reagan and Thatcher administrations, the IMF and World Bank started to apply stringent conditions to African countries. These required rigorous cutting of budgets and the adoption of strongly free market policies. To be fair, the desire to balance the books was sensible, at least in immediate terms. But assuming the market could meet people's needs, where there were lots of people too poor to interest the market, was terribly simplistic.

It's easy to understand why the promarket policies seemed so attractive. Many African states were failing to provide effective services through the public sector and there was major corruption. Something needed to change. Personally, I've no objection to the principle of market forces being used to bring efficiency to government-run services (the aid industry itself is a fine example of how inefficient the public sector can get). But it was a mistake to assume that just because the public sector was failing, the market would do better. In fact, as many Africans, including South African finance minister Trevor Manuel, have pointed out, if public institutions in Africa are too shaky and corruption too great to make state efforts a success, then there is a strong likelihood that the private sector will fail also. The ability to regulate services will be weak, and privatization in particular often leads to more opportunities for graft—through shady sell-offs and deliberate underperformance—than maintaining state ownership.

Arguably, what Reagan and Thatcherite thinking achieved in the United States and UK was a slimming of bloated states, recalibrating them to compete in the globalized modern era. What happened in Africa was a crudely applied, set-menu effort to enforce fiscal responsibility, which too often achieved little and saw economic decline continue. By the early 1990s political thinking in the West had moved on, not least as a result of voter disaffection with the social impacts of such policies. But the Fund's prescriptions for Africa and elsewhere remained broadly the same. Why? Partly because there were no African voters the Fund had to be accountable to. And partly because it's mainly finance ministries in the West that decide what policies to support on the Bank and Fund boards—they are far more attracted to policies recommending African austerity than to accepting that there's a fundamental shortfall in resources, with all the implications it brings.

As we will see in the next section of this book, the West has also in the past used Fund conditions to oblige African countries to open up their markets for trade—again a sensible policy in principle—without the reciprocal access to its own markets or the time to adjust to make it properly effective in practice. It's another example of how the Fund, created to avoid Western economic crashes and concerned primarily with book balancing, is not really fit for the general policy advice and development role it is now asked to carry out. It's not so much that the Fund's advice is always wrong, but if you run a business you don't put the accountant in charge of the whole operation. And you don't have to be a Harvard-educated MBA to know that any number of cutbacks and reorganizations won't succeed if a business—or a country—is simply not viable.

### Nonresident evil

The Bank and Fund's second self-imposed error has been their rather patronizing, one-size-fits-all approach to their work. The Fund especially is guilty of failing to tailor its policies adequately to each country's circumstances. The enormous majority of its staff sit in Washington, fly into African capitals for a couple of weeks "on mission" (during which time they expect African ministers and officials to be on call day and night), then go back and pronounce their solutions for the country's economic problems. How can they expect to understand the intricacies of a country's economy in this way? Instead they are left with long-range prescriptions that sometimes differ little between countries. It's all but akin to a doctor trying to carry out a major medical checkup by phone. After I'd been in Rwanda a while, in what was apparently a real coup, the Fund actually sent out a staff member to be resident in Kigali. Given its enormous power,

I found it extraordinary that an institution whose decisions would have complex impacts on an appallingly poor country's prospects hadn't had someone there before.

The Bank is a little better in this regard, but still inexplicably remote from the coalface of its work. The quality of intellectual analysis at its headquarters is not matched by its implementation in the country. In 2004 it went through a major decentralization process to increase its staff presence in poor countries. When it finished, there were still around 9,000 staff in Washington, against 2,500 in the field.

Of course, no institution can expect to get it right all the time. It's just that the Fund's and the Bank's errors are imposed on the finance ministries of poor countries that have little choice but to obey. Contrast this with the reaction from the Fed throughout the late 1990s, under Alan Greenspan's leadership, when the IMF argued for several years that U.S. interest rates needed to rise. Was the IMF's view seriously regarded? "I wouldn't say it had a lot of weight," said one U.S. official. It's clear that Greenspan agreed, because most of those years he simply ignored it.[18]

At the sharp end of the West's hypocrisy in Africa, it is the World Bank and International Monetary Fund whom many critics blame most for Western policies on aid. Yet it's easy to feel some sympathy for Bank and Fund staff themselves. By and large they are well-intentioned people just doing the job asked of them by their bosses: the Bank's function is to give money to countries with reasonable plans that request it (even if everyone knows they aren't going to achieve all their aims); the Fund's function is to tell those same countries to balance their budgets (even if it means cutting key social services). Why do we expect balanced advice when these institutions are still staffed almost exclusively with economists, despite the huge social and political impacts their decisions can have? Blaming them is a little like protesting outside the home of the White House press secretary, rather than having a go at the president himself.

## Wadi Halfa Wedding

Driving back home from Rwanda after the end of my posting in 2002, I got stuck for a few days in a small Sudanese town on the edge of Lake Nasser, where a ferry departs for Egypt "once every couple of weeks or so." Wadi Halfa sits on the edge of the desert, at the end of an exhilarating two-day drive through the sand from Khartoum: you follow the Nile north for the first day, pass the dark crumbling pyramids at Meroe that stand like photo-negative dunes to the side of the route, and then cut for the second into an open ocean of sand marked by white posts every five hundred yards, heading for the nearest bit of lake.

My friend Mary Louise and I were pretending to be married as we passed through Sudan to make life easier. Day meandered into day as we waited for the ferry to turn up, and as we got to know the family where we were staying, we were invited to an engagement party for a local couple. The women of the house insisted on dressing Mary Louise up for the event, complete with copious henna tattoos and a traditional "incense bath," which involved her being taken to the back of the house and made to squat over a pungent smoking hearth ("Your husband won't be able to keep his hands off you all night," they told her, incorrectly, as they infused all her clothing with the reek of Cub Scout camp). Finally ready, we all walked over the large and dusty local square that had been rigged up with huge numbers of lights, generators, a barbecue, and a band.

It was a great evening. Unbelievably friendly people, dancing, kids running everywhere, astonishingly colorful dresses against a backdrop of white walls and black night. Then came time for speeches. First the groom, then the bride's father, then the groom's father. "Where's the bride-to-be?" I asked a local man who spoke some English. "Oh, it would have been nice if she'd been here. But she studies in Khartoum and couldn't make it back for the party," he replied. The socializing continued long into the night.

Apparently this was nothing strange: the match had been made, both families were happy, and it was worth celebrating. Somewhere far off in Khartoum was the woman whose impending nuptials were the focus of it all. She may have been happy, she may not. But I couldn't help feeling that Wadi Halfa had suddenly become Washington, with the woman who ought to have been at the heart of things isolated like an African country from the arrangements being made for her future.

## Mortgaged Beyond the Hilt—A Short Guide to Debt

*Kiaribucho urafiki ni kukopa na kuazima.*
That which spoils friendship is borrowing and lending.
SWAHILI PROVERB

Being lending institutions, the Bank and Fund are closely involved in the unsustainably high levels of debt most African countries built up in the couple of decades after independence.

How did Africa's debt crisis come about? In the 1960s, 1970s, and early 1980s, African governments took out countless loans that Western governments and banks happily farmed out to them with little regard to how they would be repaid. Some went to prop up bad governments or military regimes that are now long gone, often in pursuit of cold war agendas. Some were simply wasted by the governments that received them. Others foundered on false expectations of economic growth.

Skyrocketing interest rates and bad economic policies multiplied these old debts over and over again. Many African countries reached a point where they needed new loans simply to pay off old ones. The full crisis hit when the lenders stopped lending at all, losing faith that new loans would ever be repaid, and

Africa inevitably started to default on existing payments. It was at this point that the international community, mainly through the Fund, started to apply stringent conditions for any new money.

The blame for the debt crisis is a classic example of Africa's problems. It lies primarily with the continent's governments that wasted the money. But the West was highly irresponsible to support so many corrupt regimes, and naïve in the extreme to allow Africa's debts to build up when economic growth was clearly insufficient to enable repayment. A junior bank manager who made so many bad loans without checking the borrowers' ability to repay would have been fired long ago.

Regardless of who was at fault, the debt crisis left the West in what ought to have been a terrible dilemma. On the one hand Western countries wanted to be repaid and want the principle of repayment to be maintained. On the other, they were demanding billions of dollars from countries like Uzima that were simply unable, by anyone's calculations, to meet the basic needs of their people. Should modern African governments and their impoverished people pay for the faults of previous regimes? Which comes first: repayment or basic human rights? It's not easy.

As it happened, Western finance ministries didn't seem to find this much of a dilemma until public pressure built up among Western electorates, not least through an international campaign in the late 1990s, for debts to be written off on a one-time basis. Until that point, many African countries simply continued to default and saw their debts rise and rise. Nigeria, for example, originally borrowed $5 billion from foreign governments and institutions; although it had since paid back $16 billion, in early 2006 it still owed $32 billion more (these arrears have since been liquidated, through a combination of repayment from increased oil receipts and debt write-offs).[19]

The campaign for debt relief has seen gradually increasing amounts of money written off, not least an agreement at the 2005 G8 summit in Gleneagles to write off the entire debt of the world's eighteen poorest countries, most of which are African—an initiative that has since been delivered on and expanded to other countries. Finally, Africa's debt problem is being tackled in a serious way. But it has yet to benefit all needy countries and, rather depressingly, some Western governments continue to pay for debt relief out of their aid budgets—which means as an African president that you might get some debt canceled, but you get less aid as a result. As for Uzima, it was not "poor enough" to qualify for the initial write-off, though it is now receiving some relief and should benefit further if the initiative is expanded as promised.*

## Why Even Democratic Regimes Borrow Irresponsibly

Long-term lending and short electoral terms do not go together. If you're in charge of an African country that is short of resources, with all the pressures that entails, and you know you can get a big loan, then you're very likely to take it. Repayment happens over many years and you're more focused on what you can achieve now rather than what your successors in a distant future may have to deal with. If, of course, you are corrupt, you'll definitely take the money regardless.

All this brings into question whether very poor African countries should be able to borrow at all. Most African presidents would probably not want to relinquish their ability to borrow from institutions like the Bank because they get better control over what those resources are used for than with

---

* *What about countries like Zimbabwe, which are very poor but very badly run? Even if debt is unfair, it would seem pointless to allow Mugabe's regime more money. The answer is to put aside the savings from debt relief and hold them in trust for such a time that a government is in place that will allow the country to benefit from it.*

most donor aid. But if the Bank model of large-scale systemic assistance could be maintained, with loans replaced by equally reliable grants, it would be a step worth taking. The Bank has shown some signs of moving in this direction in recent years, but African countries have, perhaps rightly, been suspicious that it is tied up with a Western agenda to gain greater control over exactly what they are allowed to spend Bank resources on.

Africa's continuing debt problem continues to grab headlines. But is debt relief more important than aid, and would we need aid at all if we wrote off all the debt? Uganda, the first African country to benefit from debt relief and a big recipient of aid, used the money saved to help double primary school enrollment and invest in its national HIV/AIDS plan, which has contributed to the country's successful reversal of HIV infection rates. It's an example of what can be achieved. Yet it's small beer compared to aid money. In 2004, Uganda received $760 million overall in aid grants, more than eight times the savings from its debt relief[20]— and hence could achieve much more with it.

The truth is that a dollar of debt relief is pretty much the same as a dollar of (good, systemic) aid. Writing off debt is important, but far more aid will still be required if African countries are to have a chance of meeting their basic needs. In many ways, debt is simply a useful rallying point for public attention, an issue where the inequity and unsustainability of Africa's plight stands out particularly clearly. It's unconscionable to make people who have almost nothing send money to people who have lots, just because they used to have some bad leaders to whom the West gave money in the past.

So how does international aid measure up to the test of all types of development aid: *whether it helps reduce poverty with lasting effect?* Large-scale institutions like the World Bank offer the right model for much aid: resources from many different Western countries are pooled into one pot and reliably distributed according to one agreed-upon set of conditions. In this sense it's much more effective than national aid, and as a U.S. or other Western taxpayer, you're mostly getting better value for money. The problems instead are in the some of the conditions attached to those Bank loans and in the narrowly ill-fitting mandate of the Fund.

Yet all debates about the quality of aid melt into the background when the issue of the *quantity* thunders into view. It doesn't matter how well you tune your car's engine: if there isn't enough fuel you'll never reach your destination. Much as I enjoyed Sudanese engagement parties, it would have been stupid for Mary Louise and me to set off in our Land Rover from Rwanda one day if we'd known we could never make it through to London. (As it was, I rolled the car in Syria and we finished the journey by bus and train, though that's another story.)

# CHAPTER 8
# AID BETRAYED

It's late afternoon in Kinshasa, and Marie is walking home from work. Today was a good day. She did some road sweeping and got just over a dollar in pay. She has perfected the hamstring-defying art—apparently achievable by African women and Olympic gymnasts alone—of serenely reaching down to hand-brush streets or mop floors while keeping her legs entirely straight and bending double from the hips, spare hand behind the back for balance. If it was a yoga move they'd call it the "cleaning with decorum pose."

Marie's country, D.R. Congo, remains more screwed up than any of its continental neighbors. Militias still run free in the east of the country killing and raping, the putative peace process is fragile, the country's institutions, roads, and few hospitals are in appalling disrepair, and most children don't attend school. D.R. Congo is a reality check, a reminder that, while more humanitarian and peacekeeping efforts would help, there is little that systemic development aid can achieve until a country sorts its own basics out.

Yet it's clear from talking to Marie that she continues to hold out hope. And, in denial of more than one hundred years of history, perhaps she's right to do so. D.R. Congo has significant potential wealth in its minerals. With some sustained political progress and some reasonable people in power, the country would clearly stand a chance. The question is whether it would receive the outside financing it needs in those first few years to make it stable enough to attract longer-lasting investment.

Could education systems be supported to gradually get every child like Jean Baptiste into school? Could clean water be made available to all, rather than being bought yellow jerry can by yellow jerry can for the lucky few? Could decent roads finally cut into D.R. Congo's unbridled jungle and enable trade to increase?

Wouldn't we all like to believe in a world where this could happen?

## A History of Lies

The biggest complaint of aid critics runs thus: there's no point spending more money on aid because it hasn't worked to date. To which the simple answer is: it's never been tried in the style and scale required to give it a chance. Aid's biggest scandal is that there is remarkable consensus about how much aid would be needed to really help halve poverty, that Western countries have continually promised to deliver these amounts, and that they have continually failed to do so.

As Marie continues the walk back to her downtrodden district and Jean Baptiste, tens of thousands of American and European aid workers, donor officials, and consultants across the continent are also finding their own way back to their homes and hotels. More than thirty-five years ago, at the 1970 UN General Assembly, their governments undertook to spend a *minimum* of 0.7 percent of their gross national income (GNI) on aid for poor countries,[21] with a commitment that each country would "exert its best efforts" to reach that figure by 1975. The 0.7 percent benchmark was based on best projections at the time of what might be needed, and widely endorsed as a sum that was realistically affordable, as well as morally appropriate.

Did they reach 0.7 percent by 1975? What has actually happened to aid levels is this:

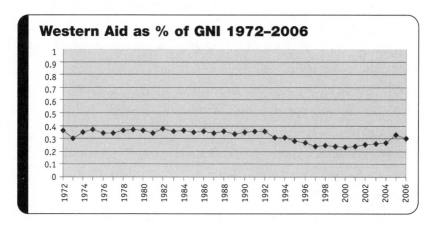

**Western Aid as % of GNI 1972–2006**

Let's be clear about this. No one in the West changed their mind about the need for 0.7 percent over this period. In fact, Western countries continued to promise they would spend 0.7 percent in countless international communiqués, including at the notable UN Financing for Development summit in Mexico in 2002. It's an extraordinary three and a half decades of unmet promises (with honorable exceptions to the regrettably small countries of Denmark, Luxembourg, the Netherlands, Norway, and Sweden). I'm not aware of any other area of modern political life where democratic Western governments have so consistently lied—both to the poorest countries of the world and to their own electorates.

## How Much Do We Need Now?

Before considering the price of these lies, it's only honest to check first whether 0.7 percent remains the amount needed. Economists rightly hate spending targets that don't change for decades, suspecting them of being arbitrary public rallying points rather than accurate assessments of need. Do we still need so much?

The welcome answer (though one avoided by some aid campaigners) is probably not. Western economies have grown hugely since 1970. Given that African economies have stagnated over the same period, the good—if ironic—news is that 0.7 percent now would go a lot farther than it did then. And thanks in · part to every poor country writing a Poverty Reduction Strategy plan, it has become easier to calculate the rough costs of all poor countries' meeting the Millennium Development Goals, including the halving of poverty by 2015. The UN's own Millennium Project estimated that the amount of aid needed from Western GNI was around 0.44 percent in 2006, rising to 0.54 percent by 2015 (as systems expand they can absorb more investment). This tallied fairly accurately with estimates prepared in 2002 (when aid stood at 0.25 percent) by an eminent panel led by former Mexican president Ernesto Zedillo—and endorsed by all Western countries later that year—which called for a doubling of aid if the MDGs were to have a chance of being achieved.

But, and the page simply isn't big enough for how big this "but" is, these estimates of very roughly 0.5 percent of GNI being needed for aid to help halve poverty are based on that aid being good quality and systemic. As we've already seen, that mostly isn't the case. The tying of aid to consultants from your own country, duplication, obsession with projects, double-counting debt relief as aid, and a lack of focus on the poorest countries all mean that aid isn't nearly as effective as it should be.

## What Your Leaders Say

You don't need to take my word for the need to increase aid. Here are some of the many VIPs who agree with me:

*"I call on all the world's nations to implement the Monterrey Consensus [which requires countries to make 'concrete efforts' towards 0.7 percent of GNI being spent on aid]."*[22]
George W. Bush, 2005 (U.S. aid in 2005: 0.22 percent. In 2006: 0.17 percent)

*"It is clear that the current volume of official development assistance will not be sufficient . . . The amounts involved look small compared to the additional wealth that world economic growth creates each year."*[23]
Jacques Chirac, president of France, 2004 (French aid when Chirac came to power in 1995: 0.55 percent. In 2006, Chirac's last full year in office: 0.47 percent)

*"Human development is both a moral end in itself and also a central pillar of our national security . . . [We must] continue to increase development assistance."*[24]
Condoleeza Rice, 2007, comparing the Bush administration's aid efforts with the Marshall Plan in Europe after World War II (U.S. aid at the height of the Marshall Plan: 3.2 percent)

*"[Increasing aid levels] is a kind of goal for the international community to attain, but it isn't a commitment by the countries. We are fully aware of the significance of that political declaration, so we have no intention of forgetting that."*[25]
Masaharu Kohno, the Japanese prime minister's personal representative on Africa, 2005 (Japanese aid in 2006: 0.25 percent, after six reductions over the previous seven years)

—   —   —

*"The numbers are roughly these: $900 billion on defence; $300 billion on agriculture; and $50 to $60 billion on aid, of which about half gets there in cash . . . unless we deal with the fundamentals, we'll be playing at the fringes."*[26]
James Wolfensohn, former president of the World Bank

## So How Much Are We Short?

Although it's difficult to calculate exactly, there is reasonable consensus about how much of current assistance constitutes the "real aid" African countries need to develop. The widely respected Washington-based Center for Global Development calculates that, on average, aid spent through westerners' taxes should be discounted by fully 61 percent to represent its real value (American aid fares especially badly, with a 65 percent discount).[27] In other words, less than 40 cents of every aid dollar we spend really helps the intended beneficiaries. Even the best-quality national aid donor by CGD's calculation (Denmark) has its aid discounted by 50 percent. In its 2007 assessment using mainly 2005 figures, CGD concluded that true aid spent by OECD countries (Europe, the United States, Canada, and Japan), even when charitable giving had been included, was only 0.15 percent of Western GNI, less than a third of the 0.5 percent needed.

The 2005 *Real Aid* report, of the Africa-based organization Action Aid, went into even greater depth. Like the CGD study, Action Aid's calculations represent a rough kind of science with a fair bit of guesswork, and its assessment of individual donors' performance sometimes varies from CGD's (best-quality donor: Ireland). But after discounting aid for factors including transaction and administrative costs, overpriced technical assistance, double-counting of debt relief, and a lack of focus on the poorest countries, Action Aid's overall conclusions were remarkably similar to those of the CGD study. Action Aid concluded that only 39 percent of global aid (excluding charity aid) can be considered "real aid"—again a discount of 61 percent.

According to some critics, these ratings may in fact be generous to donors. The UN Millennium Project, as we saw in chapter 6, believed that only 24 percent of aid actually finances real poverty-targeting investments on the ground. But regardless of exact figures, what is blindingly clear is that Western governments need to significantly increase their aid, as well as improve its quality, if we are to meet the Millennium Development Goals. In other words, they finally need to come through on their promises. It would be nice to say that we should increase the scale of aid only once the quality has improved, but the sad truth is we can't afford to wait. Systemic aid can make a real difference to Africa, and the key is in increasing this kind of aid while trying to reform the rest. Given the inefficiencies, 0.7 percent is the minimum target countries should aim for in the meantime.

### Find Out More and Hold Them to Account . . .

This table shows how much some of the larger Western countries spent in 2005—the most recent year with comparable data—along with CGD's analysis of how much constituted "real aid." I've also included Action Aid's assessment of 2003 figures, when aid levels were broadly similar, for extra comparison.

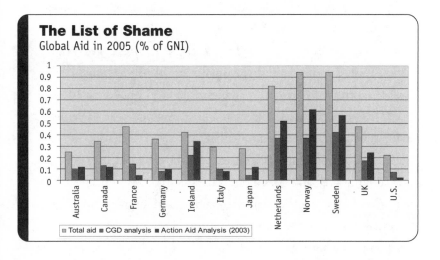

**The List of Shame**
Global Aid in 2005 (% of GNI)

Both the Center for Global Development's *Commitment to Development Index* at www.cgdev.org and the Action Aid *Real Aid* report at www.actionaid.org are really worth a look if you want to know more about how your government's aid compares to other countries', how much they spend on consultants, and so on. The CGD index is regularly updated and also gives marks for Western countries' policies on trade, investment, environmental, and other development issues.

## American Booty

It's worth taking a quick moment to examine why America's aid performance is so poor, partly as a case study but also because America is the country, above all others, that counts. Its super-size economy means that despite the fact that only Greece spends less per person, it is the largest donor by a mile, with an aid budget of nearly $23 billion in 2006. America meeting the 0.7 percent or 0.5 percent targets would be a far greater contribution to reducing poverty than anyone else could make. Yet it has no plans to do so. In fact, to give America a strange kind of credit, Washington has traditionally been much more cautious than most Western capitals about making grand promises for future aid spending it later will not keep. The OECD's best guess from Bush administration statements is that the United States will be spending only 0.18 percent of its GNI on aid by 2010.

This requires some understanding. Anyone who is familiar with the United States knows that American society is notably generous, despite the cartoon caricature of American international ignorance and parsimony shared abroad. Americans spend far more on domestic charities, faith-based organizations, and foundations than the citizens of most other rich countries. It's also important to recognize that this isn't a partisan political issue: it will surprise many Europeans to discover that George W. Bush is marginally more generous on funding than his predecessor. So when it comes to aid, how does America end up, in the words of former president Jimmy Carter in 1999, "the stingiest nation of all?"[28]

A big part of the problem is that most Americans are simply not aware of their government's lack of generosity—so the politicians and bureaucrats don't feel the heat from an electorate demanding they do more. A 2005 *Washington Post* survey[29] revealed that about half of Americans thought that more money was spent on foreign aid than on Medicare or Social Security (combined 2006 cost: $921 billion[30]—forty times more than the aid budget). A similar 1996 survey showed that the median amount of the federal budget Americans thought *ought* to be spent on aid was 15 percent—fifteen times the actual sum.[31] When informed in a 2005 survey about the 0.7 percent GNI aid target, 65 percent of Americans wanted their government to meet it as long as other rich countries were doing the same.

There is no doubt, therefore, that America's government persistently spends less on aid than its electorate wants or believes. The reality is that spending of 0.17 percent of GNI on aid (2006) is dwarfed twenty to thirty times by funding for the military. And very little of that little aid is the systemic support Africa needs. After the 40 percent or more going to consultants, much of the rest is spent through charities, leaving those charities loath to criticize administration policies for fear of losing funding. Bush, like Clinton, talks a good game—but even his much-hyped Millennium Challenge Account first had its commitments cut by Congress and has since consistently failed to translate into the intended level of spending.

One of the White House's and Congress's prime excuses is an

almost obsessive fear of corruption, which feeds off the errors of American aid's politicized cold war past and bears little reality to how aid nowadays can be sensibly processed and monitored. It is ironic then that in 2003, Congress agreed to Bush's demand for nearly $20 billion for reconstruction in Iraq, more than that year's annual aid budget for the rest of the world. Don't get me wrong: it was absolutely right that America should come up with serious reconstruction money after deciding to go to war. Yet not only did this show an ability and willingness to meet big bills when seen as necessary, but Iraq—a fractious post-conflict sectarian state with destroyed institutions, massive public distrust, huge security problems, and endemic graft—was the hardest aid environment I've ever worked in. If aid could be spent on a large scale there, it could certainly be spent in Africa's many democracies, some with records of stability established over decades.

In the end, development aid provides a philosophical challenge for American society. It has a different attitude toward the role of the state than most Western countries. America's state is relatively minimal, with federal government responsible only for a few key areas and overall tax receipts relatively small at around 32 percent of GDP, compared to, say, 50 percent for France and nearly 60 percent for Norway and Sweden.[32] Americans instead choose private giving, corporate scholarships, and so on to provide for many elements of education, health, and welfare.

The problem is that this approach doesn't map well with the needs of the poorest countries when it comes to aid. Americans don't spend nearly as much privately on aid as surveys suggest they think they do (see the table in chapter 4 for the real figures). And even if they spent huge amounts, charities and faith-based organizations don't have the structural, coherent answers Africa currently needs.

American society can maintain a substantive private role in providing for its domestic public social needs because it has a well-functioning state and a welfare safety net. Most African states do not function properly and have no such safety nets. They need them, on a basic level, before their people can progress, and American assistance needs to reflect this. The aid world—not to mention people like Lucas and Nancy, Marie and Jean Baptiste—desperately needs more American leadership. But American taxpayers, more than most of their Western counterparts, are being shortchanged and badly misled.

## Waking Up to the Men in Pink

Two of my best friends in Africa were Claire and Emma, both in their twenties. From Hereford and Shrewsbury in the UK, they had volunteered to teach English in a Rwandan school for a couple of years. The apprehension I had felt arriving in Kigali for the first time must have been nothing compared to their trepidation about their new home in the rural east of the country. After a couple of days' "orientation" in the capital from the charity that had posted them, including a documentary about the machete-wielding militias who had roamed the impoverished countryside during the genocide, they were packed off to a two-room house on the outskirts of the small town of Rwamagana. There, with no electricity, they made themselves at home as best they could by lamplight and settled in for their first night.

First thing in the morning they woke to shouts and banging right outside the door. Emma peered from the dusty window. Around twenty men in pink shirts and shorts—the color genocide suspects are made to wear when on excursions from prison—stood around the house with machetes and other tools in hand, plus two soldiers in full fatigues armed with Kalashnikovs. After some understandable hesitation, she opened the door a crack to get a decent view of what was going on. Most of the men appeared to be busy. Then one of the soldiers saw her and called out firmly, "Morning, sir."

The detachment of genocide suspects had been dispatched by the local council to build the teachers from England a kitchen on the end of their house. Prisoners were used in a similar manner for small projects across Rwanda, and, surprisingly, I never heard stories of escape. Driving among the country's thousand hills, one of the most spectacular sights to behold would be a crowd of fifty or so pink-clad men swaying shoulder to shoulder in the back of a truck as it negotiated yet another bend-obsessed road on the way to a job somewhere, or on the way back to one of the hugely overcrowded jails.

While Claire and Emma both took every available opportunity on weekends to escape Rwamagana for the bright lights of Kigali, the wooden construction caked in mud on the end of their Rwamagana house remained for them a wonderful, if weird, welcome into their new community. There should be no underestimating the extraordinary things that can happen, if people are given the right opportunities.

## The Good News?

The good news is . . . in 2005 many Western countries repledged themselves to spend more on aid. This may sound laughable, but several of them set actual deadlines by which to achieve the increases, and some are promising to make this new spending more systemic. Why did they do so? Perhaps partly because the weight of evidence and consensus that good aid really can work is becoming too much to ignore. But also because of the enormous public pressure on Western governments from their public to do so, during the Make Poverty History/One campaigns of that year.

This *could* be a significant breakthrough in the financing of aid, even if the OECD's best guess is that overall levels would only reach 0.36 percent by 2010—before any discounting for quality. The question, of course, is whether the latest promises will be kept, or whether 2005 will just prove to have been 1975 without the bell-bottoms. The last section of this book, on Change, makes a deeper assessment of 2005's new promises in a range of areas, performance so far, and what more we can do to push things further (2006 and 2007 weren't encouraging, but there are still grounds for hope). Tony Blair was so skeptical about the track record of Western leaders in keeping their promises on aid that, at the Gleneagles G8 summit, he took the unprecedented step of making Presidents Bush, Chirac, and Berlusconi, Prime Ministers Koizumi and Martin, and Chancellor Schröder—and himself—sign the commitment to double aid in person in front of the world's media. But whether the commitments are honored probably depends more on whether the public in Western countries keeps pressing our leaders to deliver.

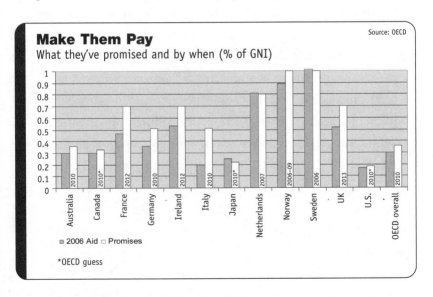

**Make Them Pay**
Source: OECD
What they've promised and by when (% of GNI)

2006 Aid □ Promises

*OECD guess

## Aid Betrayed: Band-Aids, Not Solutions

The persistent underfunding of aid is the last in the litany of flaws in the industry. To inefficiency is added insufficiency.

It's understandable that many skeptics of aid ask why we should spend more aid on Africa when it has had so little effect to date. But it is absolutely the wrong question. Did scientists give up on the space race after the first rockets blew up or didn't get far enough? They learned the lessons, refined the equipment, and ensured there'd be enough fuel to burst through the atmosphere.

It was clear in Uzima, under your leadership, that the inability to meet people's basic needs exacerbates the continent's other problems, fertilizing the ground for corruption and instability. None of those problems are the West's fault. But we find ourselves with the fortune and the responsibility to hold some of the solutions.

The confusing thing is that aid continues *not* to be delivered in the means and amounts most politicians and bureaucrats agree is necessary to make a difference (when they're not sitting in front of their checkbooks, that is). Of course, it is not 100 percent guaranteed that all systemic aid would support much greater poverty reduction: the reality is that some poor countries would prosper on it and others would not. Yet countries like Mozambique and Tanzania show that substantial amounts of systemic aid can deliver tremendous rewards in education and basic health care, not to mention reducing poverty. We have simply never tried making this level of support available to all countries that could benefit from it. This is the most extraordinary scandal of all about aid: we haven't even been trying to do what we think would work better.

It is hardly new to suggest that poor countries need significant financial help. South Korea received the modern equivalent of around $100 in aid per person per year between 1955 and 1972.[33] The expansion of the European Union has long been based on the fundamental principle that poorer members joining the club will need "structural" (i.e., substantial and systemic) funding to break through to levels of affluence mutually beneficial to all. Portugal and Ireland, to name but two countries, developed radically on the back of such financing, along with access to rich Europe's markets. More recently, all the eastern European countries joining the EU received huge levels of structural funding—far more than 0.7 percent aid spending would enable African countries to receive.

The main difference with Africa, of course, is that South Korea and EU accession countries were seen as politically and economically important. Would the aid effort in Africa really be so blatantly inefficient if it was really important for us to do better there—or if we suffered the direct political and economic consequences of its failure? There are undoubtedly things for the West to gain from Africa's progress, but these appear to be too long-term to make us sit up and smell the (imported) coffee.

In an ideal world, the West would accept a role as venture capitalist for the world's poorest countries too if it is serious about sparking growth, instead of the rather patronizing spoon-feeding of small amounts of assistance here and there. Performance to date has been weak. No venture capital firm would offer businesses such unpredictable loans and grants. No venture capital firm would apply such a wide variety of changing conditions. Most of all, no sensible venture capital firm would bother backing any organization with only half or less of the money it needs for its business plan. It would realize that the plan wouldn't work, the business wouldn't thrive, and the venture capital firm would lose its investment.

What is the cost of this failure? Africans are denied adequate help in their daily struggle to beat poverty. No, let's be more honest: *people die when they don't need to.* Western taxpayers and charity donors are not getting the results from their aid money they would hope—more simply: *not getting what they paid for;* and, though this may not be the most serious element, thousands of aid workers are left to return home each evening to the most pleasant of houses in the most unpleasant of knowledge—that they are working within a flawed system unable to deliver its objectives.

In some ways it's hard for me personally to write so critically of aid. The donor agency I was lucky enough to work for, the UK's Department for International Development, is in little denial about the scale of the problem. It has been at the forefront of international efforts to make assistance more systemic and, with a number of other donors, is thinking about how to reform the aid world's institutional system (a system usually referred to as the "international architecture," even though it bears greater resemblance to Marie's rickety shack near the Congo River).

Yet if the West's overall effort is inadequate, that is what counts. The great rhetoric all our governments speak about our generosity and the deceptively grand claims charities make for our donations in an attempt to elicit our money make us believe we are really doing something about the poverty in places like Africa, when by and large we are not. Ironically, the best intentions of thousands of aid workers then become mere Band-Aids, concealing from all our eyes the real scale of the wound.

And perhaps most irritating of all, inadequate aid means we fail once again to turn the spotlight on African governments to see whether, with sufficient resources, they could really provide for their people and make a go of the future.

If anyone feels shortchanged at this point about their aid money, they should. But they shouldn't get too depressed. It's only by understanding the wastefulness of the present that we can appreciate how to get better value for money in the future. And it's worth noting that, while we as individuals can still make a difference to a few people's lives through thoughtfully chosen charity donations, we can make a far bigger impact by improving the quality and quantity of national and international aid—as we will see later on.

Let's return to that reassuringly irreproachable president, in the beautiful sun-washed land of Uzima. With more resources than half of Africa's leaders, you are not in such dire straits as many. Yet you are fundamentally unable to meet your people's basic needs.

After those interminable presentations by the health, education, finance, and various other ministers on your very first day in office, you go back to State House for the evening, pretty down about your prospects. But overnight you remembered that you'd clean forgotten to ask anyone to talk about the aid Uzima receives. All the foreign ambassadors lining up to meet you in your new role have been at pains to boast about how much assistance their countries provide. So the following morning you nip down the corridors of the president's office to see the director of International Cooperation. Surrounded by the ubiquitous glass-doored cabinet and dark, imported desk that sit on carpeting, rather than linoleum—the flooring of choice for self-respecting senior officials on the continent—you ask for a briefing on the aid effort and how much it helps meet the gaps in your country's needs.

What do you get? Well, there are those 828 branches of international NGOs, not to mention local charities, running around in a rather uncoordinated fashion. They help in some localities but are only able to do small bits and pieces (and not all of it stuff you'd choose). Then there are more than twenty national and international aid donors, mostly trying to help more centrally, not to mention all the UN agencies. They help a bit too, with some useful consultants providing technical assistance in the ministries (as well as others wasting space). But these donors also duplicate each other chronically, demanding your hard-pressed officials' time throughout the year for those 1,000 visiting missions and 10,000 quarterly reports.

And the bottom line? For all this effort that sometimes feels rather more like a distraction, Uzima is receiving less than a third of the real investment it needs to help you halve poverty and meet the other Millennium Development Goals.

Last night's gloom threatens to settle in again as you walk back to the presidential suite. But all is not lost. You remind yourself that, in many ways, aid is really just an interim measure until growth itself kicks in, making all the people richer as well as increasing your government's revenues.

What matters in the long term more than anything is to increase trade. Again, the West is closely involved, both because it has the richest markets you want to access and because it sets most of the rules defining the terms under which you can trade internationally.

Better hope it's a better story.

# TRADE
## DUSTY PLAINS AND
## UNLEVEL PLAYING FIELDS

# CHAPTER 9
# IN THEORY

## Rabbit Stew

It's slightly embarrassing to admit how quickly I became used to life in my ample Alpine residence in Rwanda. Comfortable sofas and European style for mature African guests in one room; fake leopardskin chairs and African kitsch for young European friends in another—plus a kitchen large enough to swing a big cat in. I negotiated with the landlord to spend some of the monthly rent building an outdoor roofed area on the side of the house that enabled me to hold meetings outside without drizzle or sizzle, a simple construction of wood and local terra-cotta tiles that looked positively Tuscan to my eyes and incomprehensibly rough to the guards who sat bored by the red gates, day after day and night after night.

It was always nice to pop into the house between meetings in town and catch up with Angelina and Sylvestre. Still rather awkward about people working at my home, I would try to avoid too obviously the roles of employer and employee. But both of them were far less bothered about it: it was reliable work and they would try to capitalize on it as much as possible. Hence they were nearly always busy when I stopped by. Angelina used her copious amounts of spare time to keep up with her studies. Sylvestre, meanwhile, had taken on other work at the houses of some of my colleagues, both to keep him busy and to stop him trimming every single bush in the garden as soon as it grew an inch.

With a family to support, Sylvestre was always looking for ways to bring in extra money. He shared with the guards a small plot of land at the side of the house to grow corn and a few vegetables, and one weekend when I was out there I found a carefully hidden cardboard box concealing a rain-sodden rabbit and six pink, hairless, finger-size babies. All of them died shortly after.

Sylvestre and I discussed it the following Monday. The problem was that he couldn't afford materials to build a proper hutch: I may have boosted his official salary but it was still less than $100 a month. To spend $15 or so on materials, when there are school fees and medical costs to pay, was therefore a huge expense. Plus he didn't know how I'd react to him keeping animals (there was no way he could have kept them at home, where he owned no land and where they might have been stolen while he was out). I agreed to pay for the materials, as long as he made space for the rabbits to run around.

Sylvestre built the hutch almost immediately, given the damp demise of his recent brood. But he saw no value in bouncing, free-range bunnies and first constructed it at such a height above the chicken-wire enclosure that they couldn't possibly jump down and ever get back home again. There was soon a profusion of pink-nosed fluffy white rabbits in the corner of the garden (French pedigree, apparently). They bred just as quickly as they are supposed to, and the guards seemed glad of the distraction provided by occasional escapees, leading to protracted chases in the garden.

Once each generation had fully grown they would disappear

overnight and be carted off to the market. I would mourn their departure while Sylvestre would look at me bemused, delighted by the extra income from this rare business opportunity. He would always offer me one for the pot from each brood, an offer I could never face taking up.

**a**id, no matter how good, can do no more than help create the conditions for development. It can't deliver it. Only trade—and the economic growth it brings—can do that.

While internal trade is important in day-to-day terms, there are fairly few rich consumers in a country like Uzima, so it's hard to make big money. What really matters is selling things to wealthy markets abroad, generating an inflow of foreign currency that can then be invested back home. It has famously been observed that if Africa had done nothing more than maintain the share of world exports it possessed in 1980, average income across the continent would be around double what it is today.[1]

If there is any doubt about the potential of trade to reduce poverty far more effectively than aid, consider this: the main aim of the Millennium Development Goals, to halve the proportion of people of the world living in poverty by 2015, is actually likely to be met. The reason has nothing to do with Africa, where improvements are still minor, but is because China and India have been making huge progress in recent years on the back of increased trade with rich Western markets.

If as taxpayers we in the West seem largely unaware of the poor value for money we are getting for our aid, we seem equally oblivious that it is our patronage, as consumers, that is helping hundreds of millions of Chinese and Indians out of poverty. This may not be something we should take direct credit for—they did the hard work and we just bought things we wanted—but surely it is worth celebrating: the fastest reduction of mass poverty in the history of mankind. And, having criticized America's foreign aid, it is only fair to be honest about Americans' disproportionate role in this process. You should be proud that your business, more than anyone's, has played a key part in China's wondrous transformation, thanks to your two countries' mushrooming trade.

Yet while China and India stride on, there are increasing accusations that the West's trade terms with the very poorest countries of the world—which lack the economic might to negotiate a reasonable deal—are unfair.

This view is no longer restricted to African countries and antiglobalization protesters. Many of us have heard of huge cotton subsidies in the United States that force global prices down, preventing more efficient West African cotton farmers from getting a fair price. Or of subsidies in Europe that enable sugar beets to continue being farmed in Finland and France at two to three times the cost of sugarcane in Malawi and Mozambique, with large surpluses of the beets then dumped on international markets to reduce the market for African sugar even further.

The report of Tony Blair's Commission for Africa, prepared for G8 leaders in 2005 and whose authors included Republican senator Nancy Kassebaum Baker, denounced such trade terms as "unacceptable . . . they are politically antiquated, economically illiterate, environmentally destructive, and ethically indefensible. They must go."[2] Meanwhile, the very purpose of the most recent round of global trade negotiations under the World Trade Organization, known as the "Development Round," has been to give poor countries a better deal. President Bush announced his approach to these negotiations as follows: "Let's join hands as wealthy, industrialized nations and say to the world, we're going to get rid of all our agricultural subsidies together."[3]

No shortage of good intentions, then, just as for aid. But it is wrong to assume they are bound to translate into action. Although limited improvements have been promised on cotton and sugar, the core of the problems goes beyond the rules affecting one or two crops, while many feel the WTO process is little more than a shameful sham.

The bigger question is whether the structures through which we manage trade, as a global community, give poor countries a

## Using Protection

In an entirely free trade world, anyone could sell their produce anywhere. Tariffs (taxes on foreign imports) and subsidies (payments to your own producers) enable countries to distort trade to protect domestic producers against foreign competition; hence the term protectionism.

Although the global trend since the Second World War has been to reduce the level of both tariffs and subsidies in many areas of the economy—the process of liberalization—to this day they still affect the cost of many things we buy. The milk in your local store would be more expensive in most Western countries without subsidies—paid, of course, from your taxes—to dairy farmers. Kellogg's Corn Flakes would be pricier too, without assistance to corn producers, as might chicken, which benefits from subsidized grain used for feed. The same follows for such items as your pasta sauce (tomato subsidies) and the ground meat to go in it (beef and veal subsidies).

Conversely, the spaghetti you cook with your sauce might not cost as much without the guaranteed high prices paid to wheat producers, while many of your clothes would be cheaper without tariffs on foreign textiles, along with cashew nuts, the latest MP3 players, and your new sneakers.

real chance to help themselves. Or, just as with aid, are they fundamentally incapable of doing so? And why, if current trade rules don't work well for the poorest, can they also be acccused of ripping off Western consumers and taxpayers?

These next chapters assess how trade rules actually work, whether they are really unfair or it's simply that Africa is uncompetitive. They also find out the effect on us in the West were we to open up our markets more, including whether we'd lose our jobs, see our farm industries suffer, and pay higher prices at the cash register. It should give us a clear idea of whether we're capable of developing globalization to produce the results we want, both in our societies at home and in the world at large.

Trade is most easily split into three areas. The first covers things going out of Africa, not just exported produce but also people (chapter 10, next). The second covers things coming into Africa, including food aid, investment, and pharmaceutical products (chapter 11). The final chapter considers the effect on us (chapter 12).

But before that it's essential to cover quickly the recent history of world trade, in order to understand where things stand at the moment.

## Postwar Panacea

When American minds started turning to a new world order toward the end of the Second World War, two concerns were at the forefront of their thinking. First, Europe needed to be pulled out of the incredibly destructive cycle of conflict every few decades. Second, the damaging economic problems of the prewar years—when industrialized nations floundered in depression as a result of imposing ever more restrictive tariffs on each other's exports—should be avoided.

Both were, of course, linked. Economic growth and trade interdependence are very good incentives to keep the peace.

Their conclusion was that the world needed some new institutions. The World Bank would lend Europe money to reconstruct. The International Monetary Fund would help countries manage economic dips without having to default on debts and go into recession. And the International Trade Organization would act as trusted mediator for a gradual opening of global markets for trade.

Getting global trade agreements has never been easy, however. Unlike the World Bank and IMF, the ITO never made it into existence—largely because of fears about the impact on members' sovereignty in making their own trade decisions. Instead, America, Britain, and a number of other industrialized countries began some more modest, informal negotiations on a first round of trade reform in 1947. It ended up with what was known as the General Agreement on Tariffs and Trade (GATT).

GATT was broadly successful, and further rounds followed from the 1950s to the 1990s. Global liberalization helped drive America's great postwar growth, Europe's fast recovery, and Japan's extraordinary success. Yet this liberalization focused almost exclusively on opening up markets for industrial goods and manufactures, where the industrialized countries' comparative advantage in the world economy lay. Agriculture and textiles were excluded and remained heavily protected. In part this was because of countries' understandable postwar preoccupation with being able to feed themselves. But it was also because agriculture and textiles were where they were least competitive.

The importance of the exclusion of agriculture and textiles from significant liberalization cannot be overestimated. When African and other poor countries began to join the GATT negotiations in the 1960s and 1970s, in the aftermath of postcolonial independence, they had to sign up to the rules as already agreed upon in previous rounds.

In other words, they would be allowed to sell industrialized products such as cars into rich Western markets—of which, of course, they had none—yet gained only very limited ability to sell agricultural and textile products, which was where they were by far the most competitive. It becomes much easier to understand Africa's post-independence economic struggles when you consider that newborn countries suffering corruption and instability also found few markets to sell their produce into—a problem that, as we will see, still persists today. Southeast Asia's experience is a telling contrast: many countries there found enough money to heavily subsidize industrial areas of production, enabling them to develop before being exposed to full foreign competition and finding a relatively open international market to sell to—in addition to a larger educational base and greater urbanization. It's also significant that Asia is not divided into so many small countries, and far fewer are landlocked.

It is vital to understand Africa's difficulties in trade against this background. Further negotiations under the GATT and, more recently, the World Trade Organization, established in 1994, have not fundamentally changed the emphasis of trade liberalization on the industrialized sector. African countries, with few products of interest to Western markets and few markets of interest to Western producers, have been unable to secure terms more suited to their economies.

As we will see, the latest WTO negotiations, despite being called the Development Round, are highly unlikely to bring a significant improvement. So what effect do the current rules have?

# CHAPTER 10
# OUT OF AFRICA

## Cotton Tale

Back in the eighteenth century, many of my ancestors were living in various villages in Lancashire, England, some near the city of Bolton. They worked as house servants, weavers, and farm laborers. Britain, meanwhile, was approaching the peak of its empire, India was on the way to becoming the jewel in its crown, and demand for cotton had begun to soar.

India had plentiful, good-quality cotton. The raw product itself, picked by the poor, had little value. But when processed into textiles it was worth vastly more. The problem for the British was that the Indians were, of course, very good at processing the cotton themselves, having had a large textile industry for centuries.

In a moment of simple genius, Britain's colonial masters decided to ban the wearing of processed cotton products from India.[4] Instead, the cotton would have to be picked by hand in India and sent raw to the burgeoning mill towns of northwestern England, where it was spun into cloth by mill workers and spun into money by the mill owners. Among tens of thousands of others, my ancestors pulled up stakes and headed for work in industrialized, newly constructed cotton mills.

The trade barriers, combined with the mass-production gains of the Industrial Revolution and my ancestors' labor, meant that Britain soon exported large amounts of cloth back to many countries, including India, which was forced to allow it in almost duty free. A significant proportion of the British Empire's eighteenth-century wealth and resulting power arose from this very direct and simple distortion of global trade, while tens of thousands in India lost their jobs and large numbers probably died. My family, meanwhile, like so many, had begun a long habit of following work opportunities in a gradually globalizing world that would take them to Carlisle (for more work in textiles) and London— and eventually Rwanda.

It would be nice to think the cotton trade, too, has moved on.

## Why Trade Rules Really Matter

Just as for aid, it's important to be honest from the start and acknowledge that the main reasons for Africa's lack of trade progress in recent decades are internal: weak rule of law, corruption, poor infrastructure, and more. But think of economic growth as a traveling circus: while it's the responsibility of African countries to get the show on the road, it's the West's responsibility to ensure there's a road to travel down, because it's largely Western countries with the most desirable markets that get to determine most of the rules.

Trade rules really matter because, unlike developed Western economies, most poor parts of Africa have only a few goods to export. A country like Uzima would perhaps have one major mineral, such as copper or aluminum, and a couple of crops such as cotton or coffee. The rules determining the terms under which they can sell these products in rich markets can therefore have enormous implications for their whole economies, as do any large fluctuations in global prices.

The key test is whether well-managed countries like Uzima that are trying to address their internal problems are getting a fair chance to trade freely on the international stage. It's a test that would have been well understood by American tea importers working in Boston Harbor in 1773.


**f**oreign trade with Africa has been going on for a long time. When three wise men are said to have visited Bethlehem around Christmastime two thousand years ago, they may have arrived from the East but the gifts of gold, frankincense, and myrrh they brought to a poor child lying in a manger probably all came from rather farther south. Back then West Africa was already a key source of gold, transported across the continent and up into the Middle East. Frankincense and myrrh, meanwhile, are resins from the *Boswellia* and *Commiphora* trees common to Somalia.

Aside from a handful of raw materials, the major exports traded out of Africa today are generally simple to produce and capitalize on the continent's climatic or labor-intensive advantages. Several of those exports are also central to our lives in the West, though it's easy to forget how much. As an example, while I sit at my computer typing this I'm wearing jeans, T-shirt, and underwear that are all cotton; earlier today I drove to the gym in a rubber-tired car, and I'm currently undoing my good work there by nibbling on a chocolate bar (cocoa *and* sugar—better hope it's Fairtrade certified).

Oil is actually top of the list of Africa's exports, but in some ways its presence there is misleading. Most African countries, including the vast majority of the poorest ones, do not have significant oil reserves. Even in countries with oil and other large mineral resources, such exports are not labor-intensive in production: their high-value profits can thus easily accrue only to a small elite, which is partly why they are so often subject to corruption.

In contrast, an economy like Uzima's is likely to be mainly reliant on agriculture. Indeed, you may remember from your first day of briefing as president of Uzima that agriculture provides most Uzimans' employment, half the country's exports, and one-third of gross national income. It is progress in this area that would be most significant in reducing ground-level poverty, at least in the medium term, bypassing many of the problems of large-scale graft. Cotton is a good place to start.

## Black Cotton

Mama Idrissou is a cotton farmer in Benin, West Africa. A family man with five children, Idrissou owns only 30 hectares of land, but it is productive and the climate is pretty reliable. Back in 2003, a good year, Idrissou's land yielded about 20 hectares of cotton.

Billy Tiller is a cotton farmer in West Texas. Also a family man, with four children, Tiller farms 2,146 acres of land on the plains that are tough for cotton-growing. There are sandstorms, tornadoes, floods, droughts, frosts, heat waves, and little regular water supply. In 2003 after some particularly bad weather, only 21 of the 1,611 acres Tiller farmed for cotton were left. And he had to work long, hard hours to get even them to yield.

Fortunately, Tiller's tough year had a happy ending. Thanks to the 2002 Farm Bill, American taxpayers paid him a subsidy. The particular mechanism to work out how much is a bit compli-cated (U.S. cotton farmers got paid the difference between the real-world market price for cotton and a speculative, more gener-ous price for 85 percent of their acres based on a preidentified average yield per acre), but the end result was highly generous. Not only was Tiller paid more for his 21 acres of cotton than the cotton was worth, he was paid for nearly all the acres that went to rot too.

Back in West Africa, Idrissou also had the occasional bad season. When this happened he got little or no such help. Partly thanks to IMF advice, Benin's government wouldn't provide him with subsidies for his crop. This was sensible in that the government could hardly afford it. Idrissou knew that if he couldn't produce or sell his cotton, his family might go hungry or he might even, like some of his neighbors in recent years, go bust and have to sell his precious land.

So far, so unequal. But so what? If America wants to protect its farmers against bad harvests, isn't it entitled to? It's hardly America's fault if Benin is unable to do the same.

The problem is that Tiller and Idrissou are both selling cotton to the same world market. As it happens, it's not when Tiller has a bad year and receives lots of subsidies that Idrissou gets worried; it's when Tiller has a good year, produces lots of cotton, and *still* receives high subsidies that the anxiety sets in. That's because, even in favorable conditions, Tiller's cotton is considerably more expensive to produce than Idrissou's, leaving it uncompetitive. The subsidies allow Tiller to keep producing cotton and sell it for less than it costs him to farm it. The result is a double whammy for Idrissou: there's more competition for his cotton on the world market, which might mean he can't sell any at all, and the overall price goes down.

There are 25,000 cotton farmers in America like Billy Tiller. There are 10 or 11 million West Africans like Mama Idrissou dependent on the cotton trade, some of whose own ancestors, incidentally, may well have been taken by slave ships a couple of centuries ago to help make a success of the first American cotton plantations. Tiller is doubtless a hardworking man who is just trying to get by and provide for his family. And, as he was at pains to explain to the journalist who visited both him and Mama Idrissou in 2003, he bears no ill will whatsoever toward foreign competitors. Yet the subsidies given to him directly mean less money for Idrissou, his family, and the families of all the other West African cotton farmers.

American and (smaller) European cotton subsidies are estimated to cost West African cotton producers $250 million a year. Their exports would go up an estimated 75 percent if the subsidies disappeared.[5] This is the nature of modern, globalized trade: actions in one country have effects on another—particularly the actions of rich countries on their poorer counterparts. It's a reality, no matter how firmly we may wish to close our eyes to it.

There is another loser here: the U.S. taxpayer. In 2001–02, the total subsidies estimated to have been received by American cotton farmers were . . . *drum roll* . . . $3.9 billion. To put that figure into some context, it is almost twice the entire gross domestic product of Benin; it is more than three times as much aid as the U.S. gave all of sub-Saharan Africa in 2001;[6] and, perhaps most shockingly as far as economists are concerned, it is more than the entire value of the U.S. cotton crop that year.

It was also the equivalent of giving every one of those American cotton farmers a grant of $156,000 to start farming something else. Or indeed enough for every American to buy a couple of pristine African cotton T-shirts.

In March 2005, the World Trade Organization issued a ruling against U.S. cotton subsidies, after years of protests by African countries and NGOs. What happened next? The subsidies continued. In 2005 they were $4.2 billion.[7] In 2006, Congress did dismantle about 10 percent of the overall subsidy program, but the WTO confirmed this wasn't enough to comply with its ruling. And in 2007, the House of Representatives passed its own version of the 2007 Farm Bill, which actually reinstated some of the subsidies the previous Congress had dismantled.

What can Africa's cotton countries do in light of this? There are no tit-for-tat retaliatory measures they can impose on American exports to their own tiny markets. Besides, they want to remain on good terms to get American aid and favor.

If and when America does get around to cutting cotton subsidies again in response to the WTO ruling, it will undeniably be progress and of some help to Mama Idrissou. But it's highly unlikely the subsidies will disappear—they will just be a little smaller. Even if American cotton is forced to become less competitive internationally, West African cotton farmers will still be denied a level playing field within the valuable American market at the very least, as this is where the subsidies will still be allowed to focus.

The lesson is that even in the rare cases where the WTO rules against unfair Western protectionism, the outcome is still not the free market that African countries want if trade is really going to fire growth.

### Beef about the Milk Cows

For most non-oil-producing African countries, agriculture is the mainstay of the economy and the biggest source of foreign exchange.[8] Unfortunately, agriculture is also the sector on which the West spends by far the most subsidies. Farmers in the West receive the equivalent of $300–$350 billion a year, more than ten times as much as Africa receives in aid. The support covers all manner of crops and livestock, several of which are of interest to African farmers.

One such is cattle farming. As many NGO campaign leaflets like to observe, European cows are effectively subsidized at $803 per year, American cows at $1,057, and Japanese cows at an astonishing $2,555.[9] That equals more than $2, $3, and $7 a day respectively. Meanwhile, 300 million people in Africa live on less than $1 a day. Unsurprisingly, African farmers find it hard to capitalize on the world's appetite for beef and dairy produce.

The story is repeated for any number of exports, from olives to rice to honey. As with cattle, there is little African presence in the world markets for these products at the moment, but this is partly because there's no incentive for Africans or foreigners to invest in these areas while the global playing field remains so tilted.

The fact that the sector that matters most to African countries is also the one on which the West spends most subsidies is, of course, no coincidence. If someone somewhere else wasn't producing farm goods cheaper than in the West, there wouldn't be a need to subsidize farmers to enable them to remain competitive. Yet even judged by an objective of keeping domestic farmers in work, many subsidies are excessive. There is no logic to British, Finnish, and French farmers still farming sugar when it costs them three times as much to do so as their counterparts in countries like Mozambique (annual gross national income per person: $250[10]) and Brazil—leading to enormous subsidies from the taxpayer—especially since they could more productively farm something else. The WTO recently ruled against one aspect of Europe's sugar subsidies too, but again it will not lead to the full and free market Africa wants.

Why are agricultural subsidies so extraordinarily high? They are a historical hangover. In Europe's case—where the subsidies are highest and do most damage to Africa—they survive from the parlous aftermath of the Second World War, when farmers were

encouraged to produce as much as they could to enable a continent to feed itself again. U.S. subsidies meanwhile, though not as
large as those in Europe, endure from Roosevelt's New Deal in
response to the Dust Bowl and Depression of the 1930s. In both
cases, they have long outlived the conditions for which they were
created, and we are deep into an era of mass overproduction.

Unlike cotton subsidies, the West's agricultural subsidies are
not even on the table for significant reform in the foreseeable
future. Some efforts have been made in both America and
Europe to mitigate the most obviously damaging payments—
including in the maddeningly complex 2007 U.S. Farm Bill—but
the overall level of subsidies will remain similar. Again, it's a case
of some improvement, but nothing like that promised at the
beginning of the WTO Development Round.

I don't want to dwell yet on *why* these subsidies stay so high:
support for rural industries is an important and emotive issue for
many Western countries, and influential lobbies are at play. But
for the time being, what we can certainly accept is that they
continue to have important implications for people in Africa and
other poor parts of the world. Just as happened with cotton,
prices and demand for African farmers' produce go down and
economies are denied an opportunity to grow.

## Ambassador, You Spoil Us

An even higher proportion of Rwandans—nearly 90 percent—work in
agriculture than in almost any other African country. A year into the job,
I realized I hadn't been out enough into the countryside to see what
rural life was really like, instead of visiting offices and reading reports
about it. So I tagged along for a day with a group that was mapping
parts of the country particularly vulnerable to food shortages and
malnutrition.

This may sound crude, but it never fails to astonish how poor some people can be. During the day we visited a few homes that were unlike anything I'd seen outside refugee camps. Despite being in their own villages, these people had all but no possessions. Houses of damp mud walls with nothing to decorate them. A broken door that never shuts and no money to buy nails. Two sets of clothes if they were lucky—both so threadbare that the basic function of covering up private parts was not always met. No shoes. One cracked plastic bowl for a family. Ill health writ large on craggy faces and cramped bodies.

I had to leave the group early to return to the National Day celebrations at one of the large European embassies. Two hours after driving out of the villages I was in line with numerous dignitaries on a red carpet about to be greeted by the ambassador and military attaché (in full uniform). The people I had met that morning and afternoon did not earn the price of one soda in a day. Now it was cocktails and canapés with diplomats and ministers on the lawn. The contrast felt as big as they come.

Just as with consultants and aid workers staying in luxury hotels, there's little intrinsically wrong with westerners holding fancy parties in poor countries. Why shouldn't they? It's what their countrymen do back home, and our own societies are awash with conspicuous displays of disposable consumption. You could even argue that such events help bring money into poor economies. It's the policies of the countries Western diplomats and aid workers represent that are the real awkwardness.

Ending or amending the West's agricultural subsidies would not directly help the poorest of the poor in Africa—they live almost entirely outside the market altogether. But if their countries as a whole began to take off, they would eventually gain too. And if subsidies are combined with a serious aid effort, there's a good chance the next generation will not have to cope with so extraordinarily little while they wait for economic opportunity finally to arrive.

## Coffee with a Bitter Taste

It's fairly easy to see how Africa sometimes has its agricultural produce and cotton taken to the cleaners, because it's in competition with richer rivals. But what about when Africa is not in a direct clash with the West?

Originally from the province of Kaffa, Ethiopia, coffee was allegedly discovered when a goatherd saw his animals chewing the red berries from a coffee bush and was intrigued by their weird, wired behavior. The beans within those berries have gained global popularity and are now the second largest exported item in the world after oil, with coffee prices traded on all the major financial markets. This ought to be good news for Africa, many of whose countries have coffee as their main export.

The problem is that most processing of coffee into packaged final products is done in rich Western countries—and it's the processing that reaps most of the value. From global retail sales of $70 billion, coffee-producing countries (not all of which are in Africa) receive only $5.5 billion, or 8 percent.[11] Again, this is partly historical: the facilities to process coffee to American and European tastes grew up first in America and Europe. But what helped prevent those facilities moving into Africa to take advantage of its cheaper labor were tariffs—taxes on imports. For a long time, tariffs on processed coffee products were significantly higher than on raw coffee beans.

Trade can be a complex issue. It's too simplistic to imply—as some antiglobalization critics do—that Africa's current poverty derives directly from unjust trade arrangements. Contrary to popular opinion, African countries nowadays do not face significant tariffs on most products they want to export to the West. The world's Least Developed Countries (including thirty-three in sub-Saharan Africa) now receive tariff-free access to European markets for all of their products, and the story is broadly similar for the other key market, America, though there are a number of important exceptions, including sugar, cocoa, and cotton.[12] Yet the history is relevant: once businesses, their expertise, and their lobbies become established, it is difficult to shift them. It's fair to ask whether we are managing trade to enable poor countries to derive full benefit and Western consumers best value.

The result? A country like Germany remains the world's fourth largest exporter of coffee, despite not growing a bean. Instead, it imports loads of the raw crop, roasts and processes it in German factories, and then sells the finished products to other coffee-consuming countries. All in all, it makes far more money from coffee than Ethiopia, home of the plant and one of Africa's poorest nations, 60 percent of whose foreign earnings come from sales of mainly raw coffee.

Cocoa farmers—another mainstay of many African economies—find themselves in a similar position. The trap can be rather striking, in a Dr. Evil kind of way, as Japan's continuing and particularly high cocoa tariffs reveal: cocoa beans enter the country at 0 percent, cocoa paste at 5 percent, defatted cocoa paste at 10 percent, cocoa powder at 13 percent and finished chocolate and "elaborate" products at over 280 percent.[13] Until recently, America and Europe applied something similar. Suddenly it becomes clearer why countries like Belgium and Switzerland have such well-developed chocolate industries, besides the fact that they make it so delicious. It also explains why, although 70 percent of the world's cocoa comes from West Africa, America's two top suppliers of finished chocolate are Canada and Mexico, with Europe accounting for most of the rest.[14]

Tariffs are only half a cup of the coffee story: there's another reason why Africa too often ends up with the dregs. Though sandal-wearing aid workers may find this hard, put yourself momentarily in the polished shoes of an IMF economist, circa 1980. You are advising a poor African government how to increase exports in order to boost foreign earnings and bring in new investment. In good faith, you encourage the government to produce and export more of whatever sells well in rich markets. Coffee is top of the list for many countries.

This sensible advice was given to a large number of poor countries around the world. What is the impact of lots of countries producing more of the same products? The price falls, in a big way. In the two decades after 1980, global coffee prices fell by 64 percent.

Coffee is by no means alone. Of other significant African exports over the same period, cocoa prices fell by 71 percent, palm oil by 55 percent, and rubber by 60 percent. To this day, new crops can be subject to the same problem. Over recent years the World Bank has financed projects in Malawi to replace wetlands with shrimp farms, a potentially valuable export that finds its way to the freezer section of your local supermarket. Unfortunately they were giving the same advice to Nigeria and Ghana, not to mention a number of countries outside Africa including Thailand, Indonesia, Bangladesh, and Ecuador, so prices quickly plummeted and the rewards of the changes were never reaped as originally foreseen.[15]

## Steely Resolve

There is a clear theme developing here. It's not always that trade terms are directly unfair, but Africa struggles in general to get as much out of burgeoning global trade as do richer regions. Unsuccessful at entering into more profitable parts of coffee and other businesses, Africa is especially vulnerable to uncontrolled market movements. It's worth contrasting African countries' experience with the way Western counterparts deal with similar situations.

In March 2002 America faced a situation over steel much like that faced by Africa in the 1980s and 1990s over coffee: a significant drop in global prices, which caused problems for U.S. producers. President Bush's response was to impose tariffs on foreign steel. An African country doing the same, even if it could have afforded it, would certainly have been chastised by the IMF and World Bank, and might have had aid withheld. But even though the United States must have known it was in direct contravention of WTO rules, the Bush administration saw it as a step worth taking.

Just as interesting is the way the subsidies were eventually retracted. In November 2003 the WTO formally ruled the subsidies illegal. But it was only the threat of retaliatory tariffs on American imports by the European Union and Japan the following month that saw the steel measures actually lifted. Africa, with no markets of much interest for American products, could not have created such pressure, as we've already seen with cotton. As it happened, steel prices by late 2003 had in any case started to rise, and, come the 2004 election, Bush was seen in several Rust Belt swing states as the friend of steelworkers.

The point here is that, right or wrong, Western governments understand the need occasionally to protect their industries from fluctuating prices in international markets: it's a case of managing globalization. Opening up to international trade generally means better competitiveness and better value for the consumer, but it also means greater vulnerability to international market movements. Subsidies and tariffs (used judiciously, not gratuitously) help Western countries to manage the risks. Britain's entire dairy industry would have gone bust in the 1990s if enormous subsidies had not been used to support farmers in the wake of mad cow disease and the mass culling of herds. African countries, with the extra vulnerability of dependence on only one or two exports, do not have the same financial ability to do so.

Yet there is another vital point. What would have happened to America's steelworkers or Britain's dairy farmers if their governments had provided no help? Jobs would have been lost and many families would have suffered. But in the West we still have welfare states: no one would have died, children would still have been sent to school, medical care would still have been accessible.

African countries have little or no such welfare states. Their people are thus far more vulnerable to the fast and fluid movements of globalization's markets. So while this system of increased international trade certainly offers them new opportunities, if we run that system purely to our own design—in which we take for granted welfare states, the financial capacity to protect industries, and economic diversity that means we're not reliant on the progress of only one or two products—then it's hardly surprising African countries will suffer more than we do.

## Theft and Blatant Stealing

There is one final line of produce going out of Africa for which the continent receives little or no payment at all . . . Africans themselves.

In an era of modern travel, international qualifications, and email applications, the movement of labor is far easier than it used to be. So when a hospital in the United States has a shortfall of doctors, it advertises for more, and when an overworked, underpaid, and highly stressed physician in a country like Sierra Leone sees the advertisement, he applies to fill the shortfall. There are said to be more doctors from Sierra Leone—a destitute, war-ravaged country with especially dire health problems, including thousands of amputees and a high death rate from basic diseases like diarrhea—practicing in Chicago than in Sierra Leone itself.[16] If you are poor and can earn more than ten times your current salary in a rich Western country and provide security for your family, what would you do?

A large suburban hospital in the United States might have as many as 250 doctors on staff. In Malawi, 250 doctors serve the entire population of 13 million. Only 60 of the 500 doctors trained in Zambia since independence are still there.[17] Overall, one-third of practicing doctors in the United States trained in foreign medical schools.[18] The problem may get worse: the United States already employs about half the world's English-speaking doctors and estimates it may need a million additional health care workers over the next couple of decades to meet the rising demands of an aging population. Ironically, this is exactly the same number of new health care workers it is estimated would be required for sub-Saharan Africa to fulfil the Millennium Development Goals on health.

For doctors in the United States, read nurses in the UK (America tends to get its foreign nurses from countries like India and the Philippines, rather than Africa). Between 1998 and mid-2004, 12,115 African nurses registered to work in Britain. Yet this is a complex problem: part of the reason the shortfall in the UK existed in the first place is that several thousand British-trained nurses moved to the United States over the same period in search of the world's best medical salaries. In turn, when the UK government took steps to try and stem the flow of nurses from the poorest countries, many of the gaps were filled instead from wealthier countries like South Africa. South Africa says it spent $1 billion training health care workers who then emigrated to countries like the UK and United States between 1994 and 2000, the equivalent of a third of all the aid money it received over the period.[19] South

Africa then replenishes some of its own cadre of nurses from poorer countries like Malawi. Though it is not what anyone in the United States or UK intended, the net effect is that Africa still subsidizes the health care systems of rich countries by paying for the training of staff who then go and work there.

The story is similar for a range of professional groups, including scientists and engineers.

## Lilongwe Central Hospital

On a good day, Carlos Varela sees thirty patients in the outpatient clinic at Lilongwe Central Hospital in Malawi. But there are the seventy patients in his ward. He has no diagnostic equipment, and there is often no point in writing prescriptions because the drug cabinet is bare. He works grueling hours in a choked, fetid hospital where patients lie two and three on bare bedframes and others are crammed in on the floor, under beds, and on the veranda. For this, he is paid around $65 a month.

Dr. Varela, twenty-eight, graduated from medical school two years ago. Of the twenty-five members of his class, he is one of only three working in Malawi's desperate public health system. Three doctors have already left for foreign posts, two others are on their way abroad, and many of the rest are simply waiting to finish internships in the country's much more lucrative private clinics before they too head overseas. Nurses have made a similar exodus; there is but one nurse in most of the hospital's wards.

"I want to stay," Dr. Varela said. "If I leave the government hospital, who's going to work here? . . . But I understand the people who leave—in a few years, I will think about going, too."[20]

None of this is to suggest that there should be a blanket ban on skilled Africans from having the freedom to travel and work. The answers are not simple, begin in reviewing Western countries' health recruitment policies, and possibly take in a large, foreign aid–funded subsidy program for core African health workers.

Yet what is undeniable in an era of globalization is that the root of the problem lies in countries in the West failing to manage their needs, in this case training enough doctors or nurses, and poorer countries pay the price. If you do not offer enough places in medical schools to fill your future needs, and there are poor African countries out there whose badly paid doctors speak the same language, where do you expect the gaps be filled from? The United States has around 17,000 medical graduates in school every year—and 22,000 first-year residency slots.[21] The nature of globalization gives us a new responsibility to consider the impact of our domestic decisions on others, especially on the poorest countries, which tend to come off worst in many situations unless their needs are specifically considered.

Africa's brain drain is becoming an ever more grave issue. Yes, many of those who work overseas send money to their families back home, bringing some new resources into the economy, but it's not the same as directly participating in the development of a poor society itself through filling crucial public positions. And it is, of course, the poorest countries with the fewest career opportunities and smallest salaries that suffer most: India, Brazil, and China are calculated to be losing only about 5 percent of their highly skilled workers; Mozambique, Ghana, and Tanzania have seen half theirs leave.[22]

How serious is this? OECD research suggests that the emigration of highly skilled workers may in fact prevent the poorest countries from ever reaching the critical mass of human resources necessary to foster long-term development.[23] You may recall from your briefing as president of Uzima that one of the key aims in education was to stop young people from going off to study abroad, when so few tend to return. Well, at the moment it's not working.

Of all the produce leaving Africa, the departure of its most talented people—for no payment whatsoever—seems the harshest exchange of all.

# CHAPTER 11
# INTO AFRICA

Back near the edge of the Rift Valley in Kenya in the village of Machani, while Nancy grinds some millet and Helen sits in the shade of the small house, Lucas is working his few acres of land. Most of what Lucas grows is for the family's own consumption, but occasionally there's a little extra that can be sold at the small market in Kijabe town. Nancy told me she enjoys market days, as they're an opportunity to catch up with old friends who, at their distinguished age, "are dying off fast."

Unlike the coffee farmed on the higher slopes above the valley, nothing Lucas grows will end up sold in foreign markets. So he doesn't worry about tariffs or whatever subsidies rich countries offer to their own farmers—not that he knows anything about them. As far as Lucas is concerned—unless he was just being polite when I asked—all he thinks about places like America and Europe is that maybe someone will come one day and help them with a small project in the village or at the local school.

Yet some of the more worldly-wise vendors down at the market know there are several ways in which international trade rules can affect the daily lives of people like Lucas, from the prices he gets for his produce locally to the medicine he buys if he gets ill and the food aid the village receives if hit by drought. These rules are crucial. Because, while the most hard-nosed protection-ist might argue that Western countries can set unequal rules on access to their markets if they want (despite preaching free market values abroad), it would surely be much harder to justify any damage done directly to poor people on their own doorsteps.

More than anything else, the rules affecting what comes *into* Africa will reveal whether we're allowing advances in trade, tech-nology, and knowledge to benefit all comers in our fast-changing era of globalization.

First of all, the positive. It's easy to forget the enormous benefits that some imports into Africa have brought. In a continent that itself taught the rest of the world how to fish and use fire, not to mention giving it condoms and coffee,[24] trade's potential can be seen in four products that have revolutionized modern African life.

## Bikes and Buckets, Phones and Pharmaceuticals

- *Bicycles.* It would take only a couple of minutes for a visitor landing almost anywhere in Africa to understand how valuable the bicycle is as an affordable means of transport. It's not just the millions of journeys to work every day over distances that would not have been thinkable before, it's the use of bicycles to get produce to and from market. More often than not, if you see a bike in Africa it doesn't have a rider on top but several heavy bags of produce being pushed up a hill by a farmer who would previously have had to struggle with smaller loads on his or her back.

- *Buckets.* The bicycle is outdone in Africa only by the ubiquity of yellow plastic buckets and jerry cans. Of course, there were gourds and other containers in the past, but for cheapness, durability, and practicality, plastic is unbeatable. Nearly every household in Africa has at least one plastic bucket, whether it's used for collecting water, washing up, or storing food. Most have more. They are a truer image of Africa than a palm tree, a sunset, or a red-earth road (and, for reasons I've never been able to establish, they seem to come in only one color).

- *Mobile phones.* Prior to the late 1990s, telecom systems in Africa were poorly developed. Fixed-line networks were expensive to install, communication within countries was unreliable, and phoning abroad costly. Mobile technology allowed African users to bypass the need for fixed-line infrastructure and catch up immediately with the rest of the world. Since 2000, more Africans have begun using telephones than in the whole of the previous century.[25] Usage is increasing at around 65 percent a year—the highest in the world—and, though still out of reach of the majority, phones are no longer the preserve of a small elite. Information flows for everyone from small businesses to government have improved, families keep in touch with those abroad, and even the most apparently remote areas can be in contact with local authorities and the wider world.

- *Basic medicines.* The poster children of trade benefit to Africa are medicines. It's no fluke that Africa's population more than tripled between 1950 and 2000.[26] Much of the credit goes to basic medicines and advances in medical understanding. Far fewer mothers and babies die during childbirth (even if the numbers remain preventably high). Deaths from malaria have decreased, there is better knowledge to deal with dehydration and common diseases, and there are widely accepted procedures and formulas to treat malnourished children (as long as the means are available). There is a huge amount to celebrate.

These are only four examples. Africa is no different from any other continent that has benefited from the twentieth century's global cross-fertilization of ideas and production. New crops, fertilizers, buses to get people to work, paved roads to get cheaper produce to market, engines, water pumps, purification techniques . . .

Right now the increasing speed of globalization should mean that such benefits and advances multiply at an ever faster rate. That's why the occasions on which we fail to meet trade's positive potential, because of ill-designed rules or simple bad management, can be so frustrating. With a history taking in plastic and penicillin, how could we ever reach a point where we've invented successful, cheap-to-produce drugs to treat Africa's biggest killer disease, HIV/AIDS, but some rules on paper prevent most people from getting them?

The key to understanding much of the trade going into Africa is as a story of unintended consequences. The idea that multinational corporations deliberately try to shaft the poor and G8 leaders are in Luciferous league with them has never been credible. Yet what makes sense for us at home often has implications for others abroad. When it's inventing a bicycle, it's win-win. When it's deciding what to do with our surplus crops, developing new drugs, managing food aid, or patenting discoveries, as we will see, it can be a very different story.

## Dumped!

The best place to begin when it comes to unintended consequences is some unfinished business from the farm subsidies we examined in the last chapter: it's the well-known example of sugar.

In both America and Europe, the subsidies paid for sugar are different from those paid to cattle or cotton farmers. Instead of subsidizing farmers directly through taxes, the respective statutes effectively require that anyone wanting to *sell* sugar in those countries has to buy sugar *grown* there and do so at a fixed price.

In recent years in America, this has generally been around two to three times higher than the world price, at around 20 cents a pound compared to 7 or 8 cents.[27] (In Europe it's even more distorted, reflecting the rather obvious fact that it's a lot harder to grow sugar in the likes of France and Finland than in Mozambique and Malawi.) The cost is then passed on to consumers at the checkout line—via the sugar refiners, candy companies, and others who have to pay the higher costs—where consumers have little choice but to buy American sugar because high tariffs keep most foreign sugar out.

This is not a free market but a fixed market, of which American sugar producers are guaranteed around 85 percent. Because the subsidies don't come directly from government revenues, the sugar industry likes to claim that the system doesn't cost taxpayers a dime, yet the cost to consumers has been estimated at around $2 billion a year. American businesses that need to use sugar in their products lose out too, which is why the federal government has a program to subsidize these businesses' exports to the equivalent amount they've lost from the unnecessarily expensive sugar—funded from American taxes. Foreign sugar-producing countries lose out too, including those in Africa. These countries are allowed only limited quotas they can sell into the United States, based on historical market share, which reduces their incentive to become more efficient or invest in expansion. And, of course, they also suffer from lower world prices caused by the subsidies.

Perhaps because sugar subsidies are particularly hard to justify, sugar producers contributed more in campaign contributions to House and Senate incumbents of both major parties in 2006 than any other group of food growers, $2.7 million (it's surely always a little suspicious when an interest group backs *both* sides).[28] Their main argument as to why America should retain its distorted system is that other rich countries do the same, no matter that unilateral action would immediately benefit both American consumers and the wider economy. Yet it is true that African sugar producers suffer even more from Europe's sugar regime.

The quota that the European Union sets for the amount of sugar it will ensure is bought from European sugar farmers is, bizarrely, even more than Europe's citizens stir into their coffee and bake into their cakes. To get rid of the surplus, Europe's taxpayers are then called on to provide extra "export" subsidies that are sufficiently large to make the sugar competitive on global markets.

The effect for Africa is not only the inability to access Europe's markets (apart from another small quota) and lower prices globally; Europe's subsidized sugar can sometimes be found in African markets too, undercutting the product of local farmers and putting them out of business even on their own doorsteps. Perhaps I'm being generous in calling this an unintended consequence, but there it is. The practice is known as dumping, which seems apt because, rather like being discarded by a lover, it's not very pleasant.

There is some reassurance to be gained from the World Trade Organization here. In 2004 and 2005, the WTO ruled Europe's sugar regime illegal and there have since been cuts of up to 36 percent in guaranteed prices (that many sugar farmers have remained in business despite the cuts reveals that they never needed such large subsidies anyway). This is undoubtedly good news for most African sugar farmers. Global prices have already risen. It is estimated that a truly level playing field enabling sales to rich American and European markets would create more than twenty thousand new jobs in Mozambique alone.

But it would also be wrong to think that progress on sugar in both America and Europe is the end of Africa's problem. Export subsidies are required only if regular agricultural subsidies of the sort we witnessed in the last chapter are not sufficiently large to ensure domestic prices *already* undercut African prices. These subsidies will continue, and there will still be expensive Western products underselling African produce in African markets.

## Shopping at Uchumi

When I lived in Nairobi, I would make a weekly shopping trip to the big red Uchumi superstore on Ngong Road. The first thing to note about a shopping trip to Uchumi is that you couldn't go at night. Kibera, Africa's biggest slum, which was featured in *The Constant Gardener*, begins only a couple of hundred yards behind the supermarket, and being on foot, white, and wealthy in the dark wasn't advisable. But if it was still light, it was a nice excuse to get out of the house.

I'd walk through the small garden, and Stephen, day guard cum Swahili tutor at my house who supported a wife and three children on his official security company salary of $40 a month (which I added to—though I understand such supplementation was rare), would open up the locked metal gate and let me out onto the street. Elgeyo Marakwet Road was a popular rat run used to avoid Nairobi traffic, and a handful of young men would often loiter there, filling the road's gaping potholes with rubble and trying to intimidate passing drivers into paying for the service—though both parties knew the rubble would wash away the next time it rained.

Next I'd cross Ngong Road itself. This was no easy task, traversed as it was by demonically driven and dangerously decayed *matatu* minibuses— the main form of public transport. Matatus were rented from private owners for a fixed number of hours by drivers who would then run as many headlong, headlight-free trips along their routes in the allotted time as possible. Their only saving grace was their color, inventiveness, and variety of decoration. R. Kelly fought daily battles with Ronaldo, Black Spear, and Princess Diana to reach customers first, lights blazing from ornate back window displays that often did more to light up the road at night than the ineffective streetlamps.

Once safely wheeling my shopping cart around the brightly lit aisles of Uchumi, where much of west Nairobi's middle class did its shopping and which looked like any other supermarket around the world, I would be confused by two products in particular. The first was canned tomatoes. Kenya's fields and markets were full of tomatoes, yet cans of Italian tomatoes sold at 45 shillings, compared to 48 for the Kenyan variety.

The second product was powdered milk from Holland, complete with a picture of a smiling Dutch milkmaid on the front. This also seemed strange, as Kenya's lush highlands were crammed with healthy-looking cattle. Kenyan producers hadn't diversified into producing powdered milk to compete, even though it was heavily in demand in a country with few refrigeration facilities for the fresh variety. In the meantime, demand for other foreign milk products was boosted by continuing rumors—once clearly encouraged by Western companies—that powdered baby formula was healthier than breast milk: surely one of the most depressing examples of Africa's natural resources being undermined from outside.

The cause of these peculiarities was, of course, subsidies. Tomatoes and milk were canned and powdered and sold off abroad as a way of cutting losses on the habitual surpluses the subsidies created. And there they sat on Uchumi's shelves, expensive products from foreign preachers of the free market being sold at a loss to a poor country that didn't particularly need them, keeping local farmers out of business.

Meanwhile, the wiseguys on Elgeyo Marakwet Road continued intimidating drivers and pointlessly filling potholes, because there were no jobs for them to do. Meanwhile, the moral authority of European countries to lecture Kenya on corruption and economic mismanagement continued to look card-thin to Kenyan leaders. Meanwhile, Stephen would continue to support his family on a tiny formal salary while guarding the house of a young, inexperienced aid worker who was starting to get confused about how his aid job for a European government and his weekly shopping trip fitted together.

## Drugs and TRIPS, Uppers and Downers

Despite much progress in basic medicines and health care, which has seen African life expectancy rise by a decade since 1950, large pharmaceutical companies—known as Big Pharma by protest-ers—endure a terrible reputation in poor countries. The general image is that cheap drugs that could save thousands of lives are denied to those who need them. *The Constant Gardener* didn't help, alleging the testing of new medicines on unwitting African patients. Though shocking, the day-to-day reality is generally more complex than that. It's also more subtle.

Medical progress is a sharply double-edged sword. On the one hand, if it weren't for the riches of potential customers in the West, Big Pharma companies wouldn't research and develop extraordinary new treatments, from some of which Africa has benefited. On the other, Big Pharma's desire to protect its prof-its and its research and development budgets has sometimes meant lifesaving treatments being denied poor Africans and others in desperate need.

### Feel Better

- *Smallpox.* Most of North America and Europe were free of smallpox by 1950. In 1967 the World Health Organization (WHO) started a massive vaccination campaign to eradicate it from the rest of the world. The last endemic case of smallpox occurred in Somalia in 1977.[29]
- *Polio.* Since a global vaccination began in 1988, polio cases have dropped by 99 percent, from 350,000 per year to just under 1,800 in 2006 (most of which were in Africa).[30]
- *Guinea-worm disease.* The numbers suffering from this parasitic worm that emerges painfully from people's limbs fell from an estimated 3.5 million cases in 1986 to 25,243 reported cases in 2006 (most, again, are in Africa, particularly southern Sudan).[31]

Broadly speaking, Africa's drug habit is taken in two doses. The first dose includes medicines invented a long time ago, any patents for which have run out (such as the smallpox vaccine), or medicines for which there is little demand in the West (such as treatment for Guinea-worm disease). These drugs can be provided or marketed to Africans at reasonable prices, though we shouldn't get carried away: someone like Marie in Kinshasa will rarely be able to afford any medicine, even if cheap.

The second dose contains treatments for which there is a large Western market, such as drugs for cancer and heart disease. These drugs, once invented, are nearly all cheap to manufacture and could often save lives. But Big Pharma companies attach high prices to them, to cover both their R&D and their largest cost: marketing to Western doctors and health systems[32] (there are thought to be around 100,000 pharmaceutical sales reps in the United States chasing 120,000 family and general practitioners involved in prescribing drugs).[33] This is more of a problem than it may appear because Africans suffer from all these kinds of diseases too: people with poor diets living in bad conditions simply get ill more often. Of global deaths from heart disease, 78 percent are in poor countries.[34]

As a health minister in Africa, you used to be able to buy cheap copies of some such drugs—known as generics—because your country had no laws saying you couldn't. But as part of trade discussions in the mid-1990s, poor countries were pressed hard by their Western counterparts, home to Big Pharma headquarters, to adopt new legislation recognizing something called TRIPS: trade-related intellectual property rights. TRIPS made economic sense in theory, the idea being that companies in one country can't rip off the ideas and products of companies in another. Yet it made little sense in practice, preventing many poor countries that might have been able to afford it from buying generic drugs to treat AIDS. When those countries were given belated permission to import generics again in 2004, the conditions were so bureaucratic—in order to assuage concerns that the drugs would end up infecting Western markets—that by early 2007, not one African country had successfully managed to do so.

This was obviously scandalous. Yet what's interesting here is that it's not that we *can't* make trade work for poor countries. We can. It's just that we need to pay some attention if we're serious about getting results:

- In 2000, thirty-nine Big Pharma companies got together to prevent the South African government from passing patent laws that would have enabled them to buy more generics.[35] Their argument was that their profits would be threatened, especially in the West. Millions were denied lifesaving drugs.
- By 2003, when a public backlash against their actions had grown, many of those same companies started cooperating with international efforts to make cheaper drugs available across Africa. The rules on generics may still have been unfair, but the companies "suddenly" realized they themselves could make drugs available much more cheaply.

Should it be a surprise to us that the market will not always automatically deliver the health outcomes we want? Of course not, which is why we have developed national health systems or welfare insurance programs in our own countries (even Michael Moore would admit these could be worse). A large aid effort is now under way, belatedly, to try and get antiretroviral AIDS drugs to all Africans who need them by 2010.

Naturally, not all organizations are the same and a few Big Pharma companies have long gone out of their way to help provide key drugs to poor countries. The companies involved in making antiretrovirals will now get to be involved in saving countless lives. But in the moral versus economic conflict of medicines and research, AIDS drugs remain a reminder of how high the costs can be when trade rules that seem to make sense for rich countries have unintended consequences for the world's poor. Put baldly, countless millions of Africans have died while the means to save them existed.

Economically, it was understandable (though avoidable). Morally, it is repugnant.

## Life Support

If any further proof is needed that the way we manage trade does not always work for the poor, it comes with the discovery that even emergency food aid can end up distorted by Western trade interests against African needs.

America is the largest financer of food aid in Africa, for which it deserves great credit. Over the years Americans have fed tens of millions of people suffering acute crisis and at risk of starvation, whether caused by famine or drought, ill health, or death of a breadwinner.

Yet starvation generally occurs not because there is an absence of food—traders can always buy it in from other countries if there is demand—but because people can no longer grow or pay for it. The quickest and cheapest way to get food to the starving is to buy it from neighboring countries, or to give money to those affected so the private sector starts putting food back in the markets. Both approaches have the added benefit of supporting local economies and ensuring that farmers in the region remain incentivized to produce as much food as they can, thus reducing the risk of a repeat crisis.

Most American food aid, however, comes from America. Not only is it a lot more expensive, but it's an awfully long way away, so far that the food can't be produced in response to an emergency because it takes, on average, five months to deliver.[36] Instead, the U.S. government must guess ahead how much food aid it will require each year, before it has any idea of the need.

There are a number of winners from the American food-aid system. First are the few large agribusinesses allowed to bid for the contracts to provide several million tons of food aid each year, such as Cargill (annual turnover around $50 billion). It only

## Feel Worse—AIDS

AIDS in Africa, somewhat ironically, was spread by trade. It traveled quickly through its arteries and roads from its first known case in the center of the continent. Truck drivers, many using prostitutes, were instrumental in helping the disease move from town to town and country to country, even if it would have happened eventually in any case.

More than 20 million Africans have died so far from AIDS, at a current rate of around 4,400 every day. A further 22.5 million are infected. Africans thus comprise 68 percent of global infections.[37] But they are a much higher proportion of total deaths because they, more than anyone else in the world, have lacked access to antiretroviral drugs.

Antiretrovirals are very good value. They can be produced for less than a dollar a day and have people off their sickbeds, working in their fields and offices, and caring for their families within months. Millions of lives can be saved for a few billion dollars a year, a truly inspiring prospect of what innovative medical research and Western generosity could together achieve.

In 2007, only around three in ten Africans who needed antiretrovirals were receiving them, though even this number marked immense progress over previous years.[38] Not enough money has yet been pledged by donors to make the commitment for universal access by 2010 a reality.

You may recall that one of the most difficult challenges in aid is finding discreet, self-contained interventions that will have lasting, sustainable effect. The funding of antiretrovirals is the biggest and best such opportunity we'll ever have. It speaks volumes that we're only now just starting to take it.

comprises 2–3 percent of their overall business, but they receive, on average, 11 percent more than open-market prices for the food they produce.[39] Then there are the U.S. shipping firms that are guaranteed by law to get to transport at least 75 percent of the food.[40] This is rather a blessing for them as they're not very competitive internationally, carrying only 3 percent of America's non-food-aid imports and exports. It is not, however, good news for the American taxpayer: between 2000 and 2002, nearly 40 percent of the cash they coughed up for U.S. food-aid programs is estimated to have gone to U.S. shipping firms.[41]

Clearly, this system does not deliver as much food per dollar per starving person as food aid bought locally in Africa. As the former administrator of USAID Andrew Natsios observed, "You can't eat transportation."[42] You might think that American aid NGOs would therefore campaign against it. Yet many of those NGOs are themselves given large amounts of the food aid to distribute. The NGOs don't have to give it all away: they're allowed to "monetize" the food—i.e., sell it—and use the proceeds to fund their projects. As this is a huge source of their income (25–50 percent of the 2001 budgets for seven NGOs, including World Vision and Catholic Relief Services),[43] it's no surprise that they too have been reluctant to criticize. The charity CARE, however, finally broke ranks in 2007, announcing it was turning down $45 million in federal financing through food aid: not only was this form of aid inefficient, it said, but sometimes the imported food meant lower prices for the local crops of struggling African farmers.[44]

## Flagging Food

As ever, a little bit of history is useful to understanding America's food-aid program. Its roots lie in the heroic nourishing of a ruined Europe in the aftermath of the Second World War. But while Europe quickly recovered its ability to feed itself, American farm lobbies had gotten used to providing a large surplus and American politicians didn't mind thinking of creative ways to use it. One of the most popular solutions was to send it to poor countries unable to decide between the cold war superpowers wooing them (this was before anyone worried much about the effect of large amounts of imported food on local markets).

The cold war legacy helps explain why every sack of wheat or can of corn oil under the U.S. food-aid program has such a large Stars and Stripes printed on it. It will encourage patriots to know that, by law, the vast majority of those sacks and cans must be produced and packed in America. And the flags must be printed, of course, with American-made ink.

In 2005 the White House supported a proposal to use about a quarter of USAID's $1.2 billion food-aid budget to buy food in poor countries, rather than at home. Natsios was one of many behind the proposal, noting that if USAID could have bought food in Ethiopia during its 1984 famine, among other crises, the faster response would have saved many more lives. "Speed is everything in famine response," he said.[45] But Congress, under pressure from the agribusinesses, shippers, and some of the NGOs, refused to pass it. Their excuse in doing so was that the support of influential commerical groups was essential to retaining public political support for food aid—which is deeply patronizing to the U.S. public.

The lesson here is not that these interest groups are cynically and cruelly trying to manipulate American taxpayers' money for aid to their own benefit. They are just looking out for their own interests. The problem is that their voices resonate far louder in Congress than the voices of those the food aid is supposed to help. It would be vastly more efficient to purchase food in the region and—if that's what America wants—find a more direct way of supporting U.S.

shipping firms. As we will see in the next chapter, there are already better programs in place to help U.S. farmers.

What are the unintended consequences American taxpayers and hungry Africans end up with? A system that can be slow to respond to needs, which helps agribusinesses that don't need it (food aid is only 2–3 percent of their overall trade), and which fails to encourage African self-sufficiency. It's also a system that costs far more than it needs to: at least 50 cents in every dollar of American food aid actually ends up spent on transport, storage, and administration.

## Patently Wrong

We saw with the example of drugs and medical research that market forces will not always provide the outcomes society wants by itself, especially for the poorest. The need for some management and regulation of the market for public benefit underpins our social democracies in the West, even if political parties argue about what level of such intervention is appropriate. It's why we have legal systems to ensure fair play and publicly paid schools to educate a labor force, food standards agencies and hospitals, antitrust watchdogs, and welfare-to-work programs. Such measures are motivated both by fairness and by an understanding that they will increase society's stability and productivity in the long term.

International market forces also sometimes fail to provide the right outcomes for the international poor. It would be pointless and unrealistic to propose government and welfare systems on an international scale to solve this: our first responsibility is to our own societies, just as Africa must take responsibility for itself. But first, as they say, do no harm. Problems begin when we oblige countries to sign up to rules that make sense for us yet no sense for them. The patenting of African products and natural resources is a prime example.

Africa's biodiversity is considered by some to be its largest asset. While this is probably a romantic exaggeration, it's true that one advantage of not having developed much is that your natural and human resources lie largely untapped. The knowledge people on the continent have collected over millennia on plants, seeds, and algae is, of course, enormous and has been passed down from generation to generation.[46]

One of the West's largest assets, in contrast, is the innovation and energy of companies to research new discoveries they can bring to market. To encourage such research, patents were introduced long ago to ensure that anyone developing an original idea would have a monopoly on the fruits of that research for a fixed period of time. King Henry VI of England is thought to have given a "letter patent" to a Flemish man in 1449 for a twenty-year monopoly on making stained glass.[47]

It's fairly easy to see the conflict coming here between Africa's traditional knowledge and biodiversity and the West's rules on research and development.

As we know from what happened with generic AIDS drugs, poor countries were pressed hard in the mid-1990s to adopt TRIPS legislation on intellectual property rights, which included recognizing foreign patents (all WTO members are strictly obliged to comply). In theory, no one can steal anyone else's natural resources: there has to be proof of an original step in the research and a new discovery. But in practice, no diet food company in the West wants to market a strange cactus from the Kalahari Desert the local San people claim helps keep you going when you want a bite to eat; they want to isolate the compound that suppresses appetite and market antiobesity drugs.

The American drug company Pfizer bought the license to the *Hoodia* compound in the late 1990s from a British drug company, Phytopharm (which had first bought rights to it from a South African organization), planning to make such drugs. When the San found out, they were understandably angry and a media backlash ensued, eventually resulting in an agreement that the San would receive royalties that critics claimed would only amount to 0.003 percent of retail sales. In the end, Pfizer abandoned plans for the antiobesity drugs, so in 2004 Phytopharm sold the license instead to Dutch/British food giant Unilever, makers of Slim-Fast. They expect to bring food products made from the *Hoodia* compound to market at some point in 2008, and estimate sales close to $600 million.[48] How much more the San will really be able to fill their bellies as a result of the West's obsession with dieting remains unclear.

One other patent currently under dispute is an enzyme found in Lake Nakuru in Kenya. If you're wearing artfully faded jeans, you may be benefiting from this enzyme too. It survives caustic environments, softens fabric, and eats indigo dye, hence feeding large sales for the U.S. biotech firm Genencor, which patented the enzyme. The Kenya Wildlife Service argues it never approved access for the research in Lake Nakuru (a very nice place to go camping, though beware of monkeys stealing your food) nor receives any benefit from the discovery, and has threatened to launch a multimillion-dollar lawsuit.[49]

Most of the time, however, there has been little progress in Africans getting any reward for profits made on their traditional knowledge or natural resources. It's hardly surprising: to take on a large Western company in Western courts requires complex understanding of local law, expensive lawyers, and deep pockets. Among other natural resources patented so far are brazzein, a protein 500 times sweeter than sugar from a plant in Gabon; teff, the hardy grain used in Ethiopia's flat *injera* bread that provides the staple for almost the whole country's diet;[50] and an extract of the *Aloe ferox* plant from Lesotho, which helps lighten skin.

## Information Diet?

If you're interested in more, there's an engrossing 2006 report available online from the U.S.-based nonprofit Edmonds Institute (www.edmonds-institute.org), detailing what has apparently happened to such discoveries as antibiotics from a termite hill in Gambia, cosmetics from Africa's iconic baobab trees, and anti-impotence remedies from Congo-Brazzaville.

Of course, it would be crazy to think no one should explore and exploit Africa's natural resources: there may be wonderful new products and medicines to be derived from them. But what is required is some kind of adjusted intellectual property legislation that allows a greater share of the profit from such resources to go the countries of origin, such as happens, for example, between oil multinationals and African governments over fossil fuel reserves. To date, nothing satisfactory has emerged.

The TRIPS legislation as it stands would never have been agreed to by African countries on its own merits. It was foisted upon them because it's a particular approach that suits the West's industrialized, service economies with their heavy emphases on research and development. It is a classic case of something that works for us but does not work for them.

# CHAPTER 12
# IT DOESN'T WORK
# FOR YOU EITHER

The last completed round of world trade negotiations after the Second World War—the GATT talks that made so much progress on opening up markets for industrialized goods and services, rather than areas such as agriculture that might benefit poor countries—began in 1986. With more and more countries involved, negotiations had become extremely complex, and they lasted eight years. When the smoke cleared, it quickly became clear that poor countries had gotten a particularly bad deal. Most analysts concurred that Africa and some other regions would be worse off as a result.

Incensed, poor countries demanded immediate reforms. Instead they were persuaded to wait for the next round of trade negotiations. These would be held under a new body called the World Trade Organization, replacing the GATT system, and would specifically address poor countries' needs. Even agreeing to the terms for this new round was difficult—in Seattle in 1999, antiglobalization protesters rioted outside while bureaucrats failed to reach agreement inside. But a renewed commitment to find international consensus in the aftermath of 9/11 saw the round finally get under way at a meeting in Qatar in late 2001. It would be known as the Doha Development Round.

## Why the WTO?

The establishment of the World Trade Organization in 1994, with its permanent staff and large buildings in Geneva, was an acknowledgment of how enormously complicated trade negotiations have become. There are an ever wider number of sectors to cover, such as the burgeoning world of IT, and more and more members: 149 countries are involved in the Doha negotiations. Getting them to a point where they will all happily sign off on a highly detailed agreement is exactly as difficult as it sounds.

The key point to understand about the WTO is that it is not really an institution devoted to the spread of free trade, despite what it may say in its mission statements. The reality is that it provides a forum for pragmatic, old-fashioned battles in which each member tries to get the best political deal for itself. In general this means you want open international competition for what you're good at and much less competition for what you're not.

New trade rounds come around so slowly, and there is so much at stake for all participants, that it was probably a mistake ever to think that the needs of small, poor countries in the Doha Round would be seriously prioritized. Big, rich members still dominate, and, as a Swahili proverb observes, when elephants fight, the grass suffers . . . and when elephants make love, the grass still suffers. Beginning from the already unlevel playing field of previous rounds, the reality remains that poor countries need access to rich markets far more than rich countries need small markets.

The Doha Round has already missed a number of deadlines for completion. Yet of the last five GATT rounds, each took longer than its predecessor to be resolved: the Geneva Round began and ended in 1956; Dillon ran from 1960 to 1961;

Kennedy 1964 to 1967, Tokyo 1973 to 1979, and Uruguay 1986 to 1994. If we apply the logic of a school math exam, the correct guess might be that the Doha Round, begun in 2001, will not finish until 2011. Others question whether the round will finish at all, though in all likelihood it will: every round to date has missed deadlines and experienced crises before final resolution.

In many ways, it doesn't really matter when the Doha Round finishes, because the broad boundaries of a final deal are already on the table and it's possible to predict the likely overall impact. In 2006, the World Bank modeled a number of scenarios within these boundaries and tried to estimate the financial outcome for poor countries, taking in the limited progress being promised on Western agricultural subsidies, the effect of continued TRIPS and other conditions, and the requirements to open up markets. The good news is that larger developing poor countries such as Brazil, India, and China are likely to benefit. No accident, this: their products and consumers have now become important enough to the West that they can negotiate a reasonable deal, just as Western countries themselves will profit.

And countries like Uzima? The World Bank study concluded that most of sub-Saharan Africa is likely to be a net *loser* from the round (along with Mexico, Bangladesh, and the Middle East). A study by the Carnegie Endowment for International Peace reached similar conclusions. It only begins to look better, for cotton-exporting countries at least, if America finally cuts cotton subsidies in line with the 2005 WTO ruling.

I don't want to be too simplistic about this: there are some benefits to the proposed WTO deal for poor countries. A firmer guarantee of tariff-free access into U.S. and EU markets. A reduction in some of the Western subsidies that most distort the global price and market share poor countries get for some of their main products. Another step toward leveling out the playing field for global trade, albeit a very small one.

The reason much of Africa will suffer, however, is that the old rules were generally recognized as so unhelpful that many African, Caribbean, and Pacific countries were allowed to sell a quota of produce at high, subsidized prices in Europe. Although these quotas were small, some of them were valuable for small economies, and their value will now decline as markets are made to liberalize. While it is right in the long term that they should do so, to encourage genuine global competition, it seems cruel to remove them at a time when insufficient progress is being made on the issues that matter most to the poorest countries. Whether Africa will benefit from better access to America's markets depends mainly on whether Congress expands and makes permanent the Africa Growth and Opportunity Act, instead of just rolling it over every couple of years as currently occurs, with all the uncertainty that it brings for investors.

This leaves us with only one remaining question: why on earth might poor African countries sign up to such a deal at the WTO? It's possible they won't, but unlikely. The danger is that they might end up worse off from the collapse of an international trading system, leaving them to have to negotiate bilateral trade agreements with major powers one by one—a risk some of the richer WTO members are not slow to highlight.

## Beaten Fair and Square on a Level Playing Field

Occasionally in Rwanda the British embassy would play soccer matches against teams from various towns and villages. Despite the fact that my teammates were nearly all local Rwandan staff, these games often attracted huge attention and it was a good way to get around the country. The largest crowd I ever played in front of was for a game in a remote part of Ruhengeri province, to the northwest of Kigali. Rwanda is known as the land of a thousand hills, and three to four thousand people took an afternoon off to laze on the slopes of a small valley around a long-grassed playing field.

With the heaviest land pressure in Africa, Rwanda's hills are overfarmed. The country has only four or five major roads, making it difficult to get goods to market (the remaining roads are red-dirt tracks into which daily rain often carves fissures and where pickup trucks and buses struggle to advance). And it is double-landlocked, meaning that to export anything out of the country, traders need to go through at least two loads of bureaucracy, delays, and border taxes before their produce has even left the continent.

The vast majority of Rwandans work in agriculture. Apart from a couple of high-altitude crops such as tea and coffee, how are they ever going to compete with the large-scale flat and efficient farms of Brazil, Argentina, and Australia? The answer is that they never will—even if they develop better roads and border systems. In the long term, their best chance is to diversify their economy away from agriculture and into something else.

In 2001, the Rwandan government had a long-term vision to achieve just that, called Vision 2020. The broad idea was to develop Rwanda into a competitive global center for running IT services, similar to Bangalore in India. This would avoid the problem of being double-landlocked. But apart from that, the plan had nothing obvious to commend it. Rwanda had no comparative advantage in IT issues—back then, at least. The vision only made sense because, frankly, it was difficult to think of anything else the country might do.

On this particular afternoon in Ruhengeri province, all the locals were relaxed and had a good giggle every time the sole white boy misjudged the ball and ended up on his backside (it's extremely unnerving to have several thousand people laughing at you). And on a surprisingly level playing field they won easily, with their own imported foreign player— the local Colombian Catholic priest—putting several goals past me. Then it was back to the hills.

Rwanda is a good reminder that we need to think carefully if we are to create a world trading system in which small, poor countries can participate and benefit. It is about far more than just a few unfair trade rules. Somewhere like Rwanda needs assistance in developing new industries, over a lengthy period, before it will be able to stand stably on its own two feet in an open market. That can come with financial help and the imposition of temporarily favorable trade access.

Unfortunately, this is not even close to what we currently allow. We do permit countries like Rwanda better access to our agricultural markets than the likes of Brazil, but we subsidize our own producers so much that it's almost irrelevant. If we persist in leaving such countries so exposed, it won't be much of a surprise if they are still just as poor in another few decades—or, indeed, if conflict returns.

It is palpably clear that Africa is not able to benefit from trade as well as it might, whether because of directly unequal subsidies sustained through WTO deals, or through the unintended consequences of Western actions in a globalizing world. But what about us? Before researching this book, I assumed the reason it's so hard for Africa to negotiate fairer trade terms must be that the current terms benefit us in the West.

Far from it.

To find out the true effect on us, the easiest thing to do is to break it into three areas: how much subsidies and tariffs cost us; what would happen to our own farms if we gave Africa a better deal; and what the net impact is on our jobs and economies.

## How Much?

In July 2007 the House of Representatives passed a new farm bill, which was estimated to cost the average American family $2,590.27 over five years, or roughly $520 a year. This comes from a combination of subsidies funded from taxes—as part of an overall farm bill cost of $286 billion from 2008 to 2012—and the additional burden of inflated food prices, where import tariffs and quota systems force Americans to pay significantly more than they need to for dairy products, sugar, and other crops.[51] At the time of writing, in late 2007, the Senate was considering the bill, which the Bush administration threatened to veto for being too expensive.

Whatever the outcome, however, the sums are unlikely to be too different from the previous farm bill from 2002. This was calculated to cost the average American family $4,377 over ten years,[52] arising from an estimated $190 billion in taxes and $271 billion in increased food prices.

Europeans spend even more. In 2002, the Consumers' Association in the UK carried out some research into the average food basket. They concluded that a typical British family of four was paying around $30 more than it needs to a week because of EU agricultural subsidies, through a combination of tax and higher prices at the checkout.[53] That works out to around $1,500 a year. The Japanese have it at least as bad, spending almost as much on supporting farmers as agriculture actually contributes to the national economy,[54] including more than $600 per household on rice in 2000.[55] Whichever the country, poorer families are the most affected, as they spend a higher proportion of their income on food.

It's not just the immediate cost, however. Removing subsidies inevitably pressures industries to become more efficient. The UK Consumers' Association also discovered that its food prices were over twice those of New Zealand—a country that has largely scrapped farm subsidies. While some expenses in New Zealand are, of course, cheaper, the scale of difference is surprising: the total cost of a shopping list of fifteen food items including beefsteak, lamb chops, olive oil, and rice was around $150 in the UK and $70 in New Zealand. America would fall roughly halfway in between.

It's clear then that, as consumers, we spend quite a lot of money paying for the subsidies that harm Africa. But . . .

## . . . What about Our Farms?

Though many development campaigners don't like to admit it, the issue of what trade reform would mean for Western farmers is very important. No matter how unequal subsidies may be, reducing them could still have a serious impact on our farmers and rural communities. Few of us want to see our countryside idled and landscapes left to waste.

It is best to start with some facts. Agriculture forms a surprisingly small part of Western economies. In the United States it's 0.9 percent of economic output. In Japan it is 1.6 percent. Even in France, the leading advocate of maintaining the European Union's subsidy system, it stands at only 2.9 percent, and nowhere does it rise above 3 percent. Only 1.8 percent of America's working population is involved in farm production[56] (in contrast, of course, to sub-Saharan Africa, where agriculture provides most people's employment).

The next surprise is who the subsidies go to. There are many small-scale farmers across America, Europe, and Japan who struggle to make ends meet in a highly competitive retail food market in which prices and margins are being driven ever lower. We are strongly encouraged by media campaigns to believe that it is these small family farms that subsidies benefit. But the facts do not, on the whole, bear this out. The smallest 60 percent of European farms receive only 10 percent of Europe's subsidies, whereas the largest 2 percent receive nearly a quarter.[57]

In the United States the situation is even starker. Subsidies are smaller overall but more concentrated. Sixty percent of farms get nothing at all from Washington, while, over the last ten years, the richest 10 percent have received 72 percent of the government's support—which presumably helps explain why they are so rich.[58]

Who makes up this richest 10 percent of claimants? They are not small family farms but mostly agribusinesses that farm on a huge scale. The incentives created by subsidies are sometimes perverse and antimarket, because they encourage agribusinesses to produce the maximum crop possible even if there is no real demand for it, driving prices yet lower overall and resulting in even larger subsidies, some of which end up offloaded onto poor countries.

## The Way We Think about Farms

The way we think of farms in Western societies is unique. We like to believe in lots and lots of small, independent farmers rather than accept a process of competition and rationalization into ownership by only a few large companies, as we do for most other industries. We also favor tradition in production techniques, whereas, say with cars, we want the latest, safest, most efficient and hygienic model. I'm not sure why we feel like this, though I do too.

Yet this is clearly not what many subsidies support. With their economies of scale and large subsidies, the success of agribusinesses has fed a decrease in the overall number of U.S. farms, with large farms buying up smaller competitors and thus qualifying for more subsidies. Most European countries are experiencing a similar reduction.

Small farmers are stuck with a consumer base that wants them to pursue traditional, labor-intensive farming techniques, while they struggle ever harder to compete with modern, efficient large farms. Gaining organic accreditation is demanding, and the market for organics will not grow big enough to solve the problem. Meanwhile, we do most of our shopping in supermarkets that benefit from mass farming's cheaper prices, squeezing small farmers further. Do we really know what we want?

Some of the profits made by large American agribusinesses are used to hire lobbyists and media campaigners, who are clearly very effective. It's not just that they continue to sell us the idea that subsidies support family farmers but, according to the U.S. General Accounting Office, subsidies to large farms have tripled since 1991, while small farms have had no increase. As with most such campaigns, the lobbyists concentrate on a few key sympathetic congressmen and senators. This may help explain why just 22 of America's 435 congressional districts are thought to have collected more than half of all subsidies between 1995 and 2005: some $69 billion.[59] Incidentally, crop producers spent $15 million on campaign contributions during the presidential election in 2004, according to the Center for Responsive Politics.[60] They will doubtless spend even more in 2008.

The Heritage Foundation—hardly a hotbed of hippie aid workers, but rather a think tank so conservative it's endorsed by Rush Limbaugh—called American farm subsidies "America's largest corporate welfare program," pointing out that it is probably not the outcome that President Franklin D. Roosevelt had in mind when he first crafted subsidies to aid farmers struggling through the Great Depression. Shocked to see subsidies grow in a time of plenty, Roosevelt might also be surprised that among today's biggest and unlikeliest beneficiaries are Fortune 500 corporations including Chevron, Caterpillar, and Electronic Data Systems. They've all been attracted by the guaranteed income ensured by the subsidies.[61]

The three-quarters of Americans who support giving subsidies to small family farms might be rather surprised by all this too.[62] As might the 100 percent of American taxpayers who pay for them.

*

It's important to keep this issue in context: support for *some* farmers in Western countries is probably required if they are to stay in their fields. Yet it's clear that a lot of current subsidies do not go to support the people we want, are often heavily bloated, and, as with cotton and sugar, sustain farmers in producing a number of inefficient crops instead of moving to more naturally viable products. They also cost us an awful lot of money.

There are plenty of advocates on both sides of the political divide in America who are pressing for change and a better deal for American consumers, which in the long term could also bene-fit African farmers and businesses trying to become more competitive. But for the last few years it's the defenders of entrenched interests who've been winning. It's hard to believe the level of payments couldn't come sharply down and be more strongly focused on encouraging fresh, high-quality produce made by local farmers for local consumption. We need a debate about supporting rural livelihoods that is not distorted by corpo-rate lobbying and knee-jerk protectionism.

## The Total Bill

There is one piece of really good news here. It's not actually Africa and other very poor countries that provide a major threat to Western farmers: Africa is still too small a player. Billy Tiller, the cotton farmer in Texas, is not really worried about Mama Idrissou in Benin—his anxiety is about bigger-scale Chinese competitors. Beghin-Say, Tate & Lyle, and other European sugar processors are not so concerned by Mozambique—they lose sleep over the large sugar farms of Brazil. Chevron and other unlikely American wheat producers are apprehensive about Australian opponents, not Kenyan competition.

This reality is acknowledged in the "preferential" no-tariff access to European and American markets that most African produce is already permitted. But it's subsidies that are the real problem. It is not beyond us to design a system that reduces and removes subsidies in the key sectors of interest to African and other poorest countries, and worries less about reform elsewhere.

## The Radical Solution

Yet what if we got rid of protectionism in all areas of our economy?

In 2003 an international initiative called the Copenhagen Consensus brought together eight of the world's leading economists, including three Nobel laureates, to assess some of the biggest challenges in the world. After more than a year of research, they endorsed the findings by Professor Kym Anderson from the University of Adelaide that the world economy would gain by at least $254 billion a year (1995 prices) if everyone abolished subsidies, tariffs, and non-tariff barriers (non-tariff barriers are government measures such as import quotas, licensing standards, and other regulations—all of which have been used in the past as a backdoor way of keeping African competition out).

Most of the world's gains would come from agriculture. $110 billion of these gains would accrue to the very rich countries that currently spend so much on agricultural protectionism. That's right—the money we'd save from abolishing our subsidies and from enjoying cheaper prices at the checkout for foreign goods massively outweighs the benefits we currently get! Any jobs lost in agriculture would be easily outnumbered by wider economic benefits and new employment. Poor countries would gain too, albeit on a smaller scale as their economies are smaller.

The Copenhagen conclusions are backed up by a wide variety of sources elsewhere. A World Bank study came to a similar view. Meanwhile, the Federal Reserve Bank of Dallas reported in

2002 that saving a job in America's sugar industry cost American consumers $826,000 in higher prices at the cash register every year. Saving a dairy-industry job cost $685,000 a year. And saving a job making handbags cost $263,000.[63] There are surely many better ways of supporting employment than this.

## Trade: The Things You Really Need to Know

*Why do unfair subsidies and tariffs persist if they are bad for poor countries and bad for us too?*
The benefits of protectionism fall heavily to the few, who thus organize and lobby hard to maintain them. The costs of protectionism are spread much more thinly across the many—us taxpayers and consumers—so we can't be bothered to do much about them.

*Why do we fear liberalization if it creates more jobs than are lost?*
Those who lose jobs are real people with faces and families. Those who will gain in the future are statistics.

## Nyabagogo Market

The main clothes market in Kigali lies along the side of a main road in an area called Nyabagogo, about twenty minutes' walk from my Swiss house. It spreads downhill for a couple of hundred yards, and, walking through from the top, you first pass the more expensive stalls all packed together under a corrugated metal roof, selling new clothes, towels, and sheets, most of it from China. Next you reach the best secondhand clothes stalls with suits, jackets, and ties for men, and fancy dresses and shoes for women, plus the odd wedding dress for rent. There are a few tailors off to the side too, ready to adjust any new purchases for a small fee.

Toward the bottom of the slope is the cheaper end of the market, covered only by plastic sheeting to provide shelter from daily rain. There's a damp, musty smell here, coming from the crowded piles of T-shirts, jeans, and other items. And a constant babble of conversation between the traders, mostly women.

If you are very lucky, the items for sale at the cheap end of the market in a particularly poor part of Africa happen to coincide with what you think is fashionable back home. To the confusion of Nyabagogo's stallholders, a couple of friends and I would often go searching for secondhand American sports T-shirts that we, at least, thought were quite cool. My purchases included Newfane Soccer Club (No. 4); Plains Baseball—Sponsored by Steve's Auto; and the 13th Annual Midnight Tour—World's Largest Escorted Motorcycle Road Ride 1992.

For reasons of affordability rather than fashion, many if not most Africans now dress in cast-off Western clothing. Traveling around cities and the countryside in Africa can be a surreal experience, as you spot adults and children advertising obscure corporate conferences, dishwashing powder, and stag weekends. The process runs something like this: you stick your T-shirt in a charity collecting bin; charities sell it unsorted to exporters (using the proceeds to fund their projects); and exporters then sift it by quality before shipping it out. In one U.S. recycling factory, the best garments go to Asia and Latin America, the second best to richer African countries, and the worst to their poorer counterparts. They're then shipped and sold on in diminishing-sized bundles through local traders to end up in markets across the continent.[64]

The journey doesn't always stop there. Many clothes will be sold on again after a couple of years' wear and tear, ending up in the smallest stalls in the poorest villages. In Rwanda it was quite easy to tell the poorest of the poor simply by whether their T-shirts were so threadbare that they had holes in them.

Before the market in secondhand Western clothing grew up—the "mivumba" trade, as it's known in East Africa—some countries such as Uganda and Zambia had thriving clothes manufacturing industries. These have now died. Other countries such as Nigeria and Eritrea have avoided this fate by imposing tariffs on foreign imports. It's difficult to know which is the better option: protect your industry or allow people to have cheaper clothing. It's the sort of decision that can only be made by African governments on a case-by-case basis, based partly on how competitive they think their domestic industry might be in the long term.

I've no idea whether the soccer players of Newfane (who, from a cursory Web search, may be in either New York State or Vermont) or the fans of Plains Baseball (Georgia, or Nova Scotia, Canada?) had any idea who might end up wearing their castoffs when they threw them into a charity bin. But, fashion-victim Brit or royally turned-out Rwandan, the mivumba trade probably isn't anything to feel bad about. There's a big difference between products from overseas that seriously underprice locally available merchandise—and thus save the African consumer valuable money—and dumped goods such as European tomatoes that are only slightly cheaper than Kenyan ones, just enough to put Kenyan farmers out of business.

Your T-shirts remain, however, a highly visible reminder that Western actions can have important effects on African economies. For hundreds of millions of Africans, the very first decision they make every morning is which traded secondhand item of Western clothing to put on.

## Lose–Lose

Let's be clear about trade and the effect on us. At the moment we are paying much more than we need to in taxes and at the supermarket checkout for poorly designed subsidies, and as a result poor people in Africa are suffering too. If we changed things and provided effective support to the minority of people negatively affected in our own countries, we would have more jobs and more money, and Africans from Mama Idrissou in Benin to that immensely attractive president in Uzima would stand a better chance of sorting out their own problems. We could even use some of our savings to boost aid budgets to a level where they too will actually start to be more effective in helping millions out of poverty.

Then again, if we weren't already spending so much money on subsidies, African countries would have less need of our aid anyway.

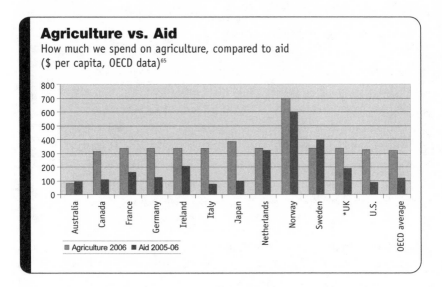

### Agriculture vs. Aid

How much we spend on agriculture, compared to aid
($ per capita, OECD data)[65]

■ Agriculture 2006   ■ Aid 2005-06

Doesn't this table look rather odd to you? We all spend far more money on domestic agricultural support, much of which harms the chances of poor countries, than we spend on (inefficiently) helping those countries we've just harmed. This is the true scandal of Africa.

Amid a global mantra of free trade, African countries are left to ponder who is really benefiting from this process. And ponder they do. President Museveni of Uganda is highly astute at saying the right things to Western donors whose assistance he needs. But it is hard to disagree when he comments to local journalists that "Uganda has in fact been donating resources to the outside world for a long time. We lost much more money through unfair trade. Ugandans are the real donors of jobs and money to the outside."[66]

It's not often that everyone from rabid free market ideologues to tofu-eating liberals is in strong agreement on an issue. The logic of competition and the free market is *not* being applied to key areas of global trade—and it is poor countries that are suffering most. Adam Smith would be spinning in his grave. And, because the lives of so many Africans are already fragile, the sad and shocking truth is that millions are joining him there early as a result.

## Market Breakdown

Sekanyo Misusela lives about an hour and a half north of the Ugandan capital, Kampala. When a journalist went to visit him in March 2005, Sekanyo revealed that he had started off a few years ago growing coffee.[67] When plant disease and falling world prices made this uneconomical, he switched to cotton. America's cotton subsidies prevented much success in this area as well, so he now grows sugar, after a brief flirtation with vanilla. Uganda's sugar industry isn't much developed, partly because of American and Europe's traditional high sugar protectionism, so instead of being sold abroad, Sekanyo's sugar goes to the capital, where it is made into a local drink, waragi.

Sekanyo's story encapsulates the difficulties African countries have in progressing in world trade. There's nothing intrinsically wrong with sugar being used to make waragi, which started life as an improvised "war gin" for British soldiers fighting the First World War in East Africa, and later became Uganda's national drink (it tastes very good with bitter lemon, even if some of the less official breweries occasionally produce bad batches that can lead to blindness—even the good stuff should be avoided if you're attending a long aid conference the next day). Yet Sekanyo is exactly the sort of entrepreneur who, in an ideal world, should be supplying and benefiting from global trade demands from lucrative foreign markets. Instead, the waragi made from his sugar helps sustain the considerable alcohol problem from which Uganda suffers, along with much of the rest of the continent— one of the less renowned aspects of African poverty.

Like Sekanyo, Uganda, despite some recent political problems, is exactly the sort of country that should be benefiting more from global trade, if any can. It has made real strides in the last twenty years to address its financial problems and for a long time was internationally lauded as well governed and highly committed to development. Yet Uganda too is finding limits to its advance. The numbers living below the poverty line may have fallen from 56 percent in 1992 to 35 percent in 2000, but progress more recently has slowed, with 31 percent still below the line in 2006. If an almost unprecedented period of sound governance and, by African standards, stability is not enough to enable proper integration into the world economy, what hope is there for other countries?

Fairer trade terms would not bring radical change to anywhere in Africa overnight, except for a few examples such as cotton and sugar. Africa's transport costs are high, its infrastructure poor, far too many of its farms are small subsistence plots, and its educational and industrial bases are weakly developed. The main beneficiaries of straightforward reduction in agricultural tariffs and domestic support would be more advanced, efficient farming countries such as Brazil and Australia.

Yet a fairer system would enable countries like Uganda and Uzima making the right reforms to see the prospect of greater benefit in the future. It would encourage more investment, both internal and external. And, just as the American architects of the post–Second World War world appreciated, it would help prevent conflict and sustain Africa's fragile stability.

## Free Trade Is a Myth

What I have found fascinating as I've researched this book is that it's not just in subsidies and tariffs on a few headline products that markets are distorted. In countless areas of trade with Africa, free market terms are not being allowed to operate. This seems extraordinary at first, because the conventional wisdom we pick up somewhere along the line in the West is that the market is a tough place and unfortunately Africa just can't compete.

Yet the areas where true market logic is allowed to prevail are rare. Take the skilled personnel we absorb from African countries, such as nurses, doctors, and the best graduates. Isn't this free trade in labor? No, a true free market in labor would mean allowing our economies to be swamped by unskilled labor as well as the professionals. Right or wrong, it's poaching.

How about the patenting of drugs: surely that is an area where Africa suffers simply because, however unfortunately, the market has no interest in providing for very poor people? This is a little more complicated, but wrong too. Patents were originally introduced as deliberate, distorting regulations in society's interest, to give inventors the exclusive ability to cash in on their inventions for a set number of years. Yet it's clear those distortions haven't been well enough designed to enable poor Africans to benefit. Major industrialized countries including Italy, Japan, and Switzerland adopted pharmaceutical patent protection only when their per capita income was around $20,000 a year. So why make developing countries adopt it at around $500?[68] If society's interest is the test, we've failed.

As for our approach to agricultural support, that is evidently not free trade either.

The truth about trade is that, managed correctly, it is a powerful force for good. But let's stop pretending the debate is about creating free trade. In a world where all trade is regulated by agreements negotiated between countries and managed through measures such as patents, taxes, monopoly legislation, and more, the concept of free trade becomes so vague as to be virtually worthless. The broad principle of reducing protectionism is useful, and what is left is a range of opinions about how quickly you do that, and how you regulate trade, to maximize overall benefit to society.

The real problem is that we are failing to consider *global* society's wider benefit when making trade rules. Why did this happen? Is it really credible that our political and corporate leaders are involved in some evil conspiracy to screw the African poor and make love to the Western rich, as some antiglobalization protesters would have us believe?

Such an account is absurd, not to mention offensive to those involved. What has happened is essentially this: as international trade has increased, trading nations have needed to put in place some rules to manage the international market process. As rich countries with the most to trade, we in the West have led the development of these rules. And we have made them mostly in good faith to improve our own economies.

Unfortunately, these rules on global trade made for our own benefit have global repercussions; they affect Africa too. African countries were not involved in any serious way in drawing up the rules but they have no choice but to abide by them. So although we never intended it, we've ended up developing a trade system that appears to suit us but that often hampers Africa.

Rather than free trade, we end up with Me trade, which too often serves entrenched interests alone. So while our aid conditionality pushes Africa to liberalize, we reserve our greatest protectionism for agriculture, the area where they have the best chance to compete. We poach qualified workers while denying free movement in unskilled labor. We fail to design patent and drug rules to ensure they can benefit those most in need of them, while exploiting the African natural resources that might be of interest to us. It is a picture unremitting in its viciousness, even if unwittingly created.

This really matters. If Africa's continuing poverty had nothing to do with decisions we in the West have made, there might still be an argument that we should do more for Africa for moral reasons. But it would be a weaker argument. Since Africa's poverty is, however, directly influenced by decisions we are making on global trade every day, and since many of those decisions are tilted unfairly *against* Africa, we have nothing less than a duty to do something about it.

## Trade Is Weird

Sekanyo Misusela is probably still farming away at his sugarcane to make waragi in Uganda, having given up on cotton and coffee. Lucas is, I hope, still tilling his land on the edge of the Rift Valley. And I am still typing at my computer wearing cotton jeans, T-shirt, and underwear. I've munched my way through several chocolate bars and drunk copious amounts of coffee. And two days ago I went to my local clinic in advance of a forthcoming trip to Kenya and got some injections from a nice South African nurse there.

But the way world trade works is starting to make me paranoid. I hate the fact that the clothes I've bought, the food I've eaten, and the coffee I've drunk make me complicit in a trading system I don't like the look of. I started to feel guilty while getting my injections that my demand on the services of a South African nurse was leaving a gap in her home country that might be being filled by a nurse from Malawi, while people in Malawi were left with no one. I even began to worry that my custom for the injections I'd had meant those drugs would be priced out of the range of most Africans.

If the major problem with aid is that the West isn't doing enough for Africa, the problem with trade seems to be that the West is doing little at all for the world's poorest continent. We explicitly fail to manage trade in such a way that they could benefit from it as well as us, the impact of this failure dwarfing the money you spend on aid. Just as with aid, we know what we need to do differently and yet we still don't do it.

The weird thing is that these trade rules that injure already fragile countries don't work for shoppers and taxpayers in the West either. The subsidies that fail Africa's farmers cost us extra in taxes as well as at the checkout line, even as Western governments are presently defaulting on their promises to conclude a world trade round in the interests of poor countries. We are dipping into our pocket with one hand to fund trade arrangements that hinder Africa, and then clumsily dipping into the same pocket to try and aid them with the other.

Not good for them, not good for us either. How on earth can that be? For the answers, we must understand properly how the era of globalization is changing the world around us.

# GLOBALIZATION
## MIGHT AND RIGHT

# CHAPTER 13
# AFRICA DOESN'T MATTER

## No Mercy on the Road to Moyale

Throughout my time in Rwanda I harbored the dream of driving home across East and North Africa once my job finished, on through the Middle East, and back to London. Planning it with my American friend Mary Louise, who was later to experience the incense bath and henna tattooing when we were stuck in Sudan, was a reminder that Africa's biggest obstacles to progress remain internal.

I bought an old Land Rover Defender in the UK and had it shipped out to Kenya, where, with all the right papers, it took three full days and visits to countless offices to have it released from Mombasa port. Many officials simply wouldn't deal with us at all until we'd employed a middleman to help us who knew the system and had "the right contacts." Then we drove up the long road to Nairobi, at night. This part of the Trans-African Highway is frightening at the best of times: crater-holed and narrow, with trucks hurtling straight down the middle, leaving you to drop as much as a foot off the side of the decaying tarmac onto the red-earth shoulder at a moment's notice. At night, and with headlights apparently a luxury, it was terrifying.

It was also bad for the car, which took an immediate batter-
ing from the on-and-off road. I could understand why a busi-
nessman I'd once met told me it cost him twice as much to have
a container driven up through Kenya and into Uganda than it did
to have it shipped from London to Mombasa. The economies of
Uganda, Rwanda, and others that rely almost exclusively on the
road to Mombasa, not to mention Kenya itself, would be greatly
boosted if the government there ever sorts it out.

The real trouble began, however, when we headed into Kenya's
barren and beautiful north. The stretch of road between Marsabit
and Moyale on the Ethiopian border runs through a scorched
wilderness famous for being patrolled by Shifta bandits. As a
result, trucks congregate each day just after dawn to make the
six- or seven-hour run in convoy. We positioned ourselves bleary-
eyed one morning near the head of the queue, thinking it would
be no problem to keep up at the front and avoid too much of the
copious dust sent up by every convoy wheel on the arid rock
road. Then the wacky races began and the trucker in front took
off at a blinding pace, leaving everyone else far behind and Mary
Louise and me shuddering to keep up.

An hour in and the engine cut out. Car mechanics was one of
our embarrassingly weak points. When another truck eventually
caught up, its driver concluded that the alternator was the problem and immediately he announced it unfixable. But he could
tow us the remaining couple of hundred kilometers to Moyale,
for a fee to be agreed. His bargaining strategy accounted for the
fact that we had no choice.

The next few hours were among the most unpleasant of the
entire trip to London. With the Land Rover tethered to the high
truck on a remarkably short leash, my head ached from the

concentration required not to crash into its rear. Our windshield cracked from the stones thrown up from its wheels. We slow-baked in our own sweat, windows closed in an effort to keep as much of the all-permeating white dust out as possible. And every time we stopped, tempers frayed beyond mending, I demanded a slower pace while the truck driver, hotwired and increasingly paranoid on the chewable buzz of *miraa* leaves, ordered more and more of his payment up front, plus a premium, or immediate abandonment in the middle of the most barren plain I have encountered. He won every time. There can have been few people more pleased to see the scratchy, unpromising buildings of Moyale finally bump into view in the dull light of dusk.

Driving on many of Africa's roads is neither easy nor cheap. It's not hard to see why it's far more competitive to be a trader in much of Asia, with its efficient infrastructure and customs bureaucracies. Yet the plight many African countries find themselves in is a bit like mine, broken down on the road from Marsabit to Moyale. They don't have all the skills to get going easily themselves; the assistance they are offered is not always helpful; and if they want to follow the road laid out ahead of them, they must do so on the terms offered by others.

Aid to Africa is inefficient and insufficient. Trade is unwittingly unfair. Western taxpayers and consumers are denied value for money for their aid and bear significant costs for unfair trade. We know most of the things we need to do better but still don't do them. The obvious question is: how did all this happen?

## Comforts and Concerns

There is a paradox at the heart of globalization. On the one hand, the expanding markets it brings, along with rapid advances in technology and communications, leave all of us potentially better off. On the other, the global nature of its forces means we feel increasingly powerless as individuals.

In America and Europe this leaves many of us feeling detached from the changes around us, with a growing sense of impotence in the face of faceless large corporations, worries about job security, and increasing disillusionment about the ability of our politicians to deliver the societies we want. In Africa, more simply, it leaves them with the persistent bum end of the deal, unable to take advantage of the increased opportunities that globalization provides. It's not so much a case of anyone deliberately shafting Africa; it's more that other interest groups are successfully following their own agendas and that no one is stopping to notice the effects. Indeed, as we gradually establish more and more trade and other rules to manage how globalization is taking place, without paying sufficient attention to African needs, we may even end up entrenching an entire continent's marginalization. Leaving it stuck, like my Land Rover, in the desert.

The reality we are left with is a dog's breakfast few of us want, and it is instructive about the whole way globalization is being allowed to evolve. During pretty much every previous phase in the history of expanding markets—such as when trading grew from local to regional to national levels—we sought to manage the market's social impacts and maximize its productiveness. This time we are allowing short-term interests to determine long-term directions, while the size of internationalizing markets is outgrowing the ability of national governments to regulate them. We are failing to help globalization realize its economic and social potential.

But who is in charge here if it's not us? Because it certainly isn't Africa or other poor parts of the world.

## What Is Globalization?

It's helpful to try and define globalization, because it seems to be used to explain such a wide variety of issues. The reason, of course, is that it actually describes a process—in literal terms, "to go global"—and hence can be applied to many things.

The most common context, however, is economic, and it should be broadly understood here as follows: *the rapid expansion of markets across national boundaries, and the social and political effects this brings.*

There are three reasons why the West's current failing of Africa is a great deal more important than was ever the case before.

- First, many African countries are now making unprecedented efforts to address their own complex problems. There are more democracies and fewer conflicts on the continent than for decades, even if our media—and, to be fair, books like this—continue to focus on the negatives. Average economic growth since 2000 of around 5 percent is encouraging (it equates to roughly 2–3 percent per person, taking in population growth).[1] Offering these countries a favorable international environment within which to fight their internal difficulties could be far more fruitful now than it would have been before.

- Second, Africa's stagnation of previous decades, matched against the West's long period of globalization-fed growth, means we could do much more to aid Africa with a small proportion of our wealth than has ever previously been possible. Developed economies grew by 50 percent between 1980 and 2001 alone, while Africa's went slightly backward.[2] Efficiently spent, our money could now fund all the key priorities to help well-run governments meet their people's basic needs and halve poverty with less than our oft-promised 0.7 percent of GNI.

- It's the third reason, however, that is by far the most important. Globalization's advances in trade, technology, and communication offer much greater potential for poor countries to lift themselves out of poverty than has ever before existed, as China and India's astonishing progress has shown. A richer West has more money to spend on the kinds of goods resurgent African economies might produce. If only we could manage globalization in such a way that African countries could really benefit, the results could be humbling.

This needs some further investigation, because our failure to manage globalization in order to allow Africa a chance to help itself isn't just about wasted opportunities now. It is also about the future world we want.

## What History Tells Us

There is a simple, if shocking, reason why the West doesn't do better by the poorest continent. Africa Doesn't Matter. Its poor markets hold little interest for Western business, and the continent provides almost no political or strategic threat to the West's stability, for the moment at least. There are thus no natural incentives to allow it a fairer deal.

What is so distinctive about Africa's plight is that marginalized groups in previous eras of expanding markets *were* a threat, and so had to be included in its benefits. These were delivered both by drawing marginalized groups into the market, and through governance arrangements such as democracy and welfare states.

*

I don't want to be too benign about previous stages of market
expansion, but the results have been pretty impressive. Back in
the eighteenth century, when some of my ancestors were working in northern English villages as house servants and farm
laborers, most transactions were still local: the blacksmith didn't
have a chain of shops across the country, most food and other
goods were procured from nearby areas, and the local sheriff or
landowner would have sorted out the vast majority of problems
whether you liked it or not. Industrialization then brought the
loss of old jobs and creation of new ones, along with migration
and changes to the social fabric of the country. Localized solutions were no longer viable, and, as my family headed for work
in the cotton mills, more political power was gradually central-
ized in London: national government to deal with national
issues.

Conditions in mills and factories were awful at first, but after a
couple of miserable generations the benefits for the workers gradually began to grow, in order to avoid social conflict from this
newly urbanized and organized labor. It was a similar story, of
course, in America, to which some of my family had fled in the
early nineteenth century, and where urbanization really took off
from the 1860s onward, with more rapid improvements in conditions. (I don't know much about these relatives. Alarmingly, I
guess it's possible I am distantly related to both soul-singing
Michael Bolton and soulless neoconning John Bolton.) Markets
hate instability (which is why businesses tend to be innately conservative). Besides which, it was also in the markets' natural interest to
see a better-educated, healthier workforce. Free schooling was
made available to all in America by the end of the nineteenth
century. Philanthropic institutions were established to look after

orphans and offer basic health care. Child labor was abolished.

The twentieth century saw a similar process. The lessons of the Great Depression of the 1930s—in which countries imposed high tariffs on each other's products, effectively sending markets into contraction and compounding economic and social losses— were largely learned. Economies grew and welfare states blossomed. Countries that flirted disastrously with communism and fascism ultimately came back into the free market fold—partly because those markets delivered in a way other systems couldn't.

As markets continued to expand, the relatively small size of American states meant that more and more trade was crossing state borders. In response, an increasing amount of federal government was put in place to help manage those markets for stability and wider social gain. A similar process was happening in Europe, characterized by small nation-states, where demands for cross-national governance were beginning to grow. The changing names of these institutional arrangements reflect the growing social demands brought by market expansion: first there was the European Economic Community, then the middle word was dropped, and in 1992 it became the European Union.

The European project in particular has been tremendously successful at helping deliver the stability necessary to underpin expanding markets and economic growth—and with it social advantage. Not only has peace held between Europe's major powers after centuries of conflict, but potential instability on its borders has been mopped up too. The likes of Spain and Portugal were brought back to democracy and fed large amounts of financing, in return for which they soon developed new and important markets for other European (and American) goods. More recently the same approach has been applied to the new accession countries, vulnerable after the collapse of the Soviet Union, and the Balkan nations.

## Why Africa Is Different

In theory, all this looks pretty optimistic. If the twentieth century brought improved conditions for the poor almost wherever our markets spread, and if our markets are now going global, then shouldn't other parts of the world soon see some benefit too, including Africa?

This is where the fact that Africa Doesn't Matter causes a genuine new problem. Unlike poor groups within our own societies, or potentially volatile countries near America or Europe's borders, Africans provide almost no threat to this new global market's stability. Africa can remain marginalized, whereas marginalized groups within national and regional markets had to be brought (or bought) in.

What it means is that Africa becomes increasingly affected by the international decisions we make in a globalizing world—especially those on aid and trade arrangements—but has little or no ability to influence them. It has no markets of its own to interest us, only a few tempting natural resources, and no major military machinery to make it geopolitically dangerous. It doesn't produce terrorists that we need to take account of (not yet, at least). Everything from aid to trade to our attitude toward conflict resolution and humanitarian relief is affected by its impotence.

In the absence of Africa's own ability to demand its interests are heard, who else can do it? Many of us as individuals in Western societies like to think of ourselves as more caring than our governments. But it's different for us too. We don't pass these poor on the street. We don't suffer from any crimes they may commit or witness the conditions they live in. It's harder for us to see what their problems are and easier for us to ignore them.

## Rwanda: The Ultimate Example of International Apathy

If anything reveals the mundane truth that Africa doesn't matter to the West, it's buried somewhere in a memorial site on a Rwandan hillside. The genocide of 1994 was well signposted, for those who bothered to look. What many don't realize is that it was no one-time event, but the culmination of more than three decades of ethnic strife, punctuated by occasional and sizable massacres: ten thousand here, ten thousand there. And the planning for the final annihilation of the minority Tutsi community had been going on for months.

It was not, of course, only the West that failed Rwanda. Her neighbors did little to intervene, but at least they had problems and ethnic tensions of their own to manage. The West had the capability to prevent the slaughter, and it had unequivocal reports from the UN commander on the ground, not to mention a number of other sources, that it was coming. When it arrived, still no one acted.

The UN Security Council went through absurdist oral acrobatics to avoid using the word—"genocide"—that would have required it to act under its own conventions. France, the most influential European power in that part of central Africa, refused to concede that a regime they'd long supported was dissolving into depravity (they'd previously helped stop Tutsi forces from entering the country). The United States, usually required to take a lead if other Western powers were to get involved, was haunted by the eighteen Army Rangers killed in Somalia the year before, and the accompanying vivid TV footage of American bodies being dragged through the dust.

With capability comes culpability. Nearly one million Rwandans died, in only one hundred days, from a population of eight million. This wasn't a vague foreign war of soldier against soldier. It wasn't even the mechanized machine-gun and gas-chamber horror of the Holocaust. It was death applied by millions of machete cuts on defenseless people by the easily defeatable: drunk, murder-high militias and the everyday citizens they attracted or induced into participation.

Today, they keep the genocide sites in Rwanda exactly as they found them, minus the actual bodies. Several of the sites are churches, where Tutsis huddled in a last attempt at sanctuary, sometimes encouraged there by duplicitous priests. Bloodied, torn shirts and dresses. Clean-cut children's clothes. A few last prized possessions, including the odd yellow plastic jerry can. Red handprints far up the walls marking the high tide of attempts to escape.

You can smell a lot of things in those sites, and you can't forget them. The sickening scent of something like badly cured leather. Man's capacity for impossible cruelty. And the West's capacity for utter indifference.

## Even Good Intentions Go Begging

How does the lack of incentives to act fairly by Africa manifest itself in more day-to-day terms? Extraordinarily, it can be so strong that even when Western leaders would *like* to do better by Africa, they still don't.

Imagine yourself as president of a Western country for a change (it's a refreshing contrast from being the boss in Uzima and easier to justify that private jet). Aid is rarely on your agenda, but when you do make the odd speech about it, you're seduced by the issues and the caring light in which new promises will bathe you. The problem is that the rest of the time it's not near the top of the in-tray, and you're under constant pressure to deliver on other priorities.

Chief among these pressures is the necessity to keep budgets down, affecting all expenditure including aid, even though aid comprises less than 1 percent of outlay by most Western governments. The difficulty is that aid doesn't have nearly the same number of powerful champions as most other areas of expenditure. Think of the criticism from various corners if you proposed cutting education, health, or the armed forces.

Yet what if you don't deliver your promises on aid? (Note: never actually cut it . . . just fall a little short on your commitments.) Well, poor countries won't risk complaining, as they're still holding out for whatever funds you do allocate; besides which, they are thousands of miles away and politically unimportant. Some charities may moan a bit, but many of them too are dependent on you for money. Meanwhile, most of your domestic media won't notice because they tend to focus on the new promises you make in speeches, rather than the actual delivery. And the public? In most Western countries, most of the public will simply remain oblivious.

If you think I'm exaggerating, try researching how many former Western leaders say they wish they'd spent more on aid while in office. Since leaving the White House, Bill Clinton has become a true cheerleader for international efforts. There's no reason to doubt his sincerity in recommending that the West do more, as he did in a speech to the Council on Foreign Relations in 2002 (and on many other occasions):

> *If you took a poll among the American people and you asked them what percentage of the budget do we spend on foreign assistance, and what percent should we spend . . . the biggest block always say we spend between 2 and 15 percent of the budget, and that is too much, we should spend between 3 and 5 percent. Now, I actually agree with them. [But] of course, we spend less than 1 percent, and we're dead last among all the advanced economies of the world in what we spend on foreign assistance . . . Most people believe we don't know how to do foreign assistance. And that most of the money is wasted. That is also untrue.*[3]

**Background:** When Clinton's administration commenced in 1992, American aid spending stood at 0.16 percent of GNI. In his last full year in office, 1999, it stood at 0.11 percent.[4] It can't all be blamed on an uncooperative Congress.

The former British prime minister John Major is another leader to have advocated more aid with the benefit of hindsight. In the course of a newspaper article in 2005, he wrote:

*It is what one does not do in life that one regrets. I know about dire poverty. I saw it in Nigeria, as a young man, during the Biafran war. And yet, looking back, I know I did far too little to end it . . . I did—year after year—protect the aid budget against the ravages of more popular claims. I did care about it, but I did not do nearly enough to end it . . . I can cite all these reasons for inaction, but none of them convinces my conscience.*[5]

**Background:** When Major's premiership began in 1990, British aid spending stood at 0.27 percent of GNI, with a nominal commitment to spending 0.7 percent. When he left in 1997, it was 0.26 percent.[6] It's the reference to "more popular claims" that seems most telling.

## Good Developments in Ethiopia

After the chaos of the towed journey to Moyale on Kenyan's northern border, and a new Land Rover alternator sent by a friend in Nairobi on the weekly European aid flight, we finally escaped into Ethiopia. There's an inevitable tendency in a book like this to focus on Africa's hardships. But Ethiopia, the land many of us in the West associate with the ultimate in African poverty, is a good reminder of how those problems are only one part of a vastly bigger picture. I can't recommend a better first place for anyone new to the continent to visit.

Two attractive female soldiers waved us across the border and we found ourselves in immediate tarmac bliss that would lead all the way to Addis Ababa. The initial section runs through desert scrub and we spent our first night camped away from the road in a dry riverbed, waking to have our morning routine impassively—and unnervingly—watched by a goatherd with an AK-47. But as the land rises, the next 200 kilometers before you reach the town of Awassa is stunningly beautiful. Large round houses line the fertile shoulders of the road, each with its own garden. Trees, grass, and grins catch in smoky shafts of afternoon sunlight. All life is lived around the road, and it's hard to imagine any country less likely to experience famine.

Driving through Ethiopia is an essentially surreal experience. Our guidebook warned that everyone and everything in Ethiopia—children, donkeys, goats, adults—ignores cars, and it proved alarmingly accurate. People walk out into the middle of the road and *then* look, startled to discover they may be about to be hit. We were even told that it is considered good luck by many old men to cross in front of a vehicle just before it passes—it's said to lengthen life. But, uniquely in my experience in Africa, you can also pull over almost anywhere approaching Addis and get a decent cup of coffee and a glass of fresh orange juice. Joy!

•

Ethiopia's roadside OJ runs out by the time you reach the rocky, poorer highlands of the north, but there are other diversions to compensate. It's a region blessed with an extraordinary architectural history, based mainly around churches and monasteries.

If one of the frequent refrains you hear about Africa is that it needs to find its own ways of adapting concepts like capitalism and democracy, the path of the Ethiopian Coptic Church provides a possible model. Cut off from Middle Eastern and European Christianity from around the tenth or eleventh century A.D., it was not to be reacquainted for nearly a thousand years. Looking at murals inside churches that are often six or seven hundred years old thus provides a strange experience. Not only is the style of art distinctive—and at least as skilled as most European painting of that era—but as a westerner you recognize only about half the stories.

Depictions of Christ carrying the cross or Moses parting the Red Sea may be familiar enough. The other half, however, illustrate legends and saints unique to Ethiopia, such as King Lalibela, who carved eleven extraordinary churches into rock in the highlands on eleven successive nights, with an angel matching every hour of labor he put in.

In the eyes of Ethiopian congregations, of course, it's the rest of Christianity that was cut off from them. The Coptic Church maintains to this day that it holds the Ark of the Covenant in the inner sanctum of a church in the city of Axum, to which only one priest has access. Every other church has a copy, which is brought out on saints' days. The thousands of worshippers amassing at these events in devout white wraps confirm that this particular version of a global trend seems to be very successful indeed.

## Global Governance: No Way

One possible answer to ensuring that globalization's benefits spread to Africa—and prevent further reliance on Western countries' unreliable goodwill—would be to strengthen global governance. This is, after all, the other traditional feature of expanding markets: they are accompanied by expanding political authority. Why not extend it now on a global scale to cover Africa? A set of stronger, democratic world institutions would certainly give African countries a fairer say on the issues that affect them under globalization, and enable them to secure a better deal.

No chance. As with everything else, the incentives to allow Africa more equal representation just don't exist. And it is clear that neither our current national authorities, nor most of us as citizens, have any desire for more international governance.

This is almost as true for Europe, whose voters seem for the time being to have reached the limit of their taste for integration by rejecting an EU constitution in 2006 and questioning closer ties with Turkey, as it is for America. Why on earth would Americans and their president sign up to stronger international institutions when they have a preeminent ability to act as they see fit, right or wrong, without it?

## International Rescue?

Unfortunately, the Western allergy to international governance doesn't just mean no new, fairer institutions. It also means that current "global" organizations are, in practice, little of the kind.

Let's start with the World Bank and the International Monetary Fund. Unequivocally, African countries are the most affected by the policies and practices of these two bodies. As you will recall from your stint as president of Uzima, it's not just the money they can provide: their willingness to work with you is also the entrée to all sorts of other donor funding. There is pretty much no chance of meeting your people's basic needs without them.

In theory, the Bank and Fund are global bodies. This is certainly how they are presented. All countries are represented on their executive boards, which make all key decisions. But look at the small print. Who actually holds the votes on these boards? The combined share of the vote of all sub-Saharan African countries adds up to around 5 to 7 percent. The people with a real stake in Bank and Fund activities do not have . . . a real stake.

This is a fundamental flaw at the heart of these two key institutions. Sure, donors provide much of the money so they are bound to demand much of the say, yet they must have an interest in effectiveness too. Not only does common sense suggest that those countries with most experience of Bank and Fund work should have some real input to their policies. But the sometimes painful reforms required in their programs are much more effectively accepted and implemented if they result from self- and peer analysis, rather than external imposition.

It's that old measure of effective aid again: ownership. African countries have been demanding a larger share of the vote on the issues that most affect them for several years now. Rather typically, America and Europe, which currently hold the vast majority of votes (and all the aces), have decided not to listen.

Denied an effective vote, African countries also lack the human resources to try to inform and influence the discussions that take place when the Bank and Fund boards consider how much and what kind of support to give them—or to cut back on. To put this in some kind of context, the office of a large European country in the Bank and Fund in Washington will have nine or ten highly qualified staff working full-time to prepare for board votes and policies, and a permanent place on the boards. Then there are large support teams carrying out and commissioning further research back in European capitals, of which I was once part (the United States, of course, has the whole of its Treasury Department just up the street). And sub-Saharan Africa? Its forty-eight countries have two seats on the boards between them, and are lucky if they have one single official from their own government among the teams there. Amid all the other demands for expensive diplomatic postings around the world, the budgets of averagely poor governments like Uzima's simply can't stretch to more.

The final irony is that while Bank and Fund programs are sometimes used by Western powers to increase pressure on African countries to move toward democracy (not in itself, of course, a bad thing), their own procedures are far from democratic. The idea is that Africa should move to electing leaders by merit, on the basis of popular mandate, in order to try and get the best man or woman for the job. Strange, then, that the leaderships of the Bank and

Fund are, by tradition, never voted on. Instead, the United States gets to choose the leader for the Bank (how else did you think that neocon and Iraq war architect Paul Wolfowitz ended up as its last president?). And Europe gets to appoint the head of the Fund.

## Obstacles to Trade

What of the World Trade Organization, often held up as an example of a more democratic institution? It's certainly true that the WTO doesn't deserve the demonization it suffers at the hands of antiglobalization protesters. Each country in the WTO has a vote, nominally giving African nations as much influence as anyone else—and much better representation than in either the World Bank or the International Monetary Fund.

Unsurprisingly, however, some nations are more equal than others. Unlike the Bank or Fund, the WTO rarely votes—it is more of a talking shop in which agreements are gradually hammered out, and no institutional design could ever change the fact that poor African countries need access to rich markets much more than vice versa. The rules may be nominally fair, but the contenders are utterly mismatched. The usual analogy is of two boxers, one a schoolboy featherweight, and one a world heavyweight: if the referee umpires the rounds according to the rules, the unpoetic reality is that Goliath never loses. David always does.

At least as significant in minimizing Africa's influence is the immense complexity of world trade discussions. Negotiations cover a vast range of areas, each of which has an implication for a country's economy. It's almost impossible to exaggerate how convoluted these issues become. The final text for the Uruguay Round, eventually completed in 1994, runs to 27,000 pages and is a complex calculation of allowed subsidies, antidumping codes, and tariff schedules.[7] There are calculations to be made concerning the possible effects of new proposed rules, large numbers of

meetings at which to assert your country's interests, and countless informal debates in the margins of meetings at which deals
can be made, frayed, or broken. That's why France has 165 staff
based at the World Trade Organization. Malawi has one.[8]

Others, meanwhile, can be even worse off:

> *Sierra Leone has no permanent mission in Geneva. Its
> nearest mission is in Brussels, with responsibility for both EU
> and WTO issues. The mission is small with only three profes-
> sional staff, including the ambassador, and in addition to
> the entire WTO agenda, it deals with UN issues as well as
> all relations with the European Union.*
> —Ministry of Trade official, Sierra Leone[9]

## What about the UN?

You may have noticed that I keep forgetting to mention all the various
UN bodies when it comes to global institutions. That's because, as I
mentioned at the beginning of the section on international aid, they have
a lot less money to spend than the Bank and Fund, and are less
influential than the WTO.

Why is that? It's because the UN is a genuinely more democratic
organization, and powerful Western countries dislike giving their money
to bodies they can less easily control. Yet, in a sign of how difficult
international governance will be—and we will surely move toward it over
the next 200 to 300 years—the inconvenient truth is also that having
many, equal bosses also makes it much harder for UN agencies to be
operationally effective.

## Might and Right

Globalization marks a new stage in the evolution of market society. Like the rest of us, Africans are ever more affected by events
and decisions made internationally, from new aid initiatives to

laws on intellectual property to decisions over the exact terms on which agricultural products can be sold in rich markets. Yet, unlike us, they have little ability to influence them.

The result? There is no precedent for so many "free" people being so affected by decisions made so far away, nor so marginalized from them.

As president of Uzima, the initial optimism of your first day in office quickly dulled. But now you've slipped into full-scale depression. Unable to meet your people's basic needs and knowing that the aid you receive is inadequate and inefficient, you tried to reach out to the governments and institutions that deliver it . . . and no one listened. There's no prospect of improved international governance, and the extraordinarily convoluted way Western countries insist on trade negotiations being conducted cuts you off from the chance to influence a system that might just work for you.

The sign on your door and the license plate on your car may read "President." And you've been receiving lots of fan mail from people seduced by the aphrodisiac of your power. But as you sit at the large desk in your large office, you reflect on how impotent you actually feel. In a globalizing world starved of incentives and institutions to ensure that the poorest countries can benefit, the only thing left still to surprise you would be if the citizens of rich countries felt strangely powerless in this new era too.

# CHAPTER 14
# SCREW YOU TOO

## Grease, Thread, and a Nail

Having your car break down in Africa isn't always bad news. Friendly assistance is more common than an aggressive fleecing. In northern Ethiopia, where we were visiting King Lalibela's eleven extraordinary rock churches—each carved straight down into a huge bed of rock, with corridors excavated around them to allow devotees to enter—the Land Rover's steering was on the verge of falling apart, only for a local driver to see us driving past and spot the problem. He ran hard after us and eventually fixed it using a nut from a hotel's plumbing system.

We were even more fortunate after we'd left the churches a couple of days later. I had already been under the car once to fix up various bits of metal from the suspension system that had started dragging from its underside—using string, rope, a chain, and a padlock. Then we heard a hissing noise. Under the car again. The vicious rocky road was wet with viscous inky oil that had sprayed out of a tube in the hydraulic brake system. I knew enough to be aware that we now had no brakes, yet had no idea how to fix it. I gave thanks we'd been heading uphill when it happened, but our plight was alarming: we were stuck on a precipitous road on the edge of a deserted valley, and the equator's fast dusk was just setting in.

Sixty seconds later a pickup crossed the ridge behind us in a hurry. The driver jumped out, told us the area was known for "outlaws," and asked what the problem was. What he did next was to reach into the pickup's front compartment and grab a small nail. Then he tore some thread from the bottom of his frayed T-shirt to wrap around it. Finally, he took some grease from a pot in the back and smeared it everywhere. And disappeared under our car.

After two minutes the broken tube was sealed, we'd filled the system with new fluid, and we were back on our way. As we were only able to drive five miles an hour because of the sheared metal chaos under the car, our guardian angel insisted on trailing us for six full hours on the long journey to the highway, while the four countrymen who made up his cargo perched uncomfortably in the back of the pickup, impassive and uncomplaining as an unseasonal drizzle set in and the foreigners held up their day.

The area where we'd broken down, in the Ethiopian highlands near the small town of Sekota, was the heartland of the 1984 famine and it was easy to see why. Almost nothing grew here. There were few roads and the ones that did exist were appalling. People weak from lack of food would have had huge distances to walk to the nearest towns, and even then there was no guarantee that aid would have arrived, due to a combination of the murderous manipulation of food stocks by the ruling Derg government of the time and the landscape's awesome inaccessibility.

Eighteen years later, here we were: two aid workers saved by the generosity and knowledge of a passerby. When we found him again the next day he refused all gifts of thanks. We put the car on the back of a truck and began the forty-eight-hour journey back to Addis for major repairs.

It seemed that our Land Rover, supposedly designed to work in any global environment, had failed in this part of highland Africa. Only effective and innovative local adaptation had enabled us to get out.

**a**frica may be on the margins of globalization. But what is happening to the Western societies in its mainstream? Perhaps rather unexpectedly, many of us feel disquieted by this market-driven modern era too.

The bland homogenization of global culture; fears over mass-produced food; decreasing trust in politicians; increasing corporate influence over public institutions; characterless main streets and malls . . . and plenty more. All these are familiar concerns we hear raised about modern life in rich countries. We seem to feel less and less in ownership of the world around us.

Yet this sense of powerlessness is strange, because power can't disappear: it can only move into new areas.

If we hope to understand why the West doesn't offer Africa a fairer deal, even though it would be better for us too, we also need to understand why we've lost some of the ability to direct our own societies in the ways we'd like. There are two characteristics of globalization in particular we must come to terms with: the diminishing of traditional democracy, and the long-term nature of the challenges we face.

## Democracy: Declining Influence

The fundamental feature of globalization is that markets have gone global, while government has stayed mostly national. The last chapter spelled out the implications of this for poor countries, but it's a significant shift for us too. Where before, businesses had to cozy up to governments to ensure they could trade and stay in the black, governments now cozy up to businesses for the same reason.

These businesses aren't just multinationals. They're also small and medium-size enterprises. Rapid advances in communications, technology, and transport mean that local American doctors can have their schedules managed in the Philippines, British lawyers can outsource conveyancing work to India, and family-owned French engineering firms can order fittings from China, confident the supplies will turn up, on time, in only a couple of weeks. If, as a Western government, you don't make your country's investment climate attractive to these businesses, they will simply go elsewhere.

The contrast with previous eras of market expansion is vivid. Until markets regularly started to cross national borders, we'd always had governments capable of monitoring, regulating, and directing businesses to society's wider interest (I don't mean directing them in an overbearing way—but the coincidence of government and business focus was clear). This is no longer the case. In the absence of global government, which will take a long, long time to arrive, businesses now dominate the global landscape in the way only governments used to be capable of. The era of capitalism with a natural incentive to some kind of social conscience may be over, temporarily at least. Our rulers no longer rule. They manage.

What are the implications of the rise of corporate power? Bluntly, if governments have to better reflect the demands of business, they have less time to listen to the desires of electorates. Leaving the nuances of party politics aside, this is a shift we as voters willingly accept: if our authorities didn't spend time listening to businesses' needs, investment would be lost and our economies would suffer.

The centrality of business needs also explains why we have less real choice nowadays when we cast our votes. Back in the 1960s and 1970s, many Western countries had serious ideological options in their major political parties, generally between liberal and conservative visions of society. Not anymore. Now we opt, more or less, for the party we think will be the best manager of our market economy. How well can they keep the business climate competitive and still provide us with some decent public services on the side?

Here, then, is the first cause of our loss of power: businesses are more influential, thus citizens are less so. Our governments are both less powerful overall *and* proportionately less influenced by us, their voters.

## Poor America!

If democracy declines in proportion to the rise of corporate influence, then America is less democratic than any other Western country. In this sense, Americans are victims of their own success. Not only does America have the most attractive market for businesses of any kind, its global dominance makes it by far the most important government to get on your side for any international commercial plans—and thus the Western country where individual voters have the least relative sway.

The result? If you are a multinational business, you'll spend vast amounts of money on trying to win the ear of the American administration. Washington now has more than 35,000 professional lobbyists, who spend at least $5 billion every year.[10] The voices of everyday American voters become ever more faint amid the rising throng.

Former national security adviser Zbigniew Brzezinski has said that all this makes Washington the most corrupt capital in the world (which is a little unfair on Pyongyang, Harare, and Rangoon, but we get the point). It's certainly true that the line between lobbying and corruption can be easily crossed. Hopefully the fallout from the Jack Abramoff debacle—which revealed one congressman, Randy "Duke" Cunningham of San Diego, to have accepted $2.4 million in bribes and evaded more than $1 million in taxes—will help sort out the problems. It cannot be a healthy system that sees congressmen and -women take more than two hundred expenses-paid fact-finding trips to that world trouble spot Paris over the five and a half years up to 2007, compared to four to Darfur.[11]

It will also hopefully remove the dirt from the American electorate's view of their leaders: a CNN/*USA Today* poll in 2006 revealed that 49 percent of Americans think their legislators are corrupt.[12]

## Stuck in the Lobby

Business is innovative. It seeks new opportunities, creates new markets, finds more efficient or more attractive ways of satisfying our desires. But when established, business can also be regressive. Once a new business has built itself up, carved a niche, it will do everything it can to protect its position, including buying out smaller competitors, lobbying governments for favorable protection, arguing against liberalizations that might threaten it, or threatening others who can't match its bulk-purchase arrangements. It wants more competition where it's effective and less where it isn't.

If all this sounds a bit theoretical, consider the rise of the lobbying industry. For nearly a year in 1996, fresh out of college and before becoming an aid worker, I worked for a lobbying company in London, Lowe Bell. Many blue-chip companies, such as British Airways and Orange, paid Lowe Bell substantial sums of money to be introduced to the right people, navigate planning and legislative processes, and receive political advice. In other words, to gain influence.

Why do they do it? Because it works. And in the last ten years, the industry has grown all over the place. In America, the number of Washington lobbyists has nearly doubled in only eight years.[13]

Lobbying can help you achieve two things: obtain support for something difficult you might want to do, such as erect a cell phone mast in a residential area, or enable you to shape future government plans that may have an impact on your business. It is an entirely honorable profession in many ways: governments will never have all the information they need at their fingertips about who might be affected by decisions they make, and lobby- ists can ensure that affected parties are able to communicate their views so that legislation is well designed.

But if governments need lobbyists to make sure they are taking account of important views, the problem is obvious: what if you can't afford to pay for a lobbying firm to explain how everything works and get you talking to the right people? After all, it's not only businesspeople who are affected by legislation. Consumers, residents, workers, charities, and all sorts of other groups are as well. Yet it's pretty much only business that buys lobbyists.

At one point a large supermarket chain wanted to build a new store on some suburban London playing fields where I'd enjoyed many cricket matches as a kid. The company spent considerable sums influencing both local planning procedures and the appeal process, and worked hard to engage support from the relevant ministry in Westminster. The local residents, who, unsurprisingly, didn't want a supermarket in their backyard (no one ever does; we just like to shop in them), had no such knowledge or ability to influence the process. You can guess who won. It wasn't cricket.

This is a tension that has always existed in democracies. Globalization's problem is that lobbying is growing, fast. And the reason it's been growing is that it is more and more successful. Since governments have little choice but to listen more to business, it is worthwhile for business to spend increasing amounts of money on designing their message nicely.

The slightly distasteful reality of it is that it's not really about how good the lobbyist is at his or her job—such as knowing how political processes work, understanding the key local institutions involved in a planning process, or identifying the key people to speak to. The best-paid lobbyists are often simply the ones with the best address book. When you pay a lot for a lobbyist, it's frequently not for their brilliant advice, it's mainly because they can access people who count. Previously, they may have been political advisers, senior bureaucrats, party officials, staffers—sometimes even congressmen or senators. Personal contacts turn straight into cash.

Between 1998 and 2006, half the senators who "left" the U.S. Senate in fact stayed on Capitol Hill and registered as lobbyists, as did more than 40 percent of former members of the House of Representatives. It's pretty much free money. Businesses will throw tens of thousands of dollars at former congressmen and -women to deliver their messages, because they know these ex-legislators can get through the door—in this case, literally: even the briefest career in Congress guarantees permanent access to the membership's restaurants, gyms, and, astonishingly, even the debating floor itself.[14]

The influence of lobbyists is powerfully seen in particular examples, whether it's the supermarket on an old playing field, or the frustration felt by the 86 percent[15] of Americans in 2006 who supported raising their nation's minimum wage from $5.15 to $6.45 an hour. The small sum hadn't been increased in nine years, before finally getting a small lift to $5.85 in 2007.

Lobbying from businesses prevented it. It is about as clear a contradiction as one can find between the social outcomes wanted by the public and the commercial outcomes wanted by companies.

Effective lobbying also explains, of course, the reason why tariffs and subsidies unfair to poor African countries persist so stubbornly. Those few groups who benefit from them—such as large agribusinesses in the case of many agricultural subsidies— spend time, effort, and big money lobbying both government and the media to retain them. As ever, if the lobbying didn't work they wouldn't do it. It's a reflection of that unavoidable problem that those who benefit from protectionism do so heavily, while those of us who bear the costs do so only lightly . . . not to mention the fact that we can't afford to pay people with influence to fight in our corner.

Then there's debt.

In 2005, Western leaders were trying to figure out ways of offering more debt relief to poor countries, thanks in large part to the Make Poverty History/One campaigns (rare examples of effective noncorporate lobbying). Some of the debt was owed to the International Monetary Fund, which had gold reserves of around $43 billion. The easiest way to find the money—and cheapest for Western taxpayers—was to sell off around $12 billion of the reserves: enough to provide substantial debt relief without compromising the Fund's fiscal security. Then the lobby enthusiasts of the U.S. National Mining Association and various gold mining firms found out.

The mining conglomerates feared a marginal hit to global gold prices that may never have happened, given the Fund's proposal to sell the gold over several years. But, in any case, it would seem fair to ask which is more important: a little instability for gold mining companies, or debt relief for hundreds of millions of desperately poor Africans? It was, of course, the lobbyists who won, and the money had to be found elsewhere.[16]

This feature of Western capitalist democracies in a global world costs African countries and Western taxpayers a great deal: not only in debt and subsidies, but in market access, preferential treatment, aid spending, and more. Government decision-making everywhere responds to influence, even if it is as innocent as someone getting in the right doorway and making a persuasive argument. African countries lack the votes, contacts, money, knowledge, and political importance needed to influence Western systems effectively. Competing demands will nearly always prevail—and political commentators talk of the crisis of democracy for good reason.

## The Myth of the Evil Multinational

Despite the bad press, few ideas are more tiresome than that of multinationals as sinning satanists. Of course, there may be Enron occasions when companies break the law, for which they should be pilloried and prosecuted. But to dismiss them as evil is fundamentally to misunderstand how capitalism works.

Going multinational is generally a measure of a company's success. It is not a form of mental megalomania. Commercial competition brings us efficiency and value as consumers, and indeed a world without Amazon, Apple, and Ikea would be more boring—and more expensive—for many of us.

Yet just as foolish is the belief that multinationals are intrinsically good in any way. Like all companies, they are fundamentally amoral. The power of competition means they will try and do things as cheaply and effectively as possible. If regulation—or consumer demand—pushes them into socially positive practices, such as observing decent health and safety rules for their workers, they will do it. If they can get away with doing the minimum and exploiting sweatshop labor, they'll probably do that too because they know their competitors will.

It is enshrined in law in most countries that a company's duty is to its shareholders. That means, as a legal necessity, they need to do what's financially best for the firm. It also means that the idea of corporate social responsibility as something naturally in a company's interest is dangerously misleading.

Of course, there can be myriad occasions on which it is financially sensible for a company to do socially positive things—whether to be seen as a friendly family firm, whether to make its employees happier in their work, or whether to ward off the threat of future litigation—such as when McDonald's un-super-sized itself. But to think it's any more than that is unwise: as perilous for CEOs to believe as the public.

•

We're hopelessly naïve—not to mention unfair—if we think companies will automatically play socially constructive roles. Or if we expect them to use their enhanced influence under globalization for society's wider interest.

Worst of all, it stops us from realizing that it is consumers who carry at least half the responsibility for the way companies act. Multinationals follow the money; that's how they became successful. If we make it worth their while to behave the right way, they'll begin to do it. With rewards points.

## Bad Timing

Our reduced influence as individuals in democracies is compounded by the second key feature of globalization: its crucial challenges are long-term, and our political and business systems do not respond well to distant demands. It's not just aid, trade, and corporate influence that are affected.

If abject, vulgar poverty is the biggest social challenge of our affluent modern world, climate change is evidently its biggest threat. Exact predictions of climate change are impossible, which is why it has been so easy to date for our heads to remain in the storm-laden clouds, instead of taking action to minimize future impacts. The wider reason for our inactivity, however, is that governments respond well to problems that have a maximum four- to five-year time scale—in other words, not longer than an electoral cycle.

As ever, it's not necessarily that political leaders are deeply cynical in their ducking of time-delay difficulties. It's that there are lots of incentives to focus on more immediate issues. This is one of the structural problems of democracy, the political system that is far from ideal—but still better than any other.

Some of the choices that the vast majority of analysts agree climate change forces us to face—such as serious reductions in our energy consumption, car-engine size, and air travel—are electoral vote-losers. In order to make such hard decisions, politicians need to be able to offer visible benefits to persuade skeptical publics, or be supported by strong counterlobbies to the vested interests involved.

## Front Line, First Wave

Who will suffer most from climate change? Rather inevitably, it is Africa. The fragility of living with little means that people like Marie, Jean Baptiste, Lucas, or Nancy have little they can afford to lose. Northern Kenya will be particularly badly affected.

The poor can least afford to meet the costs of adjusting to new circumstances—whether it's developing more resilient crop strains, building flood defenses, or diversifying economies into new produce. Many parts of Africa already suffer significant problems of drought and desertification. These are set to get worse.

## Thick Spectacle

Africa is similarly undermined by democracy's shortsightedness. Where are the practical benefits to Western countries of African progress? Um . . . well . . . it would be nice if Africa developed some really valuable markets for Western companies to sell their goods in (though even in the best scenario that will take decades to happen). And . . . that's about it. The Western business community and we consumers already get the raw materials and produce we want. In terms of short-term profits, Africa is irrelevant.

There are, of course, plenty of reasons why it *does* make sense for the West to invest more effort in Africa, and they're not just

### Domestic Checklist of Democratic Responsiveness!

Democracies respond well to some problems, and poorly to others:

*Jailing young offenders*
GOOD. Gets them off the streets. Easy quick win for political popularity. Media placated.

*Rehabilitating young offenders*
BAD. Benefits only long-term. Unpopular spending money on lawbreakers. Most do not come from influential groups in society.

*Building mass transit systems*
BAD. Require many billions of investment now, plus difficult planning processes, but completion and rewards take years.

*Repairing existing road network*
GOOD. Results visible and immediate. Pay as you go.

*Intervention in small, poor countries on edge of crisis*
BAD. Results long-term, ongoing commitment. No media attention or lobbying pressure.

*Humanitarian aid once the crisis has hit*
GOOD. Media and public demand action. Immediate results. Positive headlines.

about moral decency. Aiding a country is a lot cheaper than peacekeeping its collapse; the spread of terrorist extremism will surely expand its currently small footholds in the likes of Somalia and Kenya in due course; migration and immigration problems will continue to grow if failed states breed too. Yet none of these are strong or immediate enough incentives to reap pragmatic (re)action.

More surprisingly, perhaps, the business community shares Western democracy's problem of short-termism and narrow vision when it comes to Africa. Getting firms and financial funds to invest in African countries is immensely difficult. Some of the reasons for this are obvious: corruption, political volatility, weak rule of law, poor infrastructure, and so on. But despite these there are undoubtedly some rewarding investments to be made. In a clever hedge against future declines in U.S. production, Memphis-based cotton broker Dunavant Enterprises has invested millions in the Ugandan and Zambian cotton market, helping the latter grow sixfold in the five years to 2005, and hiring hundreds of farm trainers.[17]

The problem is that many such investments need to be quite long-term if they are going to reap big rewards. Dunavant thinks their largest profits will take ten to fifteen years to emerge. African workforces are as capable in principle as any other, but less used to working for big foreign companies, so may take longer to train. Rather than buying into existing African operations, it may be necessary to build new ones from scratch. Setting up businesses takes longer and bureaucracies are slower to respond.

Firms and financial funds don't like having to wait. In fact, CEOs and directors of listed companies usually have to report to shareholders on a quarterly basis. Results count now. The average length of tenure of CEOs has dropped overall since the mid-1990s, despite a slight recent upturn. Shares are dealt by the hour, minute, and second. Pension fund managers, who ought to be a force encouraging longer perspectives, are cautious and risk-averse when it comes to lengthy gambles—and their performance too is judged month by month, year by year, not in decades.

I know, I know. This all sounds pretty depressing. Here's a summary of the bad news about globalization.

- There are no immediate incentives to listen to Africa, leaving a democratic deficit at the heart of globalization. Never have so many people been so affected by global forces they are unable to influence.

- It's nearly impossible for leaders like the president of Uzima to find their way out. Stuck with poorly skilled workforces, weak-capacity governments, and high transportation and other trade costs, aid is highly ineffective and trade terms are not managed in ways from which they can easily benefit. And they can't even influence the terms on which that aid and trade are offered.

- Marie, Jean Baptiste, Lucas, Nancy, and hundreds of millions of others reap the daily consequences, reducing their hopes of ever moving beyond a daily diet of impossible choices.

- Meanwhile, the only people who might be in a place to better influence the design of aid and the terms of trade—you and me, who pay for them—feel increasingly impotent.

- And we are stuck in a world where the citizen's voice has diminished in competition with the corporation's, affecting everything from the size of aid budgets to global culture and the uniform blandness of our shopping malls . . .

So is there no hope?

Yes, there is, because it's within our power to change every one of the five points above.

## The Abrogation of Responsibility

The truth is, while it's fair to say that Africa struggles to meet its needs in this international environment, we in the West are not increasingly powerless at all. We have indeed lost some of the old, familiar ways to exercise our influence. But that influence hasn't disappeared. It's just moved house, and we haven't been bothered to look up the new address.

In many ways, as individuals in the West we now have the potential to be more powerful than we ever were as mere voters. The dominance of companies in so much of our everyday lives, combined with their increased influence over governments, theoretically gives us a personalized lever to use on a daily basis to help determine the society we want. Companies want to engage with us every hour, day, and week, whereas governments only want your attention once every four or five years.

Think you don't matter? Why do companies spend ever increasing amounts of money on advertising to influence our opinions, if we don't matter? Why do supermarkets stock so much organic produce nowadays, if our demands are irrelevant? Why do our governments, despite their reduced virility, persistently use focus groups to try and understand what we want?

We are still rather powerful, albeit within a framework of international capitalism that is hard to challenge. While we might feel we've lost a little sovereignty to choose what basic kind of political model we want (not a huge problem for the vast majority of us), we've certainly gained in our potential influence over distant events—including in Africa—as globalization has made the world more interconnected, with rich consumers in the West at its peak. For the most part we've allowed the power to rest in the companies that provide us with our goods. But we can claim some of it for ourselves if we want, and make them reflect our interests, rather than feel it's happening the other way around.

Something may have started back in those eighteenth-century northern English villages, and urbanizing nineteenth-century American cities, as societies changed and social and political challenges began their journey from local to national to global. As communities, we may have lost touch with the neighbors on our street. Yet we have gained something far more powerful: the ability to affect—and bring positive change to—people thousands of miles away.

Though it may not always be easy, it's about time we tried to use that ability.

# CHANGE
## ACTION HEROES

# CHAPTER 15
# WHAT HAPPENS NEXT?

The weakest part of books like this, criticizing some aspect of the way the world works, tends to be when they reach proposed solutions. They suddenly seem to go all idealistic and unrealistic, with little regard for what is politically feasible. There's little point in proposing things like a blanket end to farm subsidies, the mass rationalization of donor agencies, or the invention of a set of new, genuinely democratic world institutions: they're not going to happen.

So to hell with my own blueprint.

The good news is that, short of development utopia, most of the steps needed to give African countries a fairer chance are well known. Indeed, as I hope I've shown throughout this book, there's a pretty impressive consensus about them: the quantity and quality of aid needs to be substantially increased; the most distorting elements of trade need to be significantly reduced; and poor countries need to be allowed more control of the policies that affect them through international institutions. The real question is whether any of these will be delivered.

The main people who will decide the answer to that, because of the absurd inequalities of a globalized world, are you and me: the voters and consumers of the West.

*

It has never been truer that we know what we need to do. When history looks back, 2005 ought to mark a watershed in the West's dealings with the poorest continent. It's easy to be cynical about events like the G8 Gleneagles Summit, the politicians who attended it, and the mass popular movements and Live8 concerts that led up to it. But what was achieved was quite unprecedented in terms of campaigning success and political promises.

In March 2005, the Commission for Africa, made up of African, American, European, and Chinese leaders under the chairmanship of Tony Blair, published a comprehensive and frank report about the continent's problems and how Africa and the international community can help resolve them. It was the most detailed assessment of the challenges faced by poor countries in a generation, since a similar exercise overseen by former German chancellor Willy Brandt twenty-five years before.

In June and early July 2005, as many as 157 million people around the world joined in the Global Call to Action Against Poverty, the campaign known by various names including the One Campaign in the United States, Make Poverty History in the UK, and the Hottokenai Coalition in Japan—and characterized by white wristbands everywhere. Up to 3.8 billion (half the world's population) are thought to have tuned in to one of the ten Live8 concerts at some point. And some 38 million people signed a petition to present to G8 leaders, with the aim of pressuring them into accepting and adopting the key demands set out in the Commission for Africa report.

On July 7–8, 2005, G8 leaders and a number of their African counterparts gathered in Gleneagles, Scotland, to discuss the Commission for Africa report. The African leaders pledged to do more to address their internal problems, including corruption, instability, and lack of democracy. In turn, the G8 leaders made a pledge too. In essence, they promised that any African country making such efforts and designing credible poverty-reduction strategies should not lack either the financing, through aid, or the international terms, through trade, to give them a real chance of reaching their goals.

If you cast your mind back to being president of Uzima, this is more or less exactly the support you were crying out for. Among other things, the G8 leaders committed themselves to:

- double aid by $50 billion a year, including an extra $25 billion a year for Africa;
- end export subsidies (which often lead to dumping) and reduce other subsidies that distort trade;
- cancel up to $55 billion of debt owed by some of the world's poorest countries.

Anyone who tries to tell you this wasn't remarkable needs their head examined. It may not have been perfect, but there had never been such an in-depth analysis of, and commitment to help solve, Africa's difficulties. Getting the G8 leaders to the table to sign their promises was an exceptional achievement, and Bob Geldof, Bono, and everyone who worked on the campaigns deserve bouquets.

But not one of those involved would claim that getting the leaders to sign is the same as seeing the promises delivered.

## A Familiar Story?

At the time of writing, two and a half years on from Gleneagles, it's still unclear whether history will indeed regard 2005 as a watershed rather than just the ultimate talking shop—but it's not looking very good. Part of the problem is that many of the promises made by G8 leaders—and endorsed by other world leaders later that summer at the UN World Summit—were relatively long-term, and as we've seen, politicians don't respond well to distant incentives, even those such as being seen to keep their word. Most of the G8 leaders will not be in power by the time the promises are due to be delivered in full. The aid doubling was for 2010. Export subsidies were "probably" due for abolition by 2010 too (later changed to 2013).[1] Several of the other promises weren't even time-bound.

Progress to date has been mixed and it depends in part on whether you are a glass-half-full or glass-half-empty person.

- The debt story is good. Leaders had actually agreed to firm plans for a cut of up to $55 billion by the end of 2005, plus an $18 billion write-off for Nigeria in early 2006. Fairly little of this translates into new hard money for African governments (much of the debt wasn't being repaid anyway, so a cynic would argue these are the easiest promises for Western finance ministries to keep), but it's welcome all the same.

- At first glance, aid efforts apparently increased substantially too. But it turned out to be only because many donors were double-counting their debt relief as aid. The reality is that assistance to Africa needed to increase in 2005 and 2006 by $5.4 billion compared to 2004, but rose only by $2.3 billion. And now the gap is growing larger: to stay on track for the doubling of aid to Africa by 2010 would have required a rise of $6.2 billion in 2007—but emerging figures suggest it was more like $2 billion. Of the G8 countries, Japan and the UK are the good guys, fronting up with the cash, and Italy, France, and Germany the worst offenders, falling short (or should we say they are proving to be the biggest liars?). America delivered only half the new money it promised in 2004–06, though 2007 is looking better. America's spending promises were, however, more modest than most, and it is starting from a lower base of aid per head of population of any rich country apart from Italy.[2]

- Progress on trade has been almost nil. The WTO Doha Development Round has turned out to be little of the sort, even if it ever finally gets signed off. There's a chance that export subsidies may yet be abolished by 2013 (three years later than planned), but in any case they represent only 3 percent of total agricultural support. Europe's main agricultural subsidies look to be frozen until 2013, with no promises on what will happen after that, while in America some legislators are trying to make the new farm bill currently on the Hill even larger than the last, and 2008's presidential candidates seem eager to make nice to many of the usual protectionist lobbies.

## How Is America's Extra Aid Being Spent?

America may not be delivering as much new money as it has promised, but the good news is that quite a lot of it is being spent more effectively than traditional U.S. aid. The Bush administration still doesn't like working closely with African governments, but it is increasingly prepared to come up with the money for focused international initiatives rather than small projects. Much of the extra cash has been spent on large-scale, strategic, results-based responses to AIDS and malaria, both through the Global Fund for HIV/AIDS, TB, and Malaria and through the President's Emergency Plan for AIDS Relief (PEPFAR).

Partly thanks to U.S. efforts, more than two million people in poor countries are now receiving AIDS antiretroviral drugs, and counseling and care have been provided to more than ten million sufferers. It's a reminder that aid done well can work—and another reminder why there's no excuse for falling short on our spending promises.

The overall verdict? Well, the jury is still out, and it will take a couple more years to be clear whether the commitments are being honored. The jaded weight of experience suggests that significant successes are unlikely, and at the moment the score-card reads: Debt—good; Aid—underwhelming; Trade—bad. The positive news is there is still time to deliver (though it would be naïve to expect much on trade). Whether leaders do so or not, as the campaigns showed in the first place, seems likely to depend in part on how much pressure they are under.

## More DATA?

The organization DATA—which stands for Debt, AIDS, Trade, and Africa and counts Bono among its founders—produces a report every year monitoring the performance of each G8 country in meeting their Gleneagles commitments. It's really worth a quick look for a clearer idea of how well your government is performing. Several charities and pressure groups conducted similar studies, but DATA's is particularly useful and accessible, the brief Executive Summary most of all.

DATA plans to repeat the process every year. You can access the results at www.thedatareport.org.

## Delivering the Dream

What *would* the G8's 2005 promises mean for a country such as Uzima, if implemented in full?

You will recall that as president you had an investment gap of around $50 per person with which to provide essential services including schooling, basic health care, and access to clean water. If aid was indeed doubled by 2010—and, critically, if much of that new money was delivered to well-run countries like Uzima through their own systems, rather than in disparate projects— that financing gap would disappear completely. Poorer countries in Africa would need more, but you'd be okay. It might be the bare minimum, you would still have to manage all your internal political problems, and you would still need to achieve unprecedented levels of economic growth for several years if the Millennium Development Goal of halving poverty by 2015 is to be met. But it would be a huge change: at least you'd have a chance.

Now for a slightly more realistic assessment. If aid was doubled but followed its current pattern of inefficient structure and delivery, progress would be more modest (you may recall that the UN Millennium Project concluded that only 24 percent of aid actually finances real poverty-targeting investments on the ground). You'd get less than half the help you need to close the gap. More worryingly, the more overall sums fall short, as they clearly may, the bigger the problems will be. You'd still be left with a large number of impossible choices. And the West would never get to find out whether you could really run an effective, noncorrupt regime, given a genuine chance.

As for trade, it's rather more difficult to assess what impact the G8's promises in this area would have if fully implemented, as they were always rather vague—and widely acknowledged as the weakest part of the package (consensus couldn't be forged on something more powerful). But it's possible to imagine what some more tangible advances in trade could mean.

An end to American cotton subsidies would mean much better prices for 10 to 11 million West African cotton farmers and their dependents. An end to export subsidies and other trade-distorting support would stop Italian tomatoes and Dutch powdered milk from being dumped below price on Nairobi superstores and market stalls, creating new market opportunities for African producers. A fairer food aid regime would help sustain local capacity to produce enough food. A revision to the forced implementation of international patent laws would leave Africans better placed to benefit from the exploitation of their natural resources. An end to the poaching of doctors, nurses, and other skilled professionals would leave African countries far better resourced to address their challenges. It is thought that if Africa could increase its share of world exports by 1 percent, it would bring in three or four times as much money as it receives in aid.

Most of all, a fairer set of trade terms would leave Africa with a stronger incentive to address its own problems of bureaucracy, corruption, instability, and other barriers to trade. The prospect of a genuinely level playing field in America and Europe's affluent markets would be the firmest encouragement of all to get Africa's own economic houses in order. The high levels of economic growth required to meet the target of halving poverty—7 to 8 percent a year for Uzima—might just have a half-decent chance of being met.

## Blue-Sky Thinking, Head in the Clouds

I know I said to hell with my own blueprint. But for what it's worth, this is what a more radically reformed system might look like:

### Five points on aid

1. Western governments would be *bound* by international agreement to spend 0.7 percent of GNI on aid. This would enable the full funding of basic health, education, water, and HIV/AIDS antiretroviral programs for all poor countries that develop competent and credible national plans, as well as building up key infrastructure.
2. National aid donors would be abolished. All taxpayer aid would instead be channeled through three to four professional international aid donors (enough to provide competition without duplication). These would be based on the World Bank and rationalized UN agencies, but would have equal votes for developed and developing countries on their decision-making boards and strong in-country offices.

3. The best national aid donors, meanwhile, would survive by evolving into implementation agencies with particular skills, such as in health systems. Along with the best international charities, they would be contracted by international donors (as above) on a competitive basis to carry out specific tasks.

4. Western governments would retain small but influential development ministries, with full cabinet status. These would make annual decisions on what proportion of funding to give to each international donor, based on common reviews of effectiveness. And they would help guide the development impact of other, non-aid policies including trade.

5. There would be a properly financed UN humanitarian fund enabling the international community to respond immediately to tragedies such as drought and earthquakes without having to wait for pledges to be made and honored. This would carry out some work directly and would fund expert charities for other, coordinated work, preventing the gross underfunding of some crises and the duplication of others.

## And five on trade

1. All African countries would be given 100 percent tariff-free, unlimited access into Western markets for everything they produce (at present, only the EU offers full access, and only to the poorest countries).

2. An international timetable would be set for the elimination of all agricultural subsidies for produce most important to the poorest countries.

3. Poor countries would not have to abide by TRIPS legislation on essential drugs or other items until they reach a GNI per capita of around $3,000.

4. Western countries would be obliged to allow in as many nonskilled African migrants as they allow in skilled workers, such as doctors and nurses. This way, either the poaching stops or unskilled workers get to come and learn new skills and send money to poor families back home.

5. Foreign food aid would be abolished. Food aid would be procured as locally as possible or money simply given to those in need so the market can deliver.

## View from the Hills

Perhaps most important of all, what would fully implemented G8 promises mean for Lucas and Nancy on the edge of the Rift Valley in Kenya, and Marie and Jean Baptiste in their close-packed shack in Kinshasa, Congo?

If Lucas was lucky enough to have the combination of an effective Kenyan government and a sincere international aid community, he might get more affordable diabetic treatment and there would be free visits to a doctor for his mentally ill daughter, Helen. Freely available antiretroviral drugs should mean he loses no more children to AIDS. Long-term funding for education might mean his grandchildren stay on to secondary school, not just primary, and gain real prospects.

For Marie, increased trade and economic growth would mean a better chance of finding stable work and achieving her dream of having her own house—and less chance of her or Jean Baptiste falling into black market work or worse. Improved sanitation would mean better health. Free access to clean water would mean less money spent every week and a chance to save for Jean Baptiste's education. Free education on top of that would mean more regular and nutritious meals.

And on it goes . . .

If you want to know what G8 leaders themselves thought the Gleneagles commitments could achieve, incidentally, the following is taken from the Chair's official summary:

*The G8 and African leaders agreed that if implemented these measures and the others set out in our comprehensive plan could:*
- *double the size of Africa's economy and trade by 2015;*
- *deliver increased domestic and foreign investment;*

- *lift tens of millions of people out of poverty every year;*
- *save millions of lives a year;*
- *get all children into primary school;*
- *deliver free basic health care and primary education for all;*
- *provide as close as possible to universal access to treatment for AIDS by 2010;*
- *generate employment and other opportunities for young people;*
- *bring about an end to conflict in Africa.[3]*

NB: I note the phrase "if implemented." Do even the leaders themselves doubt their ability to deliver?

## Because We Can, Plus

As we've seen, the West's failing of Africa to date is all about a lack of incentives to manage aid, trade, or globalization as a whole in the interests of poor countries. It's not that we're anti-African, it's just that we live in a world that can be unwittingly unpleasant to people who don't matter.

The present global consensus about what the West needs to do to give Africa a fairer chance is unprecedented. It came about in large part because so many Western citizens made the simple and irrefutable point to their leaders that the current situation isn't good enough. The pressure worked and the plan the leaders laid out offers real prospects for progress, for the people who need it most.

Yet it would be wrong to assume the consensus will last. The incentives for the leaders to keep their promises are weak, and they will only be met if the people who count to politicians—Western voters—help make sure they deliver. And more is needed, especially on trade. The fact that this falls in part to us as individuals in the

West can seem awkward and unwelcome. Yet it's unavoidable and, in a sense, empowering: because we can, we must.

There is more than just a straight moral case, however. It is not only that we *can* help Africa if we choose. The fact is that it has largely been we in the West who have driven this era of globalization: we have made the rules that poor countries now have to play by. Since others are involuntarily affected by our invention, we must accept some responsibility for the consequences. Fast-rising Chinese investment in Africa will certainly help—bringing the encouragement of new export markets for Africa's mineral resources—but, for now at least, these can only be a complement to, not a substitute for, wider efforts.

The least we can do is make sure our countries, the West, are fulfilling our obligations. Then it's up to African countries such as Uzima to fulfill theirs. We need to use our political pressure, and our commercial patronage too. Fortunately, this will not require us to live saintly lives of denial and gruel, nor will it require annual Live8 concerts or the permanent sporting of white wristbands that get unpleasantly dirty after a couple months of wear.

What it does require of us is to shift the understanding of our power as individuals in a globalized world. We can no longer allow ourselves the comfortably numb nonsense of impotence. Instead we must understand our position as permanent counter-weights to forces in society that, unconsciously in an era of globalization, do not give poor countries a fair chance.

## On a Wing and a Prayer

One of my first trips in Africa, in 1998, was to Kitgum in northern Uganda, where a low-level civil war has been smoldering for nearly two decades. We flew up in a very small plane operated by a charity called the

Missionary Aviation Fellowship. The pilot began the journey by running through the safety procedures, and then led a prayer that God would deliver us safely to our destination.

The conflict in the north, still unresolved today, is between government forces and the rebel soldiers of the mad Lord's Resistance Army, who were often children abducted from their homes and brainwashed to become fighters. The danger of further abductions meant the one million or so local people lived transitory lives. They slept nights in camps for safety and tried to do a little work in distant fields during the day. Many didn't produce enough food.

Babies are especially vulnerable to malnourishment. The aid agency I worked for was funding a program of emergency feeding for the most fragile infants in dedicated clinics, with special formula milk and medical support. I hadn't witnessed the clichéd reality of small children with rake-thin ribs and bloated bellies before. Real families and real mothers, many very young. Babies with familiar names like Alexander, John, and Mercy. This was the harshest of life-and-death poverty right in my inexperienced face.

But, of course, I and my colleague, a humanitarian specialist, were there to be professional. The reason for our visit was to monitor the program and decide whether to grant the extension the charity managing the clinics had requested. Our decision proved fairly simple. Recent months had seen a significant improvement in the security situation, reasonable rains, and with them improved nutritional rates. The bottom line was that fewer babies were being brought to the clinic and nursed back to health. From our point of view, money from our limited aid budget was now saving fewer lives here than before; money that, on balance, could probably be used more effectively elsewhere. We recommended against the extension.

Somewhat to my surprise, I didn't lose any sleep over our decision. While it felt surreal and deeply uncomfortable to be in a position to play God, it was the right one. But when you learn the extent to which Western governments fail to meet their promises on aid funding, when it would cost us so little, when you know what opportunities are being missed— saving the lives of entirely innocent people—I'm no longer so sure such decisions can really be defended. We should not have had to choose.

# CHAPTER 16
# POWERLESS OR COMPLACENT?

*Kophaan tchaala dansa.*
Being alone is only good for going to the toilet.
OROMO PROVERB, ETHIOPIA

Our sense of impotence under globalization—or rather our relinquishing of responsibility for the world around us—is our own fault and our own fallacy. We have created an economic way of life that has brought us wealth, yet forgone accountability for key aspects of the society to which that wealth creation has led. As with most problems of impotence, this one is mostly in our head.

Put another way, we have stopped fulfilling our duties to the market itself in terms of helping it evolve in its own long-term interests: we let it develop without developing our own skills to manage it. Capitalism works well for societies when it is obliged to develop the social mechanisms of state, safety nets, and democracy to regulate and administer it: conscious capitalism. It does not work, for the poorest at least, when there is no such obligation and hence no such mechanisms—as with global society.

The answer to this dilemma is simple, in principle. If the "natural" incentives for Western governments and businesses to play fairer by Africa do not exist, we individuals in the West need to create some. We need to ensure, as it were, that globalization becomes not an era of comatose capitalism, but one of socially conscious individualism.

## Citizens Are Stupid

If I believed the myth of the evil multinational, decreeing that the average international business was headed by an evil genius with a forked tail and a frequent-flier ticket to Hades, I would bet he'd be sitting in his boardroom laughing manically to himself right now, in that slightly sinister way that evil geniuses do. He wouldn't be able to believe his luck that voters and consumers in the West simply do not realize the potential power they have over modern governments and businesses.

This pinstriped perfidious spirit would marvel at the way people complain about the influence of new suburban shopping malls on traditional local shops—and then do their entire weekly shopping there. He'd giggle contentedly at the way aid promises are never met largely because voters don't hassle their governments hard enough to deliver—not to mention how badly much of that money is actually delivered. And he'd delight in the way he can lobby Western governments for continued protectionism for his produce—then watch as those governments dutifully agree to it through trade negotiations because none of the taxpayers who pay the price speak up in opposition.

In all likelihood, he'd probably also be delighted that among the highest-profile public voices complaining about globalization to date have been a small sect of hooligans kicking in McDonald's windows, thus turning off the moderate masses from a rather important debate.

## The Inanity of Antiglobalization

I've never really understood how anyone can claim to be antiglobalization. You can't turn the clock back on how economies have evolved. And even if you could, you wouldn't want to.

Globalization's pace, power, and reach are what makes it so potentially vibrant in hastening growth out of poverty, as in the case of China. It can bring new investment to places that badly need it, lead new drugs to be developed that can benefit poor as well as rich, and find wealthy customers for producers in poor countries to sell to. That's not to say globalization hasn't sometimes been terribly mismanaged and caused pain and upheaval—but the issue is precisely *how* we manage it, not whether it should exist in the first place. Being genuinely antiglobalization is pointless and naïve nonsense—and, to be fair to many of the liberal groups who get wrongly labeled under the antiglobalization banner, there are only a relative few misplaced protesters who actually believe in it. The question is how to make globalization work for us.

In the interests of balance, however, global capitalism's unquestioning cheerleaders at the other end of the debate are just as off the wall. The idea that whatever globalization brings us must be unmitigated good— that whatever the market wants is always right for us too—is unambitious ignorance. Obsessed by the means, they have entirely forgotten the ends.

Antiglobalization protesters condemn themselves to a life of unfulfilled idealism. Capitalism's cheerleaders, not believing it's possible to direct the market for social gain, are the high priests of uninspired pessimism. While both groups rot in jails of their own making, the rest of us ought to be able to get on with modestly trying to make a difference: pragmatic optimists seeking to gain some control over the world around us and improve things just a little.

## Bigger Pond, Smaller Fish

The problem with working as an individual to try and regain some control over the globalizing society around us is, unfortunately, a big one: it seems an impossible task. How can I as one person change anything, especially in the face of global forces and massive multinationals?

So much about globalization and the way we ought to engage with Africa feels counterintuitive. It's counterintuitive to think that as one consumer we can make a difference, or to believe that our protest letters will help alter policy. It's counter-intuitive to accept that we need to fund systems with our aid, rather than something direct and tangible people can use like a goat. In the same way, it's not immediately obvious to us that running a car with a big engine will add to global warming. Yet this is how the modern world works, whether it feels obvious to us or not. It is millions of individuals driving cars and traveling in planes that are helping lead to the heating of the planet.

All this seems a long way from the situation my ancestor encountered working on a farm in rural Lancashire three hundred years ago, before he left for the city to spin Indian cotton. If there was a problem in his society, the village, he could go and try to sort it out face-to-face, or get the landowner to decide. The most important people in his life were visible to him, and lived nearby. Yet it's easy to forget what our ancestors' struggles have since achieved for us. Then, there was no real democracy and the word of the landlord was final. Living conditions were miserable, life expectancy was even shorter than it is in AIDS-afflicted Africa today,[4] and people had few rights—and it was all even worse if you were a woman. There's no point romanticizing it; we have far more autonomy now than they ever did.

Is the sizable problem of the small individual surmountable? It ought to be. Once every four or five years or so, most of us traipse down to a polling station to mark one vote on a ballot, even though we know millions of others are doing the same thing. We still believe in that—and it works, even if we don't always end up liking the people we elect. So why reject it anywhere else?

## The Psychosomatic Sickness of Powerlessness

What is frustrating about our fiction of impotence is that there are many ways in which we are more powerful than even a generation ago. Most obviously, our potential impact as consumers has grown hugely, as we will see. Companies are far more influential than they used to be, and—I have to side with capitalism's purists here—in many ways they are much more democratic than governments: we only get to vote once every five years, but we have direct interactions with companies on countless occasions every day, each purchase effectively a vote for the product and the way it is made.

But traditional methods of influencing are still relevant too, and this is where we should start. The idea of lobbying our governments, which make the international rules, to play fairer by poor countries may sound wearily familiar, but it is woefully underutilized. Politicians can still achieve very significant things, even if they need a bit more pressure or support to do so. How come?

One of the strange features of globalization is that, while it has reduced the power of national governments in the face of international markets, it has left those governments to make most international decisions on things such as aid and trade. This stems from, of course, fears of true global governance. Not good for poor countries perhaps, denied democracy in the decisions that affect them most, but quite a bonus for those of us wanting to influence our own leaders to act more decently.

- Aid budgets are still decided by national governments on an annual basis, and among the main considerations is the simple question: "How bad will the press be if we cut/fail to raise aid this year?"

- World trade rounds are agreed to by national governments (or the European Commission if you're in the EU), and the negotiators will only notice whether they are trampling poor countries underfoot if their paymaster publics request them to look at their shoes.
- Decisions on everyday subsidies and tariffs respond to lobbying too: it mostly takes the form of entrenched interests pressing for the perpetuation of privileges, but it will change if a public counterlobby angry at the wasting of their taxes, not to mention the injustice, starts to shout just as loud.

There's no excusing the lack of action to date by our governments and politicians, who make most aid and trade rules. Remember those unkept, unkempt promises on aid spending since the UN General Assembly in 1970? Their inaction means nothing less than the perpetuation of unnecessary misery and impoverishment for millions, and early deaths for millions more.

But since they haven't been acting, and they are *our* governments, what are we going to do about it? Unlike the poor of Africa, we do matter to our politicians. We need to make it in their interests to do what we want, rather than moan about it when they don't.

The good news, though it may be unfashionable to acknowledge, is that a lot of politicians would actually like to do better. The truth is that this is the sort of cause many of them got involved in politics for in the first place, regardless of whether you think they may since have been corrupted by the pursuit of power. But it doesn't really matter whether we think they do it for popularity, or because they want to—as long as they do it. Let's save our present-day leaders from being the Bill Clintons

## Sugar Beat

Politicians aren't everyone's cup of tea—and it's inexcusable that most have failed to act on Africa for so long—but put yourself in their shoes for a moment. Let's say you're a congressman or -woman who sits on the House Committee on Agriculture and you personally believe that the high fixed payments for U.S. sugar should be ended (the payments that cost American consumers about $2 billion a year, and cost farmers in Mozambique and Malawi far more).

It's guaranteed you will get intensively lobbied by the big sugar multinationals, who don't want the hassle of adjusting to farming something else, and probably by other agribusiness groups, who have become used to this subsidy system too. Among other things, they will:

- shower you with well-researched counterarguments;
- have you hassled by other politicians and senior official they have lobbied;
- make sure their local congressmen are asking critical questions;
- tell your party leadership they are planning to withdraw future donations;
- arrange protests outside your offices;
- sponsor media articles in your home state claiming you are hell-bent on destroying rural life . . .

. . . and so on and so forth. In the face of all this, you might still quite want to end the sugar payments. But there are an awful lot of other things on your agenda. And if you know there are few people who will stand up and support you, or promise you new votes, where's the incentive to hold firm?

and John Majors of the future, looking back and vaguely thinking, "I wish I'd done more."

This is exactly what happened with the Live8 and associated campaigns in 2005. We should get used to it: achieving social change in an era where our governments have less potency than they once did requires a wider convergence of leaders and public working together. Yet how can we stand up and ensure that the politicians are hearing our voices, if we can't get together and employ the best-connected lobbying companies to press our case?

## A Debt to Campaigning

It may sound obvious, but when we think of supporting a charity with which we agree and that does campaigning work, it is no longer a charity. It has become a lobbying organization for the social outcomes we want. This is exactly the nature of the One Campaign and other growing grassroots efforts across America, which are now lobbying politicians on these issues on a daily basis.

Indeed, many of the best aid charities have significant campaign teams. This means that quite a substantial amount of their money is not spent on putting wells in villages, books in schools, or drugs in health clinics. It's going instead on expensive office rents near government buildings, mass mailings to gain public support, salaries for staff whose sole job is to consort with politicians and civil servants, not to mention the occasional expense-account dinner to influence the people who count. And it may well prove to be money better spent than any number of goat projects or mosquito nets.

These advocacy workers and the postcard-writing, emailing, and phone campaigns they arrange can be the bête noire of many a civil servant who has to field and log all the letters, emails, and calls. But they can be very effective. Politicians really notice what they are most hassled about: after all, they need us to vote them back in next time around.

There have probably been three shifts in Western policies toward African countries over the last ten years big enough to make people like the president of Uzima sit up and take notice. These three are: moves by several donors to support African systems and budgets, not projects; the big initiatives in debt relief that began around the millennium; and the wider-ranging commitments on aid, debt, and trade made more recently at Gleneagles. The first of these shifts came about more or less because of undeniable logic that supporting and strengthening systems is essential for long-term development (not that all donors are entirely listening, including America). But the latter two would never have happened without public campaigns.

The millennium debt campaign is particularly instructive. What helped it break through in America was the energy and persuasion of Bono, along with fellow lobbyists, plus the knowledge that they represented a wide body of support. It's fair to imagine that a guy in a T-shirt and wraparound shades would never have gotten in to see Washington's power brokers without the fact of thousands of music fans and development activists wanting to know what the lead singer of U2 had to say.

Larry Summers, then Treasury secretary, amusingly claims that he hadn't known who Bono was and had only let him in because "the young women on my staff told me I had to see him."[5] But he also admitted that Bono's involvement "suggested there was a big constituency out there who care about debt." On September 29, 1999, President Clinton announced that the United States would cancel 100 percent of the debt owed to it by the world's poorest countries (admittedly, this was only a start, as those countries' really big debt was to international institutions such as the World Bank—but it was an important start). And just over a year later, and much, much more lobbying, Congress finally approved it.

## America's Millennium Challenge

Historically, whatever relatively small sums of American aid have been targeted to Africa have failed to help foster the long-term development of local systems. Sometimes aid has been subordinated to the foreign policy aim of supporting friendly leaders. Often there has been a reluctance to back inevitably weak local capacities, leading to aid being spent unsustainably, if sometimes picturesquely—hundreds of schoolchildren in one West African country, for instance, were recently issued bright new American backpacks and colored pencils, to use in schools that remain teacher-less, destitute, and decrepit.[6]

What hasn't helped is the number of different parts of the federal government that have, over the years, gotten their hands on some of the aid budget. By 2005, more than twenty-six separate parts of the government were managing and implementing U.S. foreign assistance programs (and more than 20 percent of official development assistance was being managed by the Department of Defense).[7] It is not realistic that aid can be spent strategically and coherently by so many different agencies.

The Bush administration's new Millennium Challenge Account (MCA), announced in 2002, was created to address the inefficacy of much American aid. Money would go only to those countries that could be certified as meeting strict standards of accountability and efficiency, thus incentivizing political and economic reform. As long as those standards were met, benefiting countries would be entitled to manage refreshingly substantial investments themselves, according to their own priorities. In July 2007, by way of example, the MCA agreed to a $507 million program to help Mozambique build roads and improve access to safe drinking water.

Though enacted with rare bipartisan support, in practice the MCA hasn't proved as promising as its principle. By December 2007, $4.8 billion had been approved for specific long-term projects in fifteen countries in Africa and elsewhere, but only $155 million had actually been spent, partly due to insufficient bureaucratic capacity.[8] The shame is that this has led Congress to cut future allocations before the MCA has had a real chance to prove itself. It means some African countries that have undertaken sometimes painful reforms to qualify for the program will now not be allocated resources, causing a lack of faith in the process.

Overall, the MCA is undoubtedly a move in the right direction, offering much improved value for money for American taxpayers. What needs to happen now is for disbursement to speed up, for Washington to rationalize the rest of its aid system, and for some kind of similarly coherent aid program to be created for countries who desperately need assistance but who are not yet sufficiently well-organized to qualify for MCA support.

## Live Bait

The debt campaigners took many lessons from their millennium effort and applied them ten times over in the run-up to 2005, Gleneagles, and the Make Poverty History/One campaigns. How could they land the much bigger catch of increased debt relief, doubled aid, and reformed trade? The interesting feature here was that the British government, holding the 2005 G8 presidency, was genuinely committed to a radical change to Western policies affecting Africa. Yet even these British leaders recognized that their own willingness was never going to be enough to get the whole summit to sign up to the steps required.

Bob Geldof, Bono's equivalent in the UK (in campaigning terms, if not musical), had worked with Tony Blair, Gordon Brown, and others in the British government to get a radical package to the table. He had long resisted proposals to revisit the 1985 Live Aid concerts that had turned a generation's attention to an African problem for the first time—the horrific famine in Ethiopia—worrying that the celebrity circus that came with a grand new set of gigs might distract from the gravity of the issues. He also wanted to avoid any implication that 2005 was just about getting charity donations, as had been the case twenty years before. But with only a couple of months to go before the summit at Gleneagles, the messages coming back to Britain were clear: other G8 leaders, including America, were balking at the full package, and the summit risked ending in a watered-down anticlimax.

If they were going to budge, these leaders needed to overcome the pressures for business as usual in their finance ministries, trade ministries, central banks, and legislatures. There simply weren't enough incentives for them to do so. Only in April did Geldof finally agree to arrange the Live8 concerts. Two months later, up to half the planet tuned in at some point. And a few days after that, the G8 leaders all signed on the dotted line, in front of a phalanx of photographers.

## Culture Change

What do millennium debt relief and the 2005 promises for Africa tell us? Mentally rebranding campaigning charities as lobbyists is important, but it underplays the true significance of large public campaigns in an era of globalization. What we need to accept is that key policies affecting poor countries will not change *unless* we make a fuss.

It is not simply that our governments can't always be trusted to do the right things, leaving us to protest when they fall short. The fact is that such promises will *never* be made in the first place, nor subsequently kept, without significant public pressure.

Once we accept this, there's no choice but to come to a shocking and unpleasant conclusion. If this is how it works, then it has not just been Them to blame for failing Africa and other poor countries to date—it's Us too for not having made them do it.

In a globalized world without incentives to play fairer by Africa, it truly is up to us to deliver.

## Faith in Lobbying

I was reaching the end of my time in Rwanda. Though I was excited about the upcoming drive home through East and North Africa and the Middle East, and looking forward to spending more time with family and friends back in London, I was sad to be leaving. I had gotten used to the climate, perfected a Sunday morning pineapple and coffee breakfast instead of a fry-up, and found the perfect place to hang a hammock under the Swiss-style eaves of my incongruous house. Most of all, I would miss my committed and hardworking colleagues in the office, and I'd miss Angelina, Sylvestre, and the guards back at home.

Angelina inherited quite a lot of home furnishings as I packed up, to add to the clothes left with her by female friends who'd come to visit. Sylvestre and the guards got a few bits and pieces too. But for all of them, the current resident leaving meant the end of a known quantity and the uncertainty of his replacement, with all the lack of job security that implied.

On my last evening in Rwanda, I walked down the short drive by the side of the kitchen to exchange leaving presents with the two night guards at the gate. For nearly two years, they had kept watch over all the comings and goings at my house. Work functions, friends to stay, girlfriends, late-night parties.

They believed in lobbying: they gave me a Bible.

## Possible Choices

Corporate lobbying firms can only dream of being able to organize events with the public participation and profile of the One Campaign or Live8. While it is true we would love their high-paid, high-access lobbyists, they would die for our numbers. Yet it's obviously unrealistic to maintain as large an effort as 2005 every year. Yet, when political leaders realize that there is among their voters a large, permanent constituency for change, they will themselves start to consider the international implications of day-to-day decisions they make.

This requirement for public participation to deliver social change in a modern, market-dominated world is by no means restricted to global poverty. Activists are today's action heroes. We need to understand that individual effort, by thousands of people working together, is the only way we are likely to achieve the societal outcomes we want in areas where business and the mainstream media do not take an automatic interest. There are plenty of examples, regardless of whether one supports the particular causes or not: evangelical Christian groups gaining greater censorship of what goes on U.S. TV; French students going on strike until new labor laws are rescinded; Spanish, Italian, and Japanese protesters (eventually) obtaining the withdrawal of their countries' troops from Iraq.

Quieter, longer-established groupings can prove equally influential: the pro-Israeli lobby in American politics; the green lobby in Germany; the protectionist farm movement in France. Politicians in democracies are nothing less than obsessed with what we think—hence all the opinion polls they commission and the focus groups they convene. The only thing is, if we want our views listened to, we do actually have to voice them: we can't expect someone to guess what we think. In a lobby-rich, rich-lobby society, we need to accept that someone on the other side of the argument will almost always be putting up contrary views. This is especially so when we are up against what may be a corporation's or other entrenched lobby's well-funded interest.

The most influential campaigns tend to be those that are long-lasting and continue beyond single events: in other words, when political leaders are left in no doubt that the lobbies are not going to go away. All we can do is try. In an era of globalization, on issues that we really care about, it is self-defeating not to do so.

## Taking Action

It may be easier to be told we should give a donation to something rather than give our time to it. But if one thing is clear, it is that giving money to charities that do good works in Africa is not the solution. The best of those charities can certainly make important and wonderful differences to individual people's lives. Yet they will not address the really big issues.

So what can each of us do?

### Quick Note on Humanitarian Aid

Whatever you think of aid charities—and I believe the good ones *are* worth funding—it is particularly important that we continue to help fund humanitarian agencies in times of crisis. Until sufficient and permanent international funding is set aside to respond immediately to urgent needs, we will continue with the absurdity that many people suffering from earthquakes, floods, and famines will receive help only if generous individuals in richer countries feel concerned enough about the pictures on their TV screens.

No magic techniques here. The key is in leaving our country's decision-makers in no doubt that we wish to see policies affecting Africa improve—in particular the quantity and quality of aid, and the approach to reforming trade.

### 1. Write!

There's a rough sliding scale of effectiveness when it comes to written material. If you send a preprinted campaign postcard on behalf of a charity, it will simply get collected and counted as one of a number. Ditto if you put your name to a prewritten email through a campaign Web site. But the more personalized and detailed a letter is, the more it will be noticed, and the more consideration it is likely to get in response.

### 2. Sign petitions

These have become much easier to organize in recent years, through the Internet. Many good campaigning Web sites organize petitions on several different subjects over the course of a year (see below). Though less effective person-by-person than letters, petitions are becoming an increasingly important form of campaigning, and we should probably get used to putting our names on them, for issues we care about, on a regular basis.

### 3. Protest

If petitions get some notice, prewritten emails and postcards a bit more, and personalized letters quite a lot, then participating in protests and demonstrations gets more still. For a start they are good visually, so the media is more likely to pick them up. Essentially, decision-makers know that the more time you commit to something, the more you must care about it (inconvenient for those of us who want to protest quickly, but unavoidable). The past masters at media-savvy protesting, ironically, are French farmers, who have been known to release thousands of sheep onto the Champs-Elysées and to build fruit and vegetable pyramids in the shadow of the Louvre. The pictures, of course, went around the world.

### 4. Organize local events

Getting fully involved as an activist and helping organize local events—whether speeches or debates, barbecues or fasts—is obviously more powerful than any of the above. There are two particular benefits. First, there's a good chance you'll be able to get your local paper to cover the event. Second, if you subsequently write to your local congressman on behalf of a wider group, your letter will carry significantly more weight as they will know you represent a larger constituency of people.

## 5. Lobby your own friends

This is potentially more important than any of the above. We can only change the West's engagement with Africa by using our numbers. If there is value in you writing, protesting, or whatever, there's five times as much value in persuading five other people to do the same.

## 6. Donate to campaigning charities

Our voice is most important, but our money can help too. Some charities and other organizations do request financial contributions to help support their campaigning work.

## 7. Vote

The thing that will really make our leaders listen is if they believe they will lose or gain votes according to the international policies they adopt. Even though it may not be the decisive factor in our vote, we should make it one of the key issues. More important, when candidates come knocking on our doors or speaking at local hustings, we should ask them what their policies are and give them a hard time if we're not happy. And challenge them as to whether they've actually delivered in the past.

## Lastly … become better informed

The more we know, the more we can do. And the harder questions we can ask, the more our leaders will be clear that we care.

## Benevolent Multinationals

A number of campaigning charities and other bodies now provide extremely good Web sites to advise and guide people on lobbying our leaders. They also coordinate campaigns on particular issues at appropriate times—such as just before a congressional vote or a large international summit. Some of the best sites are:

**National sites**

| | |
|---|---|
| www.one.org | —the definitive campaigning site plus lots of links |
| www.data.org | —good information plus holds the G8 to account |
| www.cgdev.org | —in-depth analysis of development issues |
| www.jubilee-usa.org | —the latest on debt |

**International sites**

| | |
|---|---|
| www.whiteband.org | —home site of the Global Call to Action Against Poverty |
| www.maketradefair.com | —Oxfam International's trade campaign site |

But there are plenty of other excellent Web sites out there, with useful information and already campaigning on issues that may be particularly close to your heart. There's rarely been a better reason to Google.

# CHAPTER 17
# PROFIT IN VIRTUE

*Drive thy business, or it will drive thee.*
BENJAMIN FRANKLIN

Pressing politicians is essential because they make the key decisions on aid and trade terms that affect Africa. Yet there is a far more direct way we can contribute to the continent's growth: by shifting the incentives of businesses to trade and invest there more.

You might guess from reading this book that I am not exactly a free market fundamentalist. But neither am I a dreamer. Capitalism works, inasmuch as it creates wealth, better than any other kind of economic system. Without wealth, we cannot create social "goods," such as schools, roads, police, courts, hospitals, and so on, let alone foreign aid budgets.

The reason it works is that it is uniquely responsive to demand—as long as we have money. Fortunately, in the West, most of us do. The challenge is now that we need to use that responsiveness not just for personal taste and value, but to achieve some of the social outcomes we want from a business-dominated society—our own personal contribution to ensuring that African countries are better able to benefit from an international trading system that persistently fails to bend in their direction.

## ConsumerVoters™

Every time we buy something—some food, a shirt, a mortgage—we are effectively voting for it, choosing it above all sorts of competitors. Put crudely, whereas my ancestor in Lancashire would have had to buy his beer from the one landlord in the village, even if he hated him, my choice of drinks and venues can be eye-blurring. This gives us considerable power. Yet, by and large, we don't use it.

We are, of course, aware that our choices are important to companies: it's why they spend so much on advertising and marketing. But we underestimate how much it is really the case. Without our money, companies are precisely nothing. As such, they are far more vulnerable than government administrations, which can ride out a couple of years of low popularity. If everyone stopped buying Coca-Cola (though personally I like it and it's very popular in most of Africa, where it contains extra sugar), the company would crash within a month. Indeed, this is more or less what happened to the fur industry, albeit over a slightly longer period, once those high-profile and spectacular antifur campaigns began in the 1990s.

Our failure to realize our clout in a consumer-fixated world is, in truth, the most baffling aspect of modern life and at the root of our powerlessness. If we want social change in heavily business-influenced societies, we must harness business to help achieve it. We're every company's bottom line, their lifeblood; yet most of us act and complain as though we are subservient to their power. It is almost as if we have no self-respect, no sense of value for the money we've earned through our own work. Why on earth would

I give my business to a company whose practices or policies I don't approve of? Unless we don't have much cash—and frankly, most readers of this book will not fall into that category—we can afford to make our choices on more than price alone.

When we elect governments and they perform badly, most of us will acknowledge some kind of responsibility for putting them in power in the first place, even if only to the extent of "I wish I hadn't voted for them." It ought to be the same with companies: when we buy something we are not just voting for that product, but effectively endorsing how it has been produced and what that company does with our money—including the way they treat their staff, who they give political donations to, and what they lobby government about.

Where do the sugar barons of Florida and Louisiana get their money to press governments to maintain their massive subsidies? From the sugar they sell us. Where do the cotton farmers of the Midwest pay for their Washington lobbyists from? From the jeans and T-shirts we buy from them. Where did sportswear manufacturers in the 1990s get the money to pay their board members big bonuses while paying sweatshop workers in Southeast Asia a paltry few pennies? That's our cash they're using!

We need to start taking at least a little responsibility for what our money ends up doing. To give it an appropriately gimmicky label, we need to become ConsumerVoters™.

That's the theory, anyway.

## You Don't Matter?

If you ever thought your choices are unimportant to companies, this is how much they spent trying to influence those choices through advertising in 2006:[9]

- $163 billion was spent on advertising in the United States ($23 billion was spent on aid).[10]
- $34 billion was spent in Japan (including more than $3 billion on cosmetics and toiletries).[11]
- $26 billion was spent in the UK ($3 billion of which went on regional newspapers).[12]

Meanwhile, $22 billion was spent in Germany, $13 billion in France, $11 billion in Italy, and $10 billion in Canada.

## Davids vs. Goliath

There are three ways in which companies survive and thrive:

- by being the most competitive (producing good-quality things we need at good prices);
- by being the best at convincing us that we want their particular product (unless Nikes *really* are better than Adidas this year); and
- by influencing the government to impose rules that suit their operation.

The most successful do all three. However, we consumers do not have to be influenced by at least the first two of those three ways, should we so choose. We can instead make our choices on any number of other criteria, such as where the product comes from, how it is likely to have been made, or who the shareholders are.

Now, no one is suggesting we have to find out everything about every product we buy. None of us has that kind of time. But companies will work incredibly hard to keep our business. While they will encourage us to want what they make, they will also make what we want—if enough of us demand it.

Goliath was huge, but he had a weak point, and David had a

pebble and a slingshot. On reflection, however, it would have been an awful lot more productive if, instead of killing him, David had rounded up thousands of friends and forced Goliath to do their bidding. In fact, an altogether better model is Gulliver: it's time we whisked him up and started to carry him where we want to go.

## She Loves You, Yeah Yeah Yeah

One of the reasons we need to keep watching how our companies and politicians engage with poor countries is that their professed good intentions can so easily dissipate when it comes to the heat of the moment—whether it's a matter of deciding how much they can really "afford" to pay foreign factory workers; in last-minute trade discussions when governments are also trying to protect national interests; when facing pressures to cut overall government budgets; and so on. Disturbingly, it's a problem that apparently afflicts many westerners themselves in Africa, who can forget their supposed high principles when push comes to shove and act in disgraceful ways.

The most obvious example are the vacation habits of so many Western men and women—but most especially middle-aged men—who turn up in Africa and sleep with prostitutes. It is excused in all sorts of ways—"she is my girlfriend, not a hooker, and I'm just helping her out"; "we genuinely like each other"; "the girls are so poor and could use the money" (well, in that case just give her some . . .). The really pathetic thing is that some of these guys are obviously thinking, "I can really be myself with these girls"—who just happen to be half their age, twice as attractive, and with whom they have nothing in common—in a way they feel they can't back home. I've got more time for the men who at least acknowledge it is a straightforward business transaction.

The hypocritical aspect to all this is that most would think it wrong to go to sex workers at home. But it's a vacation, the girls are so attractive, it's very cheap . . . and principles go out of the window. It's rather like a friend of mine in Nairobi—one of the loveliest and most caring people you could hope to meet—who harshly fired his guard for being in the shower early one morning instead of at the gate. Later it transpired that he'd sacked the wrong guard (the day and night guards having just swapped shifts)—and yet still he made no attempt to undo his error. Stable jobs are hard to come by in Nairobi, and a whole family's livelihood can sometimes rest on such a cursory decision. My friend wasn't racist in any conventional sense—he'd never have treated anyone of any color that way back home—but it's extraordinary how people and countries will behave when they think no one's looking and they can get away with it.

Many of Africa's prostitutes are extremely beautiful, not to mention witty and well educated. It's simple economics. There's a much larger group of people prepared to sell themselves (or with little choice but to do so) than in Western countries, because poverty is so abject and widespread, creating lots of competition.

Perhaps worst of all are the men who lead these girls on for an evening, enjoying their company, when they have no intention of actually going home with them and handing over some money. I remember about half the members of a soccer team I played for doing this when we ended up at an incredibly dubious bar called New Florida's in Nairobi one night. The girls have a hard enough time as it is. They don't need people who go through the supermarket filling up their cart but never intend to make it to the checkout.

## Organic Growth

There are, thankfully, more positive ways to spend our money. The rise of the organic movement in the last twenty years has been remarkable. Back in the mid-1980s, it was a tiny niche fixation for what were sometimes perceived as a bunch of Luddite health freaks. Then it took root.

Using only natural fertilizer, organic food sales in the United States had grown to $6.1 billion by 2000, then tripled to $17.7

billion by 2006. The sector is forecast to grow at 20 percent for the next few years.[13] In Germany, Europe's leader in organic consumption, there are 17,557 organic farms and the market stood at $6.5 billion in 2006.[14]

The organic sector long ago outgrew the health food stores where it had started. But supermarkets didn't start stocking organics because they thought it was, like, a really right-on concept. It was because there's profit in it.

Fairtrade looks as though it is following a similar path. Certified Fairtrade goods guarantee an agreed, reasonable level of income for poor producers and are often accompanied by social or environmental initiatives to help their wider communities. Despite being a relatively recent phenomenon, the global market has expanded rapidly to more than $2.2 billion worldwide and seems set to grow and grow. In the United States, now the largest Fairtrade consumer, sales were $700 million, an increase of 45 percent on the previous year.[15] Where only three years ago there were 150 Fairtrade products available to consumers, there are now going on 2,000, from coffee and chocolate to wine and soccer balls.[16]

The growing organic and Fairtrade markets are proud examples of consumers exercising their power, making their choices of what to buy because of wider considerations than simply price. And this power can also work through deciding what *not* to buy. There are several cases: from the backlash against sportswear manufacturers over sweatshop labor in the 1990s that made them improve their employment standards (though quite possibly not enough); to the fuss about the use of child labor to weave rugs in India; to public boycotts of McDonald's because of industrial farming techniques and marketing to children (yes, there would be even more McDonald's outlets without these protests).

Sometimes we can be too cynical as societies: all these consumer campaigns made real changes in how things were done—perhaps not as much as we would have liked, but real changes nevertheless. Indeed, it can sometimes be easier to get multinationals to act ethically than our no-chain local stores and restaurants, because the multinationals are so worried about their public reputations. McDonald's in the United States has insisted that its eggs come from hens with larger space to grow than the legal minimum—whereas most local diners probably just use regular battery eggs (and they would apparently go further if customer demand required; in the UK, McDonald's now uses free-range eggs). All its restaurants in New England now sell only Fairtrade coffee.[17] Wal-Mart-owned Sam's Club converted its store-ground coffee to Fairtrade in 2006, whereas a local store may not stock any. Likewise, Adidas, Nike, and Reebok probably uphold better labor conditions for their factory workers than the cheapest, nonbranded sports lines. Those Nike workers may be fearful of their bosses; but their bosses are fearful of us.

There's plenty of mileage for us as consumers here: corporate leaders are increasingly catching on to the idea that, in an ever more competitive environment, one way to differentiate your product from someone else's is its ethical credentials. And the fear of negative publicity remains. In the words of Warren Buffet, "It takes twenty years to build a reputation and five minutes to ruin it."

## Global vs. Local

Climate change is deeply concerning. Many people may feel there is a difficult trade-off between buying more African exports and buying locally produced goods to minimize "food miles" and the environmental cost of transportation. In Europe this concern is set to undermine what had been a growing market for vegetables and flowers grown out of season in countries like Kenya, especially for those items then flown fresh to Europe's consumers by plane. It's relevant in America too, where the issue of transportation costs has been used, for example, by some of the domestic cotton and sugar lobbies as another reason to justify their large subsidies.

The reality is often much more complex than it looks. Africa produces things that suit its climate. Cotton and sugar grown in Africa tends to use less fertilizer—which is highly carbon-intensive to produce—than those crops grown in America. Cut flowers grown in Kenya and flown to Europe still have a lower carbon imprint than most European cut flowers, because of the high energy required to keep Europe's hothouses lit and warm.[18]

In any case, would a boycott of goods flown in from Africa be fair? We've seen in this book the difficulties African countries have had in getting decent international trade terms. And it is unequivocally true that the average African creates vastly less environmental pollution every year than the average American or European. So now we're going to squash their chance of economic growth while we continue to fly off on our vacations, drive our car around, and put the central heating on so high that we have to open the windows?

How about we keep buying African produce—but maybe walk to the store for a change when we do it?

What the growth of organic and Fairtrade markets reveals is that, while many of us still *feel* misguidedly impotent in the face of multinationals, many consumers in Western countries are already using their powers of choice. They are demanding products made to standards—ethical or health-related—that they are personally content to consume. It's only a short step from exercising this choice to realizing quite how politically powerful it makes us. It's *we* who should take credit for the growth of organic and Fairtrade markets, not supermarkets or anyone else.

Having this kind of impact over large corporate purchasers or producers of African goods is tremendously important. Multinational corporations invest upwards of $300 billion in developing countries annually—more than three times the global flow of aid.[19] It's obvious the potential positive impact this could have if more such investment flowed to Africa, in addition to the other, larger developing countries that currently dominate. Indeed, it's a safe bet that a large number of corporate executives in all sectors would like to feel that their work was more socially productive, as well as bringing them home the bacon. But capitalism encourages competition and is ruthless, leaving little or no room for sentiment or sympathy.

I'm not saying that companies and their employees have no responsibility for their actions and that anything legal under the letter of the law is okay. Far too many people have excused far too many things to themselves with that line. But the responsibility to make companies more socially useful lies also with governments to legislate so that the ways those companies act are constructive, not destructive. And it lies with consumers to decide whether or not they want to buy the product in the first place.

We can, as their clientele, create a virtuous circle whereby we demand the product to be made in more ethical ways or procured from more ethical sources—or more environmentally friendly, or whatever—and then they can enjoy going out to produce it. It's not corporate social responsibility, it's community–corporate cooperation.

Despite the growth of organics and Fairtrade, this "ethical" market is still relatively small. Many people continue to complain about book chains that put local booksellers out of business—but still buy their paperbacks at the chains. We're alarmed by the *No Logo* stories of the way high-end coffee franchises ruthlessly pay their baristas the minimum wage even after years of employ-ment—but we still get our coffee there. *If* this is stuff we're seri-ously concerned about (and I'm honest enough to admit I like my coffee-chain cappuccino as much as the next person, though I do always ask for Fairtrade), then let's at least act on it.

## A Sunday in Kigali, Banging Your Head Against the Wall

Since I've already raised the oldest trade of all once in this chapter, it seems appropriate to consider an infamous Rwandan example of the patronizing relationships that can still exist between the West and Africa, even at a personal level.

The Canadian writer Gil Courtemanche wrote a novel called (in the English translation) *A Sunday at the Pool in Kigali*.[20] It is set in the run-up to the genocide, and its early pages contain probably the most convincing account I've read of how the hysteria could ever have built up in Rwanda's capital to enable such butchery to begin. But its imagining of the relationship between the protagonist (a middle-aged Canadian journalist) and a young Rwandan waitress at the Hôtel des Mille-Collines tells us far more about the preoccupations of the author, and many male expatriates in Africa, than about the country itself.

Gentille, the waitress, "whose name is as lovely as her breasts, which are so pointed they abrade her starched shirt dress," is a timid young Tutsi. She and our hero fall deeply in love immediately, despite barely having exchanged a word. They have sex and fall asleep naked under a tree in the hotel's garden, which only the most ardent exhibitionist would attempt on that small and visible plot of land. He reads her some Parisian poetry, her soul is awakened. They both climax again. Later on they are naked in front of her father, a very traditional man in a distant village, but somehow this is okay too.

For good measure (and I'm not sorry for spoiling the story), the book seems to have a fascination with sex-death as well. The protagonist's first African friend to die expires from AIDS, but only while receiving a blow job from a prostitute while his mother looks on devotedly and approvingly. Another friend dies at a militia roadblock, though not before being been forced to perform oral sex on his mutilated wife for the first time ever (they both die at the apex of ecstasy, the machete coming down on him as he climaxes inside her). Is this genocide porn?

I hope I don't come across as too prurient. What irritates isn't the sex, it's the perpetuation, through the patronizing and unequal relationship between Gentille and our hero, of the image of expatriates as exploiters. Trying to put some kind of romantic literary gloss on it doesn't change the fact that it's still a middle-aged white guy getting a better, younger lay than he would at home. The meeting of minds is utterly unconvincing—but, as a study of a certain Western mind-set, the novel is unintentionally all too accurate.

There are, needless to say, plenty of genuine and equal relationships between Africans and outsiders. But relationships and fantasies like these only confirm the general perception of many Africans that westerners are in their continent to use, not to share.

## Fair-Played

Purchasing Fairtrade products is, of course, one of the most obvious ways of encouraging further trade with Africa. But how effective is it, and how long-lasting?

Fairtrade is not sustainable in the long term. Rather like charity aid, it helps but it isn't the answer. (The basic idea is that poor-country producers are paid a guaranteed price, above the market rate.) What Africa needs is to become competitive in its own right, on a level playing field, rather than rely on false subsidies from people paying extra.

It's also true that the real benefits for Africa's producers will come from goods being processed there, rather than simply exported as raw materials. A vast majority of African Fairtrade coffee, tea, and chocolate is manufactured and packaged in America and Europe, which means, even after the markup, that

## Buying Blue-Sky

It's true that it's difficult to find out about the ethical standards to which products are made—it's not always that easy even to find out where they're from. There's no way we can be expected to go into a supermarket and make informed choices about everything we buy. But the more "ethical" purchases we make, the more items get produced to those ethical standards—and the more their ethical credentials, such as the Fairtrade tag, are displayed on the labeling.

In the long term, I want to be able to walk into a supermarket and know that everything I buy is produced to a reasonable standard—whether it concerns treatment of animals, environmental pollution, or labor conditions—rather than having to pick things out consciously. I want to know that whatever product I choose, including those I choose for the practical reason that they are cheapest, I won't be complicit in the unfair exploitation of someone else.

We are now at the beginning of this process. One fast-growth area has been a great expansion in the nutrition guidelines on children's food packaging. The question is how quickly we can make this kind of addictive food habit develop.

sometimes only 5 percent of the final price goes to the country of origin.[21] This needs to shift: it's still not Africans who are making the most from Fairtrade.

Yet, all the while that trade rules remain unfair, buying Fairtrade *is* an effective personal statement that you do not wish to be complicit in the unjust trade arrangements around us. I must admit to getting irritated by some of the misleading charity-style paraphernalia around Fairtrade: it's not just for hippies, it is classic direct action to make up for the deficiencies of globalized markets and it sends a clear message. It's also a good way of protecting people such as coffee farmers from heavily fluctuating prices on international markets, which can hit those living without welfare safety nets hard, by guaranteeing a minimum price.

> *All of us have to go shopping—*
> *and Fairtrade is simply shopping with respect.*
> KWABENA OHEMENG TINYASE, HEAD OF THE
> KUAPA KOKOO COOPERATIVE, GHANA

## Retiring the Unpleasant

Perhaps the biggest impact we can have with our custom is to think about where we invest our money. It is a gaping hole for a bit more control.

Socially responsible investment has grown enormously over the last ten years. SRI means that, before buying shares in a company, an investment fund will check the activities of that company against social and environmental criteria—and not invest if they don't pass those criteria. Different funds do this to different levels of robustness; most simply check only that the company does no significant harm. A couple of decades ago the issue for many people was simply that they didn't want their money invested in companies involved in apartheid South Africa. But now it has grown to encompass wider considerations, such as environmental sustainability, human rights, and arms trading.

Nearly one in ten dollars under professional management in the United States is now involved in some way in socially responsible investing. The sector is projected to grow to $3 trillion by 2011.[22] This is huge money. Yet, standing back for a moment, in many ways it's more extraordinary that the proportion is only 10 percent, rather than 100 percent. Why on earth would anyone want to have their hard-earned pension or other savings backing companies doing things they don't necessarily like? Especially when that money could be promoting less damaging ways of doing business, as well as earning for retirement?

What's nice is that there's profit in this too—a classic example of the virtuous circle we can create between consumers and corporate managers to achieve positive ends. The Social Investment Forum discovered that SRI assets grew 4 percent faster than overall managed assets in the United States in the decade up to 2005.[23] And it is clearly a market that will continue to grow.

The more we use it, the more options we will get for how we can have our money invested. This is a wonderful way to exercise personal choice: are you particularly concerned with animal rights or environmental degradation, encouraging emerging markets or backing local firms, or not investing in unsavory foreign regimes or in military manufacturers? Ethical banking is a growing field too.

What is the impact of directing our money in this way? Companies wanting to adopt more ethical practices will find it easier and cheaper to get investment, compared to companies that do not act in such a way. It's simple, and powerful—and if more of us did it, it would be more powerful still. If we can get near to 50 percent, it will mean that virtually any company seeking investment will have little choice but to consider their social and environmental impacts, before even approaching potential backers.

## Making a Difference—Retail Therapy

What the market does and the effects it has are ultimately the distillation of our purchasing decisions. We don't buy what we don't want. It's about time we extended such decision-making to the way things are produced, and where, as well as to the product itself.

Influencing companies is generally a lot less onerous than influencing governments, because they give us so many opportunities to get our message across every day. So here are some suggestions about how you can spend your hard-earned money.

### 1. Buy
If you want more African products to be sold, buy more of them. More investment will flow into Africa.

### 2. Don't buy
If you discover something you dislike about the way a company acts, don't buy its products until they change.

### 3. Feedback
Next time you're in a store, mention to the clerk that it'd be nice if they stocked more African products—and ask that the message be passed on to the manager. Or ask what their sourcing policy is (it almost doesn't matter if you don't really listen to the answer—they'll remember you asked). The more regularly you can ask these kinds of brief questions, the better.

### 4. Encourage the wearing of labels
Every now and then, tell someone in the shops you frequent that you'd like to see better labeling on their goods about production and labor standards, or country of origin.

### 5. Double the value
Change your bank account and mortgage to an ethical bank, and your pension and savings to ethical investment funds. Get a better return, in all senses.

### 6. Get awkward

If you want to be a little bit more active, go into a coffee shop and ask if they serve Fairtrade. If not, leave. If they say yes, ask why all of it isn't fairly sourced. Put them on the spot.

### 7. Get really awkward

If you can find the time, fire off a few letters to your supermarket and other firms, asking what their ethical and social sourcing policy is. Or simply ask, "How do I know that what I buy in Wal-Mart/Kroger's/wherever has been produced to reasonable standards, that the actual producers are getting an okay price, and that there hasn't been exploitation?" That'll get them thinking.

### 8. Get your friends involved

Just as before, all the above is many times more effective if your buddies do it too.

# CHAPTER 18
## GUILT OR GLORY

*Let your politicians know you are watching every step they take. They made promises—now they must make them good.*
NELSON MANDELA

*No one could make a greater mistake than he who did nothing because he could do only a little.*
EDMUND BURKE

During my last month in Rwanda, I joined a visit by some officials from the Ministry of Education to a typical school that donor support was beginning to reach. Perched on top of a steep hillside, the classrooms, each with breathtaking views, ran in single file along the ridge and were arranged by age group. The headmaster introduced us to the final class, which he said was made up of seventeen- and eighteen-year-olds. They looked thirteen or fourteen at most.

Despite having worked a few years in aid, I was shocked at such a visible show of poverty. Short lifetimes of malnutrition had led to stunted growth in some, a delay in reaching puberty for others. It was as telling as the bent old men and women you would sometimes see walking in the countryside, whose craggy faces suggested a long lifetime of endurance, fortitude, and grandchildren, but who turned out to be easily younger than my parents. Poverty is so malign it can even be physical.

When the students in that classroom asked me what foreigners were doing to help their country, I could give them an immediate answer about my country's aid program and our support for education. But I wondered what the wider reply was, and whether I could honestly claim that the West was really trying to help places like Rwanda face up to their immense internal problems.

Since I left Rwanda in 2002, a lot has changed in terms of international attention to the West's ineffective, unwitting, and unfair policies toward Africa. The work of the Commission for Africa and the Make Poverty History/One campaigns have finally put many of the key issues on the table, and discussing the finer details of development work no longer has to be a case of ignoring the elephants in the room. This is encouraging. Yet there is no guarantee that the initial commitments made will be followed through, nor that the future development of globalization will occur in the interests of those who could most benefit from it.

Africa needs a larger and far more coherent aid effort from America and other Western countries. It needs us to stop trying to control every penny ourselves, instead supporting poor countries' own systems and providing finance through the most efficient, pooled mechanisms. Africa needs a set of international trade terms that genuinely assist ambitious farmers and businessmen and women who want to earn their way out of poverty, support their families, and see their countries' economies grow. And it needs us to ensure that those rules are clear and predictable, to

provide an extra spur for Africa's leaders to reform their own onerous business bureaucracies.

You may feel that the solutions I have set out in this book to
reach these goals are insufficiently grand: that this incremental
effort to change the decisions our governments make and shift the
ways the market does its business is inadequate. But the nature of
an imbalanced, globalized society leaves us little practical choice.
This book isn't written for government leaders, it's for you and
me as citizens and consumers. As influential individuals in a world
system, we must ensure that voiceless individuals have the chance
to determine their own futures. If we don't, who else will?

## Remote Control

The vexed story of the West's engagement with Africa is part of
a wider problem facing modern capitalism. We think we are
powerless to effect change. It's tempting to believe we can't
change much about our societies, and instead take advantage of
the reasonable standard of living globalization gives us, switching
on our iPods and multichannel TV and shutting out the feeling
that we're becoming gradually more marginalized. There may
even be a chance we'll go down as the generation that suffered a
social regression, returning to an era of public powerlessness not
seen in the West since the enormous changes sparked by the
Industrial Revolution.

Ultimately, we find ourselves halfway to creating a paradox.
On the one hand, globalization's uncontrolled energy has enabled
us to stand on the cusp of being the last generation in human
history to live with abject, mass poverty on our planet. On the
other, unless we direct and control it a bit more from here on in,
its "natural" forces will themselves prevent us from making the
final leap: we may not fully be able to capitalize on capitalism.

## Captain America

Nowhere matters more to changing the West's retrograde relations with Africa than the United States. Indeed, nowhere has a greater influence on global business or such a powerful say in international institutions. And nowhere is there a society better aware of the importance and value of personal responsibility.

I am an Americaphile. I know it as an empowering, effective, competitive society. It has beliefs in the rights of the individual that are the envy of most of the rest of the world. Yet it also suffers from two myths about Africa, for which both liberals and conservatives are equally responsible. The first is that you can't do much to help the continent (that's right, the country that took on fascism in Europe and then won the cold war is unable to help countries that actually *want* its intervention). The second is that Americans are doing a great deal already.

While it's no excuse for other countries and their citizens to cease their own efforts, the world desperately needs American leadership if we are serious about changing the way globalization, aid, and trade affect the prospects of poor countries. It is more important for consumers and voters to exert their power in the United States than anywhere else: lucky them, as they can achieve most. A breakthrough could come quickly, because once more Americans understand how little help they are currently providing, especially in foreign aid, they will surely demand that their government meets their expectations. As Harry Truman said, "Give Americans the facts and they'll do the right thing."[24]

There are some promising signs, both in faith-based groups and a new generation of young activists, but much more is needed. Bill Clinton recently observed, "Nobody will ever get beat for Congress or president for not doing it. We have never created an effective political constituency, but it is coming."[25] We must hope so.

## Cashing In

What's the likelihood we as individuals will really take the kind of action and responsibility that Africa needs from us?

There's no point in being naïve: there is a big chance we

won't, in America or elsewhere. It is more than possible that the aid and trade hopes of the early millennium will soon fold into the usual fudge of unmet promises, that the inevitable failings of some African governments will continue to be seen as an excuse to trust none of their counterparts, and that business as usual will, in time, return to drowning out the development demands of Africans and campaigners alike.

Yet grounds for optimism are there. The issues have a higher profile than ever before. The public in many Western countries has announced quite clearly that they would like to see a better deal for Africa. Consumers are gradually making more ethical demands with their money, and an increasing number of businesses are beginning to respond.

Frankly, none of this would be convincing enough to make me believe change is likely if it wasn't for one additional factor: the unfairness toward Africa is bad for us too, from the poor value many of us get for our aid money, to the extra we pay in our tax bills on subsidies and the higher prices we face on other products at the checkout line. This is significant. It means we have a common cause with Africans in demanding a better system.

The most successful social and consumer changes of recent times have usually stemmed from self-interest: the organic market and the anti-GM movement alike have grown quickly because people are motivated to act by things they believe directly affect them, their health, and their pocketbook. If unfair tariffs and subsidies mean an average American family is surcharged more than $500 a year through a combination of tax and higher prices at the cash register, it's obvious we have a stake in seeing change here too. Charities and campaigners should not be afraid to have a louder debate about how we lose, as well as Africa.

Saving our lost money would easily cover the extra cash needed to raise aid spending to an effective level. It would comfortably allow the revered president of Uzima to meet his or her financing gap. And the freer trading environment created would increase the incentives for Uzima's budding entrepreneurs to brave the world marketplace themselves.

## Globalization's Dire Straits

Later on the same day I visited the hilltop school with the astonishing views, I drove on to the town of Gisenyi, close to the border with Marie's country of D.R. Congo. My embassy colleagues were sponsoring a Rwandan culture festival, and a large crowd had gathered by the shore of Lake Kivu for the general amusement and free music. Some of the local dignitaries were clearly irked by the embassy's insistence that local street children be allowed to attend. But no one seemed to be enjoying themselves much as a number of rather tedious speeches were followed by a disappointing local band playing low-tempo, low-volume versions of Congolese *soukous* classics.

Then the band stopped and "Sultans of Swing" by Dire Straits came on the PA system. And everyone, from the scruffiest street kids to mayors and ambassadors, got up and started dancing with each other. Against all odds, years after I had first complained of Kenya's radio soundtrack of Phil Collins, Rick Astley, and Michael Bolton, it was the ultimate exponents of white middle-aged rock who brought harmony to one small town in a vibrant but run-down part of Africa.

Globalization can have some unexpected effects. And after seeing that, despite the embarrassing Rwandan TV footage that followed of me dancing dreadfully in a suit, I'm inclined to believe almost anything is possible.

## Success and Successors

It is important to keep all this in perspective. We can't save the world, and it would be misleading to suggest that Africa's poverty is our fault, or that our current failure to manage international affairs more in the interests of the world's poorest countries is the prime cause of their problems. African countries face many huge challenges of their own, and only they can address them. But we can help with a number of others.

What makes me feel most uncomfortable is not the school of stunted children on a Rwandan hillside. It's when I think of my friends in Kigali, a city that may be full of raw and degrading poverty but is also home to a growing middle class of well-educated, relatively affluent Africans. What can we in the West possibly do that this energetic middle class could not? Well, that middle class doesn't control the trade rules, many of which affect the poorer rural population. It can't influence the price of AIDS drugs. It can't deliver Rwanda better access to Western markets. It can't substantially boost government funding for primary education and basic health care.

- We cannot get Africa out of poverty. Yet we can help give Africans a better chance to do it themselves.
- We cannot say an end to poverty is going to happen. Rather, we can help a serious reduction in poverty to become a possibility.
- We cannot force African countries to be better run. But we can help create the conditions in which those running well can thrive.

In the long term, Africa's prospects must eventually be bright, if only because it will eventually be the world's only remaining repository of cheap labor. The question is whether people like Marie and Jean Baptiste—or rather their children or grandchildren—will have to wait fifty years, say, to see that marked development in their country and continent, or whether it will take two or three hundred. It's a question that will define life expectancies, determine how many millions of children die from preventable diseases, and how many aspiring traders continue to struggle to provide for their families. It will also help influence how quickly African countries can move on from corruption and how many unnecessary civil wars, coups, and famines they will experience in the interim.

## Glory

What I have not had space to do in this book is spend nearly enough time describing the progress now taking place in many parts of Africa: the Mozambiques, Tanzanias, Senegals, and others that in recent times have all managed to start creating virtuous circles of stability, growing transparency, economic growth, and a reduction in the numbers living in absolute poverty.

Then there's the average economic growth of 5 percent over the last few years, albeit on the back of high global commodity prices. The increasing proportion of children across the continent now attending school. The growing numbers of HIV-positive Africans now accessing antiretroviral drugs—even if those numbers remain far too small. This is undoubtedly a promising time for the continent.

What we should be focusing on is creating an international environment that gives African countries a real chance to flourish. And then letting them get on with it.


■ think back to my drink with Marie by the busy, potholed road ■ in Kinshasa, and to sitting in the afternoon sun with Lucas and Nancy outside their small house near the edge of the Rift Valley. In many ways it feels simply . . . embarrassing that what we do or do not do has the ability to help or hinder their prospects. I wish it were not the case.

In an ideal world, what we do and don't do would be simply irrelevant to the kind of life Jean Baptiste will grow up to lead, or the challenges Lucas and Nancy's extensive family will face. In that ideal world, aid would be coherent and sufficient, and trade terms would accept the need to give the poorest countries an easier route into international markets. We could feel no responsibility for what people like Marie, Lucas, and Nancy do with their own lives. Yet much about Western countries' relationship with Africa is so dysfunctional that it will only change if we as Western individuals stand up and do something about it.

## Our Story

If it would be wrong to claim that the West is in any significant way to blame for Africa's past and current poverty—even if we have failed to be much of a help to date—it will be different in the future.

Globalization gives African countries greater opportunities to develop than before. Their chances of doing so will increasingly be defined by international rules, especially on aid and trade. Given that the ability to influence those rules lies predominantly with us as individuals in the West, from now on we will be complicit if Africa's circumstances fail to improve.

It's not really a question of who has the influence, it's a question of whether we choose to use it. Changing our societies in this era of big powers and small individuals will not be easy, but it can be done. Either we are part of the solution or, regrettably, we become part of the problem.

It's guilt, or, in a way, it's a kind of glory. We can no longer be the complacent, comfortably numb generation. We must become responsible for ourselves and our society once again.

# ACKNOWLEDGMENTS

All the opinions expressed in this book are my own, and do not represent those of any group of people or institution I've worked with.

There are many people to whom I owe thanks. First among them are my colleagues in the DFID office in Kigali: Jean, Boniface, Vedaste, Jean-Marie, Faustin, Josephine, Kalayu, Chris, Liberal, Netty, Gerard, Mark, Rupert, and Caroline. Working with them, in Rwanda, was the opportunity of a lifetime, as was getting to know Rita and Damascène. I hope I've done some justice to the issues we dealt with.

Dave Fish and Barbara Kelly gave me the chance to go to Rwanda in the first place. When I got there it was a true privilege to work with Donald Kaberuka, and several others inside and outside the Rwandan government, nearly all of whom had already experienced more event and upheaval in their lifetimes that I am, thankfully, ever likely to in mine. Emma Day, Claire Burgoyne, Rick Erlebach, Karin Christiansen, Mark Allen, Ulrika Jonsson, Sarah Hague, Donata Garrasi, and many others made it a lot of fun along the way.

This is a good chance to say thanks again to Alex Evans for

inviting me to Kenya in 1996, my first visit to Africa, and to his parents, Bridget and Nick, for subsequently having always offered a welcoming home and challenging chat. Also to Soiya Gecaga, Lara and Ninian Lowis, Tom Fletcher, James Grayburn, and Kate Hemmings, among others, for the entertaining exploration of Nairobi nightspots and upcountry beauty spots, while my colleagues in the offices in Nairobi and Kampala offices made the daytimes more enjoyable and educative still.

Lynne-Marie Simmons, Chris Foot, James West and Abi Johnson, and Casper and Esa Preysing all provided warming hospitality abroad during the writing of this book. Amy Eldon and Lucy Woodward both helped inspire it, in different ways. I owe loads to Mary Louise Eagleton, who gave me great advice, somewhere to stay in Kinshasa, and, most important, shared an amazing journey overland from Mombasa to London. My brother, my sisters, and my friends at home all helped keep me sane when I was struggling with the writing, which was all too often.

In addition to some of the people above, I received very helpful advice and comments from a number of friends and old colleagues. They are responsible for none of the errors and misjudgments in the book, but the mistakes would have been more numerous without them. Among them are Daniel Davis, Laura Kelly, Hetty Kovach, Mick O'Doherty, Mike Eldon, and Marcus and Alice Evans. My agent, Jessica Woollard, has directed me tirelessly through the confusing world of publishing and helped focus my work. I'm grateful to Jeannette and Richard Seaver at Arcade for believing in the book, to Tessa A ye for her diligence, and particularly to Cal Barksdale for his insight, tolerance, and improvements.

There are three people I'd like to thank in particular. Dad, for his advice, example, and support. My mother, who gave me counsel, a place to work and sleep, and just about everything else. And Fen Grey, for being incredibly patient—and, most of all, just for being there.

The people I'm most nervous about reading this book are colleagues I've worked with over the years, from whom I've learned a great deal, and whose passion and commitment are consistently impressive. I know the story I've set out is broad brush, and lacks some nuance and detail. But I don't think it will be possible to reach the goals aid workers and many others are aiming for, unless we can build increased public support for better aid and trade policies: I hope this book can play a small part in that.

# APPENDIX 1:
# NATIONAL AID DONORS[1]

The number of national aid donors has grown from five or six in the mid-1940s to at least fifty-six today, which is partly why the coordination of aid is so difficult. In 2007, the World Bank offered the following "partial list" of donor countries. The vast majority are active in Africa, and many carry out work through more than one of their own aid institutions:

| | |
|---|---|
| Australia | Libya |
| Austria | Lithuania |
| Belgium | Luxembourg |
| Brazil | Malaysia |
| Bulgaria | Malta |
| Canada | Mexico |
| China | Netherlands |
| Chinese Taipei (Taiwan) | New Zealand |
| Cyprus | Norway |
| Czech Republic | Pakistan |
| Denmark | Poland |
| Estonia | Portugal |

| | |
|---|---|
| Finland | Romania |
| France | Russian Federation |
| Germany | Saudi Arabia |
| Greece | Singapore |
| Hungary | Slovak Republic |
| Iceland | Slovenia |
| India | South Africa |
| Indonesia | Spain |
| Iran | Sweden |
| Ireland | Switzerland |
| Israel | Thailand |
| Italy | Turkey |
| Japan | United Arab Emirates |
| Korea | United Kingdom |
| Kuwait | United States |
| Latvia | Venezuela |

# APPENDIX 2: UNITED NATIONS AGENCIES IN AFRICA[2]

**UN agencies with an office in most African countries:**

| | |
|---|---|
| FAO | Food and Agriculture Organization |
| OCHA | Office for the Coordination of Humanitarian Affairs |
| UNAIDS | Joint United Nations Program on HIV/AIDS |
| UNICEF | United Nations Children's Fund |
| UNDP | United Nations Development Program |
| UNHCR | Office of the United Nations High Commissioner for Refugees |
| UNIDO | United Nations Industrial Development Organization |
| UNFPA | United Nations Population Fund |
| WFP | World Food Program |
| WHO | World Health Organization |

## UN agencies with regional offices across Africa:

| | |
|---|---|
| ECA | Economic Commission on Africa |
| ILO | International Labor Organization |
| OHCHR | Office of the High Commissioner for Human Rights |
| UNIFEM | United Nations Development Fund for Women |
| UNESCO | United Nations Educational, Scientific and Cultural Organization |

## Other UN agencies with development projects in Africa:

| | |
|---|---|
| IFAD | International Fund for Agricultural Development |
| MAS | Mine Action Service |
| UNCTAD | United Nations Conference on Trade and Development |
| UNEP | United Nations Environment Program |
| UN-HABITAT | United Nations Human Settlements Program |

# NOTES

## INTRODUCTION
1. Fukuda, Dyck, and Stout, "Rice Sector Policies in Japan," USDA, March 2003, www.ers.usda.gov. See note in chapter 12 for full information.

## POVERTY
1. World Bank Development Indicators 2005 data.
2. Statistics from *Times Concise Atlas of the World*, 8th edition.
3. UNAIDS.
4. Jeffrey Sachs, *The End of Poverty*, 196.
5. Malaria and diarrhea statistics from WHO World Health Report 2004, estimates for 2002.
6. Commission for Africa report, 2005.
7. Tim Radford, *Guardian* (UK), October 2, 2003.
8. Assessment based on Web search of news and wildlife sources; no comprehensive statistics available. Lions in Tanzania, one of the main centers, kill approximately sixty-five people per year, classed as extremely rare.
9. WTO, 1996, quoted on www.worldvaccines.org.
10. Source for much information in the last three paragraphs: Thomas Pakenham, *The Scramble for Africa*.
11. David Lamb, *The Africans*.
12. This paragraph draws directly from Ryszard Kapiscinski's brilliant book *The Shadow of the Sun*, 35 ff.
13. David E. Bloom and Jeffrey E. Sachs, "Geography, Demography and Economic Growth in Africa," Brookings Papers on Economic Activity 2 (1998).
14. David Lamb, *The Africans*, 45.
15. UN Human Development Report, covered in *Guardian* (UK), July 9, 2003.
16. UNCTAD as quoted on www.data.org.
17. Based on P. Starkey et al., *World Bank* (2002), quoted in Commission for Africa report.

18. Sources: World Bank Development Indicators 2004; World Bank Web site; OECD.
19. Tony Blair, writing in *Guardian* (UK), March 12, 2005.
20. DFID Country Profiles: Uganda, at www.dfid.gov.uk.
21. Unless otherwise stated, the data in this chapter is taken from World Bank World Development Indicators 2007 online, figures from 2006, and from the IMF Regional Economic Outlook for sub-Saharan Africa, April 2007. All key economic figures, including gross national income, GNI per capita, and government revenue, as well as population and land area, are derived from data that excludes South Africa. This is because South Africa is both large and significantly more affluent than most other African countries. A few other sub-Saharan African countries are also relatively affluent—Botswana, Gabon, Mauritius, Seychelles—but are not so large as to create significant distortions to average statistics. Most other figures, such as on health, education, transport, and so on, are taken from data including South Africa, as the statistical distortion created by its inclusion is not significant in any of these areas. With the exception of AIDS statistics, South Africa's presence, if anything, will have a positive effect on most statistics—i.e., make problems appear not quite as bad as they really are.
22. World Bank World Development Indicators 2004 CD-ROM, figures from 2002.
23. World Bank Africa Basic Indicators Factsheet, 2003.
24. IMF Regional Economic Outlook for sub-Saharan Africa, April 2007.
25. American Friends Service Committee, quoting Malawi vice president, at www.afsc.org/pwork/0106/010606.htm.
26. BBC news at www.aegis.org/news/bbc/2002/BB020511.html, taken from a World Bank report.
27. Robert Page, "Health Spending Exceeded Record $2 Trillion in 2006," *New York Times*, January 8, 2008.
28. Commission for Africa report, 2005, 369 (draft).
29. UNHCR: Estimated number of asylum seekers, refugees, and others of concern to UNHCR as of January 1, 2004: Africa: 4,285,100. Europe: 4,242,300.
30. Africaaction.org. Precise annual figures on debt repayments tend to emerge only eighteen to twenty-four months after the event.
31. See Sachs, *The End of Poverty*, 294: he claims that most low-income countries have government revenues of 10 percent. When supplemented by grants and borrowing, this is at least more than the 5 percent GDP/6 percent GNI most low-income countries spend on MDG areas.
32. Robert Page, *New York Times*.

## AID

1. OECD/DAC 2005, figures for 2004.
2. OECD/DAC figures aid through taxes, average aid flows 2005–06, published December 2007. Aid through charities from OECD/DAC 2006 figures, against UN population figures.
3. OECD Aid Statistics, 2005 figures—Total Net Flows from DAC

countries by Type of Flow.
4. Quoted in article by Jeevan Vasagar, *Guardian* (UK), January 3, 2006.
5. OECD/DAC. Net disbursements of ODA for 2004–05, based on net disbursements and broadly adapted to exclude effect of multilateral contributions. Note: when donors' aid includes "amounts unspecified by region," overall percentages of aid to Africa rise to around 40 percent.
6. OECD/DAC.
7. UK Department for International Development Web site, www.dfid.gov.uk.
8. *Time* (Europe edition), October 3, 2004.
9. www.aidharmonization.org.
10. Last few figures from www.worldbank.org.
11. OECD/DAC estimates. Other statistics in this paragraph are from Action Aid report, *Real Aid*, 2005.
12. Action Aid, *Real Aid*, report.
13. Hilary Benn, UK secretary of state for international development, speech, February 2004.
14. Center for Global Development, 2007.
15. OECD/DAC quoted in Action Aid, *Real Aid*, report.
16. "The United States and the MDGs: U.S. Contributions to Reducing Global Poverty," Interaction, the American Council for Voluntary Action, 2007.
17. Action Aid, *Real Aid*, report.
18. Michael M. Phillips, "Federal Reserve Often Tosses Out IMF Advice on Economic Policy," *Wall Street Journal*, September 30, 1999.
19. Editorial, *New York Times*, November 24, 2005.
20. *Time* (Europe edition), October 11, 2004.
21. "Each economically advanced country will progressively increase its official development assistance to the developing countries and will exert its best efforts to reach a minimum net amount of 0.7 percent of its gross national product at market prices by the middle of the decade." UN General Assembly Resolution 2626 (XXV), October 24, 1970, Paragraph 43. Note: GNP is now commonly replaced by the essentially similar GNI.
22. George W. Bush, speech to UN High-Level Plenary Meeting, New York, September 14, 2005, at www.whitehouse.gov.
23. Jacques Chirac, speech to World Bank Shanghai Conference, "Scaling Up Poverty Reduction," May 26, 2004. See www.elysee.fr/elysee/elysee.fr/anglais.
24. Condoleeza Rice, remarks to InterAction annual forum, April 18, 2007.
25. Masaharu Kohno, quoted in *Guardian* (UK), February 2, 2005.
26. James Wolfensohn, press conference at World Bank spring meetings, April 22, 2004, at www.worldbank.org.
27. www.cgdev.org/doc/cdi/Index_2005.xls.
28. Jimmy Carter, address at Principia College in Elsah, Illinois, quoted from "Who Rules Next?" *Christian Science Monitor*, December 29, 1999, www.globalissues.org.

29. www.publicagenda.org.
30. www.usatoday.com/news/nation/2004-10-03-debt-cover_x.htm.
31. *Washington Post* survey, see www.nap.edu.
32. OECD figures—Economic Indicators for DAC Member Countries in 2004.
33. Nancy Birdsall, president of CGD, testimony to the Senate Committee on Foreign Relations, May 17, 2005, www.cgdev.org.

## TRADE
1. Oxfam.
2. Commission for Africa report, 2005, 256.
3. George W. Bush, interview by Trevor McDonald, ITV1, UK, July 4, 2005.
4. Several sources, including article by Karl Marx, *New York Herald Tribune*, July 11, 1853, at www.marxists.org.
5. Commission for Africa report, 2005, chapter 8, based on World Bank data.
6. OECD.
7. Oxfam, *Recipe for Disaster*, report, April 27, 2006.
8. Intermediate Technology Development Group, at www.itdg.org.
9. *Guardian*/Action Aid, September 8, 2003.
10. World Bank Development Indicators, 2004 data.
11. CFA report, 276, based on research by Page & Hewitt, 2001.
12. Ibid.
13. Ibid.
14. Progressive Policy Institute, www.ppionline.org.
15. Eileen Maybin and Kevin Bundell, "After the Prawn Rush: The Human and Environmental Costs of Commercial Prawn Farming," *Christian Aid*, 1996.
16. Noreena Hertz, *I.O.U.: The Debt Threat and Why We Must Defuse It*, 165.
17. Editorial, *British Medical Journal*, July 2, 2005.
18. Leana Wen, "Where Are the Doctors?," *New York Times*, June 25, 2007.
19. Migration News, at www.migration.ucdavis.edu, 2004.
20. Taken directly from article by Stephanie Nolen, *Globe and Mail* (UK), April 28, 2004, at www.globeandmail.workopolis.com.
21. Celia W. Dugger, *New York Times*, October 27, 2005, article taken from research by the *New England Journal of Medicine*.
22. Larry Elliott, *Guardian* (UK), December 6, 2004.
23. Ibid.
24. Fire is thought to have been first used by *Homo erectus* around 1,420,000 B.C., in Africa. Evidence of fishing with bones for hooks exists from around 38,000 B.C. Condoms were used in Egypt from around 1850 B.C. There is a useful list at www.krysstal.com/inventions.html. Also www.avert.org/condoms.htm. The first record of coffee being used as a drink is thought to be "of beans exported from Ethiopia to Yemen where Sufis drank it to stay awake all night to pray on special occasions. By the late fifteenth century it had arrived in Mecca and Turkey." Article by Paul Vallely, *Independent* (UK), March 11, 2006, www.news.independent.co.uk.

25. International Telecommunication Union, see http://news.bbc.co.uk/1/hi/world/africa/3686463.stm, May 5, 2004.
26. www.geohive.com.
27. Editorial, "America's Sugar Daddies," *New York Times*, November 29, 2003.
28. Clifford Krauss, "Seeing America's Future in Fuel," *New York Times*, October 18, 2007.
29. Many sources, e.g., www.dermatology.about.com.
30. Global Polio Initiative.
31. Carter Center, Health Program Information, www.cartercenter.org.
32. Jeremy Laurance, *Independent* (UK), September 28, 2005.
33. James T. Robinson, "Changing the Face of Detailing by Motivating Physicians to See Pharmaceutical Sales Reps," *Product Management Today*, November 2003.
34. Sarah Boseley, "Dying for a Profit," *Guardian* (UK), September 8, 2003, www.guardian.co.uk.
35. Ibid.
36. Sophia Murphy and Kathy McAfee, *U.S. Food Aid: Time to Get It Right*, Institute for Agriculture and Trade Policy, www.tradeobservatory.org. DATA/UNAIDS.
37. DATA/UNAIDS.
38. WHO.
39. Murphy and McAfee, *U.S. Food Aid*, 27.
40. Ibid.
41. Christopher B. Barrett and Daniel G. Maxwell, draft manuscript of *Food Aid After Fifty Years: Recasting Its Role* (London: Routledge, 2005). Quoted in *U.S. Food Aid* report above.
42. Quoted in article by Natasha C. Burley, *New York Times*, September 22, 2005, at www.nytimes.com.
43. Barrett and Maxwell research, cited in article by Celia W. Dugger, *New York Times*, October 13, 2005.
44. Celia W. Dugger, "CARE Turns Down Federal Funds for Food Aid," *New York Times*, August 16, 2007.
45. Barrett and Maxwell, draft manuscript of *Food Aid After Fifty Years*.
46. IRIN article on Earth Summit, August 30, 2002, www.irinnews.org.
47. Unconfirmed—taken from Wikipedia at www.en.wikipedia.org/wiki/Patent.
48. Jay McGown, "Out of Africa: Mysteries of Access and Benefit Sharing," Edmonds Institute, 2006, www.edmonds-institute.org. Also "The Commodification of a Cactus," *CSW Update 2007*, UCLA Center for the Study of Women.
49. Anthony Barnett, article in Observer (UK), September 5, 2004, www.observer.guardian.co.uk.
50. IRIN article on Earth Summit, August 30, 2002, www.irinnews.org.
51. Fran Smith, "How Much Will the Farm Bill Cost the Average Family?" July 20, 2007, openmarket.org.
52. Article by Brian Riedl, December 10, 2001, at www.heritage.org.
53. Press release July 10, 2002, at www.which.net.
54. Devinder Sharma, "Protecting Agriculture," in *Foreign Policy in Focus*, February 5, 2003, www.globalpolicy.org.

55. Drawn from Fukuda, Dyck, and Stout, "Rice Sector Policies in Japan," USDA, March 2003, www.ers.usda.gov. (OECD Producer Support Estimate for rice farmers in Japan was $20.42 billion in 2000. Circa 45 million households in Japan = circa $450 per household. Japanese households spent 1 percent of income/$340 on rice in 2000. Price savings of at least 50 percent could be achieved with abolition of tariffs on foreign rice.) Also mentioned in article by Steve Moody, Japanese Department, Brigham Young University, www.japan-101.com.
56. USDA Economic Research Service, 2002.
57. Charlotte Denny and Larry Elliott, article in *Guardian*/Action Aid, September 8, 2003.
58. Environmental Working Group (U.S.), farm subsidies database, November 1, 2005, www.ewg.org.
59. Ibid.
60. www.opensecrets.org/industries/indus.asp?Ind=A01.
61. From reasononline, magazine of the Reason Foundation, at www.reason.com/0602/fe.dgsix.shtml.
62. 2004 poll by the PIPA/Knowledge Network. See Heidorn article below.
63. Susan Sechler and Ann Tutwiler, article in *New York Times*, June 26, 2006, www.nytimes.com.
64. Research from www.pbs.org at www.pbs.org/independentlens/tshirttravels/film.html.
65. All figures from OECD statistics. The comparison is imperfect but broadly accurate. Aid per capita is drawn directly from the OECD's own figures, based on aid as a percentage of GNI. Agriculture support per capita is derived from OECD estimates of total support as a percentage of GDP, divided by OECD population figures. Figures for consumer support to agriculture are based on GDP per capita, whereas aid figures use GNI per capita, which is slightly different. But this only gives a margin of error of up to 10 percent, which is not enough to significantly change the overall picture.
66. *Monitor* (Uganda), May 15, 2004.
67. BBC News Online, March 14, 2005, at www.news.bbc.co.uk.
68. Nancy Birdsall, Dani Rodrik, and Arvind Subramanian, article in *Foreign Affairs*, July/August 2005.

## GLOBALIZATION

1. World Bank Development Indicators 2005.
2. UN World Economic and Social Survey 2006, table 1.1.
3. Bill Clinton, remarks to Council on Foreign Relations, Yale Club, New York, June 7, 2002, at www.clintonfoundation.org.
4. Isaac Shapiro, "Trends in U.S. Development Aid," Center on Budget and Policy Priorities, May 9, 2000, www.cbpp.org.
5. *Guardian* (UK), July 6, 2005.
6. DFID Statistics on International Development.
7. Larry Elliott, "It Will Take Years to Revive Trade Talks," *Guardian* (UK), July 31, 2006.
8. UK Department for International Development, *Trade Matters*, December 2005.

9. Beatrice Dove-Edwin, "Life in the Merry-Go-Doha-Round," in *Trade Negotiations Insights* 5, no. 3 (May/June 2006), www.icstd.org.

10. Editorial, *Guardian* (UK), January 9, 2006.

11. Oxfam, "The View from the Summit-Gleneagles G8 One Year On," www.oxfam.org.

12. Information in this and the previous paragraph is drawn from Gary Younge, "Like Arsenic in the Water Supply," *Guardian* (UK), January 9, 2006.

13. Editorial, *Guardian* (UK), January 9, 2006.

14. Information in this paragraph is drawn from an editorial in the *New York Times*, August 8, 2005, based on evidence from Public Citizen, at www.nytimes.com.

15. Pew Research Center, "Maximum Support for Raising the Minimum," April 19, 2006, www.pewresearch.org.

16. The information in last two paragraphs is from an editorial in the *New York Times*, June 3, 2005.

17. G. Pascal Zachary, "Out of Africa: Cotton and Cash," *New York Times*, January 14, 2007.

## CHANGE

1. UK Web site for Gleneagles G8 Summit, at www.g8.gov.uk—section on Africa.

2. From www.datareport.org.

3. Chair's summary, Gleneagles G8 Summit, July 8, 2005, at www.g8.gov.uk.

4. Wrigley and Schofield's *Population History of England* shows that life expectancy at birth rose from thirty-five to forty years between 1781 and 1851—still less than Africa's current expectancy of forty-six.

5. Noreena Hertz, *I.O.U.*, 9.

6. Communication to author by senior USAID official.

7. "The United States and the MDGs: U.S. Contributions to Reducing Global Poverty," Interaction, the American Council for Voluntary International Action, 2007.

8. Celia W. Dugger, "U.S. Agency's Slow Pace Endangers Foreign Aid," *New York Times*, December 7, 2007.

9. World Advertising Trends 2006, at www.warc.com.

10. OECD.

11. www.dentsu.com.

12. Advertising Association, at www.adassoc.org.uk.

13. *Nutrition Business Journal* estimates based on Organic Trade Association's 2006 Manufacturer Survey, annual *Nutrition Business Journal* surveys of manufacturers, and other sources, at www.ota.com.

14. www.organic-europe.net, quoting research by Professor Ulrich Hamm of Kassel University.

15. Andrew Downie, "Fair Trade in Bloom," *New York Times*, October 2, 2007.

16. Lucy Siegle, "Dilemma as Ethics Enters the Mainstream," *Observer* (UK), March 12, 2006.

17. Peter Singer, *The Ethics of What We Eat* (New York: Rodale, 2007). Also in interview with Patrick Barkham, *Guardian* (UK), September 8, 2006.
18. Initial research by International Food Policy Research Institute, www.ifrpri.org.
19. Emerging Market Economics, "Pro-poor investment," paper prepared for DFID, August 2002, at www.emergingmarkets.co.uk.
20. Gil Coutemanche, *A Sunday at the Pool in Kigali* (New York: Vintage, 2006).
21. Andrew Purvis, "Ethical Eating: How Much Do You Swallow?" *Observer Food Monthly* (UK), February 26, 2006, quoting Neil Kelsall, marketing director of Malagasy.
22. Celent (financial consultancy), www.celent.com.
23. Social Investment Forum: 2005 report on Socially Responsible Investing trends in the U.S., at www.socialinvest.org.
24. www.one.org.
25. Bill Clinton, speech in Davos, January 27, 2005, quoted in *Guardian* (UK), www.politics.guardian.co.uk.

## APPENDICES
1. www.unsystem.org.
2. "Aid Architecture: An Overview of the Main Trends in Official Development Assistance Flows," World Bank Development Committee, March 29, 2007.

# BIBLIOGRAPHY

Bakan, Joel. *The Corporation: The Pathological Pursuit of Profit and Power.* New York: Free Press, 2004.

Bhagawati, Jagdish. *In Defense of Globalization.* New York: Oxford University Press, 2004.

Commission for Africa. *Our Common Interest: Report of the Commission for Africa.* 2005.

Courtemanche, Gil. *A Sunday at the Pool in Kigali.* New York: Knopf, 2003.

Easterly, William. *The Elusive Quest for Growth: Economists' Adventures and Misadventures in the Tropics.* Cambridge, MA: MIT Press, 2001.

———. *The White Man's Burden: Why the West's Efforts to Aid the Rest Have Done So Much Ill and So Little Good.* New York: Penguin Press, 2006.

Gill, Peter. *Body Count: How They Turned AIDS into a Catastrophe.* London: Profile Books, 2006.

Gourevitch, Philip. *We Wish to Inform You That Tomorrow We Will Be Killed with Our Families.* New York: Farrar, Straus and Giroux, 1998.

Guest, Robert. *The Shackled Continent: Power, Corruption, and African Lives*. New York: Smithsonian, 2004.

Hertz, Noreena. *I.O.U.: The Debt Threat and Why We Must Defuse It*. New York: Collins, 2004.

Kagan, Robert. *Paradise and Power: America and Europe in the New World Order*. New York: Knopf, 2003.

Kapuscinski, Ryszard. *The Shadow of the Sun*. New York: Knopf, 2001.

Klein, Naomi. *No Logo: Taking Aim at the Brand Bullies*. New York: Picador, 2000.

Lamb, David. *The Africans: Encounters from the Sudan to the Cape*. New York: Random House, 1983.

Pakenham, Thomas. *The Scramble for Africa: White Man's Conquest of the Dark Continent from 1876 to 1912*. New York: Random House, 1991.

Sachs, Jeffery. *The End of Poverty: Economic Possibilities for Our Time*. New York: Penguin Press, 2005.

Stiglitz, Joseph. *Globalization and Its Discontents*. New York: W. W. Norton, 2002.

———. *Making Globalization Work*. New York: W. W. Norton, 2006.

Wilkinson, Rord. *The WTO: Crisis and the Governance of Global Trade*. Oxford: Routledge, 2006.

Wolf, Martin. *Why Globalization Works*. New Haven: Yale University Press, 2004.

Wroe, Martin, and Malcolm Doney. *The Rough Guide to a Better World and How You Can Make a Difference*. London: Rough Guides, 2004.

Wrong, Michela. *In the Footsteps of Mr. Kurtz: Living on the Brink of Disaster in the Congo*. New York: HarperCollins, 2001.